Minarets
on the
Horizon

MUSLIM PIONEERS IN CANADA

Murray Hogben

MAWENZI
HOUSE

Published with the generous assistance of the Canada Council for the Arts and the Ontario Arts Council. We also acknowledge the support of the Government of Canada through the Canada Book Fund and the Government of Ontario through the Ontario Book Publishing Tax Credit.

Cover design by Sabrina Pignataro

Cover images: Mohammad (Sam) Asiff peddling goods to Alberta farmers from his horse cart in 1930s, photo courtesy of Fisal Asiff; fmajor/Mohamed Al-Amin mosque, Beirut, Lebanon, stock photo /iStockphoto

Author photo credit: Bibijehan Henson

Library and Archives Canada Cataloguing in Publication

Title: Minarets on the horizon : Muslim pioneers in Canada / Murray Hogben.

Names: Hogben, Murray, author.

Description: Includes bibliographical references.

Identifiers: Canadiana (print) 20210148004 | Canadiana (ebook) 2021014873X | ISBN 9781774150320
  (softcover) | ISBN 9781774150337 (EPUB) | ISBN 9781774150344 (PDF)

Subjects: LCSH: Muslims—Canada—History—20th century. | LCSH: Immigrants—Canada—History—20th
  century. | LCSH: Pioneers—Canada—History—20th century.

Classification: LCC FC106.M9 H64 2021 | DDC 305.6/970971—dc23

Printed and bound in Canada by Coach House Printing

Mawenzi House Publishers Ltd.
39 Woburn Avenue (B)
Toronto, Ontario M5M 1K5
Canada
www.mawenzihouse.com

To my wife Alia without whom the best parts of my life would not have occurred,
to our children Noorjehan, Ameera and Omar,
to our grandchildren Bibijehan, Shakoor, Isra and Reza,
to our son-in-law John Douglas Henson,
and to all the pioneers, recorded or not.
May God be pleased with them all.

Contents

The Carpet-Weaver's Excuse

BACK IN 1979, I TRAVELLED ACROSS MUCH OF CANADA TO RECORD interviews with some of my Muslim coreligionists, with the aim of documenting their experiences as immigrants, the challenges they faced, and their current conditions. At that time we numbered just short of 100,000, and the Council of Muslim Communities of Canada (CMCC) and the Canada Council had decided that such a survey would be worthwhile.[1] But as time passed, I lost faith in myself to ever carry out this daunting project without the aid of institutional support, which I did not have. In 2011, an arson attack destroyed all of my tape recordings, partial transcriptions and paperwork. Fortunately much had survived in cyberspace. This was enough to compel me to pick up the project again. I added more material to it and completed it, though forty years later. However, I have long been concerned about memory lapses by myself and my ageing interviewees and about possible misunderstandings between us that could have affected the accuracy of this history.

As the famous poet and astronomer Omar Khayyam (1048–1131) wrote, in the rendition of Edward FitzGerald titled the *Rubaiyat* (1809–1883):

> The Moving Finger writes; and having writ,
> Moves on; nor all thy Piety nor Wit
> Shall lure it back to cancel half a Line,
> Nor all thy Tears wash out a Word of it.

To mitigate such a final and unforgiving judgment on my book, I make a plea for indulgence, using the oriental carpet-weaver's excuse. According to a story, the weaver should make sure there is an obvious mistake in the work, because to weave a perfect carpet would be to challenge the perfection of God. In that sense, because of errors, I hope that God will be pleased with my efforts.

PART I

Introduction: The Project Since 1979

"MOSLEMS!"

That was the word that the leader of our 1950s high-school clique picked as a useful derogatory term for "losers"—any outsiders who weren't part of our little group. Growing up in Ottawa, we had never met or seen a Muslim (the preferred spelling) before. What were Muslims like? Sinister Arabs besieging gallant French Foreign Legionnaires in a desert fort? Veiled harem women? Gunga Din?

A few years on, while I was finishing a bachelor of arts degree in English literature, I encountered Islam firsthand when I met a young Indian Muslim woman, Alia Rauf. She made such an impression on me that I became a convert in 1956, married her, and went on to become an active, practising Muslim and spokesman.

In 1961, there were less than 6,000 Muslims in Canada. Today there may be up to 1.5 million of us spread out across this country. As the secretary of the Muslim Society of Toronto in the 1960s and later of the Islamic Society of Kingston, I worked with Muslim groups into the 1970s and became connected to the Council of Muslim Communities of Canada (CMCC), which was founded in 1979. It was then that, with funding from the Canada Council, I began a project to record interviews with Muslim men and women from across the country about their lives as immigrants. In its final form the project, and this book, has become a record of the lives of Canada's pioneer Muslims.

The word "pioneer," in the first place, refers to Muslims, or their antecedents, whose lives began in late nineteenth- and early twentieth-century Syria (which included present-day Lebanon) and Albania. They were the earliest Muslims in Canada. That was long before the liberalization of

Canadian immigration policy in the late 1960s. A cursory reading of the evolving immigration acts from 1869 through the 1962 Order in Council shows a gradual move to eliminate overt racism in the laws. Finally, the 1967 Order in Council established the points system, which excluded race, ethnicity, and national origin from the conditions of admissibility to Canada. Education, professional skills, work experience, and knowledge of English or French were emphasized in the interests of Canada's economic and labour requirements. Although immigration officers retained some discretion, South Asians and others were no longer limited by quotas. An ever-increasing number of Muslim immigrants began arriving, and their families expanded.[2]

To be clear, I am using the word "pioneer" in this work to mean those Muslims who had immigrated to Canada from the late nineteenth century onward through to those arriving before the critical year 1967 from a variety of countries, or were born here.

In this book, I am using "Muslim" to refer to all who self-identify with Islam to some degree to census-takers, friends, and others. The term includes those who practise the tenets of the faith with more or less rigour and sincerity, and also those who connect only culturally with other Muslims on occasions like weddings and funerals.

My only regret is that I haven't had more time or energy to add other voices, those of more women and ethnicities and that cover a wider geographical area. This long-delayed work is far from perfect—as I have admitted in my apologia. But my sense of obligation to old friends, the Muslim pioneers whose stories must be told, and the wider Canadian Muslim and non-Muslim communities, compels me to stop here, with the hope that others will carry on this work.

1. *Through the Looking Glass*

I BEGAN THIS COLLECTION OF MUSLIM LIFE STORIES WITH MY personal, rather embarrassing anecdote about "Moslems," because it typified the lack of knowledge or understanding most Canadians had about Muslims and Islam in the mid-1950s. Even now, at the end of the second decade of the twenty-first century, the larger public remains unaware of the virtues and humanity of ordinary Muslims and their religion and customs. There is suspicion, to go with ignorance, about the religious positions and political attitudes of moderate Muslims, let alone the fundamentalists. Many Canadians, including moderates, feel a well-justified revulsion for the headline-grabbing excesses of violent extremists like al-Qaeda, the Taliban, Boko Haram, and the so-called Islamic State. Unfortunately all Muslims are often tarred with the same unforgiving brush.

I encountered Islam in its moderate, most beautiful form, and that is how I became a Muslim.

I was born in Toronto in 1935 of loving parents from Edinburgh, Scotland and raised in a somewhat Scottish Presbyterian home. It wasn't until I first met Alia Rauf, daughter of Dr Mohamed Abdul Rauf, the Indian High Commissioner to Canada, at Carleton University in 1954–55 that Islam appeared in my life.

Alia was a young, beautiful and fascinating, pink-sari-clad student from India, and she was for me—and still is—the most wonderful and interesting woman in the world. Somewhere near the beginning of our story she gently pointed out that there was no use my falling in love with her because she couldn't possibly marry me, a non-Muslim. Faced with a potentially life-altering situation, I pleaded ignorance and asked for more information about her faith. As a result, our platonic relationship blossomed and led me to learn about Islam and make the *shahada*, or statement of belief, to her, and more formally to others later on: "I bear witness that there is no god but God, and I bear witness that Muhammad is the servant and messenger of God."

Alia's explanation of Islam emphasized its simplicity of beliefs and duties rather than the narrowness and prohibitions of late twentieth- and early twenty-first-century Islamic literalism. Headscarves, *sharia* courts and guilt-by-association with Middle Eastern and other *jihadi* atrocities were not on either of our radar screens. I was drawn to Islam's core belief in one single, indivisible God, propounded by a series of prophets from Abraham through Jesus and ending in the Meccan Prophet Muhammad. I also liked the demands of the Five Pillars, the diversity of the believers, and the art and architecture of their homelands.

In the spring of 1957, I graduated with a BA in English and carried on in the fall to earn a more practical one-year journalism degree, graduating in the spring of 1958. By then I had managed to win her father's very reluctant approval to marry Alia, who was to be sent away overseas, if I waited for a year and completed various practical conditions, like having a job, an apartment, and trans-Atlantic plane tickets.

After graduation, still single, I joined the Canadian Broadcasting Corporation in Toronto. There, as a keen new Muslim, I spotted the likely Muslim name of Tahir Bokhari, a sound technician listed on a TV show's credits.[3] When I met him, nervously I asked him if indeed he was a Muslim like me, and he was. Originally from Pakistan, he introduced me to his friend Rabbani Malik and his wife and in turn to an Albanian Canadian, Fatime Kerim (later Shaben), and her children, and to another Muslim convert Walter Howell and his Canadian-born wife Violet, who was of Lebanese origin. They were among the first Muslims that I met in 1950s Toronto. Others included Khaliq Khan and his soon-to-be wife, Brigitte, and Ali Tayyeb and his wife Husna (née Mulla).

In 2014 Ali and Husna Tayyeb's son Vezi wrote a wonderful "Lives Lived" essay in the *Globe and Mail* about his mother's life, soon after she died at eighty-six in Toronto. She had been born in Barabanki,

India in 1927 and earned a BA degree in English literature at Aligarh Muslim University. In 1948, soon after the Partition of the South Asian Subcontinent, she took a train to Pakistan, so that she and Ali could get married. On the way it was attacked by a Hindu mob, and she was saved by a Hindu couple who hid her under their seat. Ali was a surveyor in northern Pakistan and they settled in Rawalpindi. In 1950, Ali came to Toronto as a student on a scholarship, one of the first Pakistanis to arrive. He went on to become a professor of geography at the University of Toronto. They had three children, a daughter, Afroze, and two sons, Vezi and Shiraz. Ali Tayyeb died in 1976 at the age of fifty-four.[4]

The Tayyebs and Howells were among the little Muslim family that I had joined by the time Alia and I got married in May 1959 and settled in downtown Toronto.

Today, at least half of Canada's one million-plus multi-ethnic Muslim ummah (community) congregates in Greater Toronto. Mosques with domes and minarets appear on the skylines and plain little Islamic centres are scattered all over the city. But when I converted to Islam, there were only a few hundred Muslims in Toronto, and until the early 1960s we didn't even have a place to pray.

However, there had already existed a small Albanian Muslim Society of Toronto. Their *imam* for events like weddings and funerals was an elderly and very gentlemanly shopkeeper, Regep Assim. He, with some relatives, had started and operated High Park Sweets on Bloor Street West, just east of High Park. They began as candymakers, because as Muslim immigrants they couldn't readily get jobs. Several of them later also co-owned a restaurant and the Kingsway Club, a dance hall where Eid prayers were held at least as early as 1957.[5] These Albanian store-owners and tradesmen opened their hearts to us newcomers. Their association became the Muslim Society of Toronto in 1957.

In 1961, we opened the first Toronto mosque, at 3047 Dundas Street West, in the working-class Junction area. We called it the Islamic Centre, and it was shown in the Eid greetings card I drew at the time. It was celebrated for a while as Mosque One in the early 2010s on the Tessellate Institute's website, www.mosqueone.ca. The building was largely bought

Author's Eid card with drawing of Muslim Society of Toronto's Islamic Centre, mid-1960s.

and paid for by generous Albanians. However, we were not the first Muslims in Canada to found a mosque, this having been done previously in Edmonton in 1938, and in London, Ontario in 1957.

Our mosque was a glass-fronted storefront building, a former leatherworker's shop, but after cleaning up the front room we could say our prayers on a spread-out bedsheet or two. What distinguished our first Muslim Society of Toronto home were some "Islamic" or domed arches which I drew and which we painted on the back wall of the front section where we held our small Sunday meetings. The paint was donated by one of our more successful members, a young Bosnian chemical engineer named Hassan Karachi, who had come to Canada in 1949 and founded Niagara Protective Coatings in Niagara Falls.

Our weekly congregational prayers were held on Sunday instead of the traditional juma, or Friday, because we were all studying or working. We would hold a meeting in the front room with some sort of

Sunday school at the Islamic Centre, Toronto, with teacher Alia Hogben, mid-1960s.

appropriate talk as *khutba*, or sermon, and take up a collection, usually change or small bills, which we would hand over to Mr Assim to help cover expenses. Those praying would then adjourn to the long workroom at the back for prayers on strips of rough matting. We stood—men in front and Alia and the women just behind, by tradition—and bowed and prostrated ourselves following Mr Assim.

Alia and others taught Sunday school classes for the children in the apartment upstairs and we celebrated the two Eids, Eid al-Fitr and Eid al-Adha, with assorted foods and cheerful dubke dancing, typical of all the old Ottoman lands. It was a wonderful time of friendship and building something new in Canada.

Following the return home of Pakistani graduate student Syed Badrul Hasan, his wife Fatima, and their children, I succeeded to the post of secretary of the Muslim Society in about 1961 and held it until the late 1960s. One of the highlights of my time as secretary, while I was working for the CBC, was that I was able to meet Malcolm X before his appearance as a mystery guest on CBC's *Front Page Challenge*. I introduced myself and invited him to return, if and when possible, to speak to our little community.

Malcolm X had become disillusioned with Elijah Muhammad`s Nation of Islam. In the spring of 1964, he joined orthodox Sunni Islam. He travelled to Mecca that summer and performed the traditional hajj, or pilgrimage. Sometime in late 1964 Malcolm informed me that he was returning to Toronto to meet the Barbadian Canadian author Austin Clarke, who had just published *The Survivors of the Crossing*, and would be free to see us later that day. He duly arrived to meet Clarke and afterward I took him to our Woburn Avenue house for dinner. He then spoke at our centre, an event that went tragically unrecorded. But there remains a photograph of this tall, charming man holding a big Islamic calligraphy print, taken with a group made up of Bosnians, Pakistanis, Indians, Arabs and myself, all smiling.[6] One of my brothers-in-law, Raheem Rauf (deceased 2020), drove him in a snowstorm in his Volkswagen Beetle to the Toronto airport and he was gone.

Soon after, one dark winter night, our home was broken into before we returned from work, but nothing was taken. Our old brown leather briefcase with the week`s collection and all our society paperwork was left untouched under our coats, which were hanging in the cold front hall. I suspect that it was the work of the police, who still considered Malcolm X

Malcolm X, who spoke at the Islamic Centre, Toronto, in late 1964, with author on his right and Dr Rahman Syed, in bow tie, on Malcolm's left. Photo courtesy of Amjad R M Syed.

a threat to white authority.

Very soon after that, in late February 1965, Malcolm was killed in Harlem, by assassins from the Nation of Islam, it has been claimed, or possibly the FBI.

It is unfortunately a fact that as in many—probably all—religious groups large or small, frictions do arise over personalities, doctrine, and customs, whether in Harlem or here, and so it was with the fledgling Muslim Society of Toronto. Differences over the need for office-bearers, elections, and membership fees led some members to split off in 1969 to form the Islamic Foundation of Toronto and start their own centre. Initially it was located on Rhodes Avenue.[7]

By that year, the growing Muslim Society had bought a former Presbyterian church on Boustead Avenue and refurbished it as the Jami Mosque. We took out the church pews, covered the floor with broadloom, and gave the few stained glass windows to the departing churchgoers. Things were moving along well as the community grew into the new enlarged space. But then, as before, differences arose following the arrival of an overseas missionary group called the Tablighi Jamaat. They often stayed at the mosque for nights on end, setting up house and cooking meals. Their *amir* began preaching rather simplistic sermons and

Seitali Kerim, left, and Murray Hogben at Muslim Society of Toronto Sunday meeting. Late 1960s.

once scolded Alia and the other women for wearing nail polish. One day a member of that group reached out and pulled a curtain in front of them. As matters went from bad to worse the activist Muslim Students' Association[8] bought the mosque from the Muslim Society of Toronto, which was having trouble keeping the peace there.

During this painful process, Mr Assim, ever God's helper, died in late 1972 after falling from a tall ladder while trying to chase pigeons from a high front window of the Jami Mosque. He died equally of a broken heart, according to his cousin Seitali Kerim, because the mosque, which he was instrumental in founding, was now in the hands of a much more conservative group. I greatly regret that I never thought of recording Mr Assim's story.

Feeling alienated, Alia and I increasingly dissociated ourselves from the Muslim Society of Toronto. My doctoral studies in history in Canada and England were also taking up most of my time and energy. In 1973, my PhD thesis completed, we left for Kingston, where I became an assistant professor of history at the Royal Military College of Canada, and then at le Collège militaire royal de Saint-Jean, Quebec. When I had failed to find a permanent opening in my field by late 1979, I became a reporter and columnist for the *Kingston Whig-Standard,* and held that position until retirement in 2000.

Meanwhile, however, our Islamic activities had never stopped. Alia and I became members of the Islamic Society of Kingston, and I was made its secretary, in which capacity I became involved in the planning and construction of the Islamic Centre there. On Fridays for some years I volunteered as a Muslim chaplain at Kingston Penitentiary and other area prisons. Unfortunately, Alia and I eventually clashed with the more traditional leaders of the Islamic Society and their adherents over the issue of the women's entrance in the new mosque and where the women should stand for prayers. This led in time to our being driven out of the community. It was only years later that I began to attend Friday prayers at the Centre again, though irregularly.

In 1972 I had become involved in the founding of the Council of Muslim Communities of Canada (the CMCC). Through the CMCC I met a diversity of Canadian Muslims. In 1979 I was able to make a trip across Canada, encouraged by my friend, the late Muin Muinuddin, to meet some early pioneer Muslims and others in order to prepare a study of the early Muslim presence in Canada. In 1980, again because of my association with Muinuddin and the CMCC, I was included among the ten Canadian Muslims invited to Iran by the Islamic Republic for the commemoration of the first anniversary of the new state and the four-teen-hundredth anniversary of the birth of Islam. It was a memorable as well as a discouraging experience because our vague hopes for some posi-tive changes from within Islam were coming to nought before our eyes.

To complete my list of involvements, for more than thirty years I spent a week at a summer camp teaching Islamic arts and crafts to Muslim girls and boys as well as introducing them to canoeing. I retired from this activity in 2019. The camp, known as Camp Al-Mu-Mee-Neen (the Camp of the Believers), was an inspiration of the CMCC; after 2013 it became Camp Deen (the Camp of the Faith).

Meanwhile, Alia had become a member of the Canadian Council of Muslim Women (CCMW), another project of the CMCC. In 2002, following her retirement from the Ontario Ministry of Community and Social Services, she became the first full-time executive director of the CCMW. As such, she attended—and I joined her when we could be manage it—various Islamic women's conferences and study groups in Canada and abroad, becoming internationally known as an advocate of women's rights in Islam. She retired from her position in the fall of 2018.

For me, one of the most interesting parts of becoming a Muslim was that it opened doors to other countries and experiences. We travelled more after our three children had grown up. These various trips included to India, Britain, Europe, and Tunisia. Once we spent two weeks in Morocco, a trip that epitomized my own faith when I went through the arched doorway into the blue-tiled, eleven-hundred-year-old Karaouine Mosque in Fez. I had somehow "arrived." Since then I have always felt at home in Morocco during subsequent visits and have prayed in many of its ancient and beautiful mosques. By now I have visited mosques from Casablanca to Cairo, Istanbul to Damascus, Muscat to Delhi, Agra, and

Hyderabad. I have also visited the Al-Aqsa and Dome of the Rock in the Old City of Jerusalem.

One matter that continued to haunt me over the years was that I had not yet put together my collection of stories of the pioneer Muslims of Canada. In the following chapters I have at last fulfilled my intention. Here I should also acknowledge the inspiration of journalist-historian Barry Broadfoot (1926-2003), who wrote several notable oral histories by interviewing average Canadians about their experiences in peace and war.[9] For me, his interviews made history come alive. You will be the judge of mine.

PART II

Introduction: By the Numbers

THE PRESENCE OF MUSLIMS AND ISLAM IN THE AMERICAS IS A relatively new academic subject. The Europeans who arrived after 1492, conquering all other peoples in the New World and then adding African slaves to those under their heels, were the ones who wrote the histories. They did so, of course, with little sympathy for their subjects or regret about their treatment of them. But increasingly in the twentieth century and even more so in the twenty-first, the stories of the defeated, enslaved, and marginalized are being found under the rubble of European conquest.

The presence of Muslims, whether pre-Columbian Arab and African sailors or post-Columbian slaves in North and South America, is now being chronicled by a number of writers. Hassam Munir, a Toronto-based student of Islamic history, mentions the possible pre-Columbian arrival on the North American continent of Muslim Mandingo traders from West Africa.[10] The essay "Muslims of Early America" by Sam Haselby ponders why they were forgotten.[11] His account explores the Muslim presence before and during the Spanish conquest via slavery and brings to light the lives and contributions to America of individual Muslims. Haselby cites Sylviane A Diouf, who suggested that at one time there may have been "hundreds of thousands of Muslims in the Americas." Of the ten million African slaves sent to the Americas, some 80 percent went to the Caribbean and Brazil. Some of those slaves were Muslims.[12]

Omar ibn Said (ca 1770–1863), a West African-born Muslim and scholar, was kidnapped and crossed the Atlantic to be enslaved in North Carolina. The manuscript of his autobiography, written in Arabic in 1831 and now at the Library of Congress, has been published as *A Muslim American Slave: The Life of Omar Ibn Said*. A highway marker in Cumberland County, North Carolina now commemorates Said's life.[13] As well, there is an intriguing novel, *The Moor's Account* (2015) by the Rabat-born, prize-winning author Laila Lalami imagines the life of the black Moroccan slave Mustafa Al-Zamori, known as Estabanico, who was one of four Spaniards who survived a 1529 expedition that began in Florida and ended years later in New Mexico.[14]

Another recent study, *Muslims and the Making of America* (2016), by former Canadian and now Los Angeles-based Amir Hussain, opens with a brief history of Muslims in America before moving on to chapters on Muslim contributions in music, sports, and culture. Hussain devotes a good deal of space to the boxing legend Muhammad Ali. He argues:

> Muhammad Ali's life gave the lie to the "problem" that this book seeks to address, that Islam is viewed in a three-fold way: as new to America; as foreign to America; and as comprised of adherents who are violent, "un-American," and a threat to our nation. The reality, sketched in this book, is that Muslims have helped us to be *more* American, to be *better* Americans.[15]

Because of the mass importation of African slaves to the United States but not to Canada, the history of Muslims in Canada is quite different from that of the United States. Moreover, just as there are ten times fewer Canadians than Americans, the quantity of published sources on Islam in this country is considerably smaller.

In telling the story of my own arrival as a convert to Islam in the late 1950s, I have in effect painted myself into the much smaller canvas of the history of Muslims in Canada. According to a 1961[16] estimate, there were 5,800 Muslims living in Canada. But there had been Muslims in Canada for more than a century before that, albeit in small numbers. One of the first black Muslims in Canada, Mahommah Baquaqua, arrived in Upper Canada via the Underground Railroad in the 1850s.[17] An educated man, the West African-born Baquaqua had been enslaved and sent to Brazil, but he later escaped from a Brazilian ship moored in Manhattan harbour. In 1854 he was living in Chatham, an escaped-slave settlement in southern Ontario. It was there that (like the West African-born Muslim scholar, Omar ibn Said), he wrote and published an account of his life, *The Biography of Mohammah G Baquaqua*.[18]

The first Muslims to be officially counted in Canada were James and Agnes Love of Upper Canada (now Ontario) in the mid-nineteenth century.[19] Listed as "Mohametans" and ethnic Scots, they arrived in Canada in 1851. With the birth of their first child, also named James, in 1854, they became a family of three. In all, the Loves bore eight children, including a daughter, Elizabeth, born in 1864, and Alexander, the youngest, born in 1868. The Canadian census of 1871, just four years after Canada's Confederation, listed thirteen Muslims, including another family, John and Martha Simon and their children. The Simons, according to Munir, were emigrants from the United States, the children of East European immigrants, probably Ottoman subjects.[20]

It is important to note that while my concentration here is on the Muslims of Greater Syria (which until the collapse of the Ottoman Empire included present-day Lebanon) and their descendants, the vast majority of these Syrians who emigrated to Canada in the late nineteenth and early twentieth centuries were in fact Christians, according to emeritus University of Alberta sociology professor, Baha Abu-Laban. Even the vintage photo on the cover of his important book, *An Olive Branch on the Family Tree: The Arabs in Canada*, shows a group of presumably Syrian schoolchildren and their teachers in Canada, with a priest.

Abu-Laban states that the late nineteenth and early twentieth-century Syrians are estimated to have been 90 to 97 percent Christian. His research suggests that this was so because "Syria had the misfortune of being geographically very close to the Sublime Porte (the Ottoman Turkish court and government in Constantinople) and thus was subject to firmer control than other dominions of the Ottoman Empire." Syria's Muslims, he continues, were closer to their powerful Turkish colonial rulers than the Christians in a variety of ways and not exposed to as much Western influence and intervention. Syrian Christians also were more comfortable in a massively Christian Canada than their Muslim brethren.[21]

In the late nineteenth century, before the Great War of 1914 and the subsequent fall of empires that resulted in mass movements of peoples, Muslim populations were found largely outside North America. They lived from Morocco in the west, across North Africa and the Middle East—much of the latter in Ottoman hands—across Persia and the Russian Caucasus and Central Asia right up to British India, Burma (where my wife Alia was born), the Dutch East Indies, Indo-China, the Philippines, and even Fiji. There were also Muslims, of course, in various parts of Africa.

Baquaqua, the Loves, and the Simons were unusual. Many early Muslims in Canada were "Syrians" (really Lebanese), in addition to whom were a few Ottomans—Albanians and Bosniaks. Often they were escapees from the dreaded Ottoman army draft and poverty, hoping to make a fortune in North America and then return home. Muslims represented only a small proportion of Arab immigrants. In the pre-1939 period, about 90 percent were Christians escaping religious persecution throughout the Ottoman Empire and its successor states;[22] many of them later brought their families to join them to a more welcoming land.

According to Abu-Laban, from the early twentieth century to mid-century the Arabs as a group were largely identified as "Asians." This classification rolled them in with the Chinese, Japanese, and Indians, who were not welcome in Canada. Abu-Laban cites the Superintendent of Immigration's two Privy Council Orders of 1908 restricting the immigration of those who had not arrived directly from their homeland—that is, those who had stopped anywhere en route from Asia, for example Hong Kong. The superintendent's PC 926 added a $200 landing fee for Asians other than the already restricted Chinese and Japanese. Abu-Laban adds, "Although PC 926 was aimed at immigrants from India, British Columbia's biggest concern, the Superintendent of Immigration in Ottawa interpreted it to include Syrians, among other Asian groups. This measure effectively restricted Syrian immigration to Canada."[23]

Later restrictions, Abu-Laban says, continued to discourage Syrian Arab immigration—as the figures recorded in the census years 1911 to 1951 reflect—and immigration was very slow until they began to be considered as "Europeans" when sponsoring relatives. Finally, after the Second World War, the Canadian government yielded to growing pressure, local and international, to open its doors wider to immigrants from elsewhere than the United States and Western Europe. Further regulations designed to reduce discrimination on the basis of race or national origin were passed in 1962 and 1967. Collectively, these regulations allowed citizens of Asian and African countries, among others, to sponsor more relatives and provided nationals of these countries with more access as independent immigrants.[24] Abu-Laban also notes that on average 150 Arabs—Christians and Muslims—were admitted annually to Canada from 1946 to 1955, the number jumping to 446 from 1956 to 1960. From 1961 to 1970 the number went to an annual average of 2,884,[25] due to the change in the immigration laws.

Most Syrian-Lebanese coming to North America landed in New York, Halifax, or Montreal before spreading out. For many (invariably men), with little education or useful languages, their initial calling was as peddlers. They were set up in business by "some good soul in New York," or "a Syrian wholesaler in Montreal, who tagged each of the items in English and Arabic," or "Jewish wholesalers" and sent off with a large pack on the backroads of rural North America.[26]

On the website *Mysteries of Canada*, Bryan McKay describes how in the early twentieth century, the "Syrian peddler" was a well-known figure for many rural families who couldn't readily reach scattered stores or wait for mail-order catalogues to eventually provide what they needed. Some peddlers had unique collapsible packs that could be compacted as goods were sold. McKay writes, "The Syrian peddler had his wares with him. Small tools, cooking utensils, sewing materials, fabric, bedsheets, and dry goods were common, and sometimes foreign produce was also offered. This consisted of spices, salt and pepper, and seed. Many producers took their chances with seed for Syrian corn with varying results."[27]

These pioneers started out on foot, in snow or rain or summer heat, and once they could afford it, on a horse and cart. In the same manner as many of Canada's early Jews, some were eventually able to establish a store or other enterprise, even a bar. They travelled from the Maritimes

Mohammad (Sam) Asiff peddling goods to Alberta farmers from his horse cart in 1930s. Photo courtesy of Fisal Asiff.

and Quebec in the East to the Prairies and the developing Northwest and on to the Pacific coast. They were amazingly resilient and mobile, and generally well connected, with widely scattered relatives from their homelands.

The other major element in the very slowly growing Muslim population of Canada were the South Asians, initially on the West Coast. The first immigrants from South Asia were Punjabi men, mainly Sikhs with some Muslims, who arrived in British Columbia from British-ruled India and went into the timber industry. They began landing in Vancouver in 1903, but that very British province already had discriminatory practices against Chinese and Japanese immigration, which it now extended to Indian immigration. In 1908 the federal government responded to BC's hostility to Asian immigration and banned people not arriving by continuous journey from their countries of origin. This ban also restricted Arab immigration. Notoriously, a Japanese freighter, the *Komagata Maru*, sailed into Vancouver via Hong Kong in 1914, just before the Great War, with the 376 Indians on board hoping to settle in Canada. They were not allowed to land and after two months sailed back to India.

Canada's provincial and federal governments began very gradually to lift their restrictions on South Asians after Indian independence in 1947 and the resulting division of "India" into India and Pakistan. (Pakistan was later split into present-day Pakistan and Bangladesh.) However, only 150 Indians, 100 Pakistanis and 50 Sri Lankans were allowed into Canada each year. Not all of them, of course, were Muslims. The restrictions on Muslim Arabs were not eased until the lifting of the earlier discriminatory, "continuous journey" rule in the 1960s. Unlike the original Syrian Lebanese pioneers, two-thirds of the South Asians arriving from the late 1960s on, including Muslims, were educated or professionals.[28]

Officially at least, the Muslim presence in Canada at the start of the twentieth century numbered only in the double digits. Economist and statistician Daood Hamdani's research into census records found that in 1901 there were only forty-seven Muslims spread across this vast land. It is possible, of course, that these figures underrepresent the reality, as so many of these Muslims were on the open roads as peddlers or living in isolated trading posts in the North—or were justly nervous about being singled out as Ottoman Turks. By the 1911 census, the figure had shot up to 797, yet by 1921 the number had fallen back to 478. Many of these citizens of the former Ottoman Empire, against which Canada and the British Empire had been at war, may have returned to their homelands or possibly were deported.

During the War, Muslims were regarded with suspicion, as were Ukrainians and other citizens of the former Austro-Hungarian and German empires, and many of them were interned. The historian Hassam Munir has noted that a large group of "Turks" were arrested in Brantford as "enemy aliens" in 1914. Shipped first to Kingston, they were then sent north to a work camp. According to Bill Darfler, a Brantford researcher, a Brantford businessman who had been selling plows in Constantinople (now Istanbul) had recruited a few hundred Armenian Christians and Turks (possibly Kurds) to work in the factories of the bustling Ontario town. In November 1914, they were all rounded up, entrained to Fort Henry in Kingston, and sent to Kapuskasing. The total number of interned "Turks" here was 205, according to the *Canadian Encyclopedia*. There is apparently no record of where they went after the war.[29]

On November 11, 2017, the Muslim chaplain at the Royal Military College of Canada, Capt. Ryan Carter, held memorial services for the Muslims who had died in Canada's wars. They included the only known Canadian Muslim casualty of the First World War, from the Battle of Hill 70. He was Pte Hasan Amat, twenty-three, from Western Ontario, originally from Singapore and one of the twenty-two Muslims who served.[30]

With the end of the First World War, Canada's doors again opened to immigrants, until the job shortages of the Great Depression of 1929 closed them once more. In the census of 1931, only 645 Muslims were recorded. In 1931 the Canadian census ceased listing Muslims as a group, perhaps because of the relative smallness of the numbers. Muslims were not separately coded again until 1981, following the request of the Council of Muslim Communities of Canada.

In the post-1960 years, after the lifting of immigration barriers, the more readily accessed postwar world gave thousands of Muslims from everywhere the opportunity to spread their wings in the West, including Canada. Hamdani estimates that the number of Muslims had risen to 1,800 in 1951, to 5,800 in 1961, and to 33,430 in 1971.[31] In 1981 the Muslim population had reached 98,165 and included Canadian-born Muslims. In 1991 the number had jumped to 253,265, and in 2001 to 579,640. The Muslims who were now coming to Canada were often from the educated elites of their struggling homelands.

Despite the uncertain accuracy of the voluntary National Household Survey of 2011, it indicated that Muslims then numbered 1,053,945. Canadian-born Muslims represented 28 percent of that total. The rising numbers of immigrants include refugees from civil wars in Syria, Iraq, and Afghanistan, plus those fleeing hardships in northern Africa.

Population of Muslims in Canada[32]	
1854	3
1871	13
1901	47
1911	797
1921	478
1931	645
1951	1,800
1961	5,800
1971	33,430
1981	98,165
1991	253,260
2001	579,640
2011	1,053,945

2. Vancouver: Pacific Coast Arrivals

IN 1979, I VISITED RIAZAT ALI KHAN AND HIS FATHER AMANAT ALI Khan, who was then ninety-five years old, in Vancouver. As we sat there, Riazat undertook to translate from Punjabi his father's recollections of his early years on the West Coast, with explanations when necessary.

Amanat Ali Khan came from the village of Halwara, district of Ludhiana in Punjab, India, in 1912. He came because he had heard that Canada and America were good countries and there was a lot of money to be made there. He had relatives who had come before him so he came and joined them. Most of his relatives had come during the years 1906, 1907, and 1908 but the history of our people started around 1904 in this country when the immigrants started to arrive.

Immigration to Vancouver had stopped around July 1908, but until then people in large numbers had come from our village. It was cut off in 1908 and people couldn't land here anymore. From 1908 to 1910 they went in great numbers to San Francisco because they couldn't land here. [In those days] the Sikhs were in greater numbers than the Muslims in Vancouver as well as in San Francisco, but among the Sikhs, Hindus, and Muslims no one had as many people as from our village, which was about 100 percent Muslim. The percentage of Sikhs [among the South Asians coming into Canada] was about 58, the Hindus were 2 percent and the Muslims 40 percent. The reason for this disparity in percentages was that the majority of the immigrants came from East Punjab where Sikhs and Muslims were predominant in agriculture and the Hindus were mainly shopkeepers. The reason the Sikh and Muslim farmers came was that they were hardworking people . . . and they knew that with hard work they could make a lot of money in America.

[Soon] immigration was cut off in San Francisco as well, so by the time he [my father] came [in 1912] they landed in Seattle, which was still open to our people. The ships came from Manila straight to Seattle and anyone who was coming in those days had to have a six-month stay in Manila in the Philippines to qualify to come to the USA; that immigration [route] stayed open 'til approximately 1913 when immigration to the West Coast stopped . . .

Some immigrants who had gone back to India for a visit came back in 1913 to Vancouver together with some new ones around November 1913 . . . the *Komagata Maru* came in early 1914. My dad was [in the Vancouver area] working at Fraser Mills—which is known as Crown Zellerbach of Canada in Coquitlam, right on the banks of the Fraser River. That was the largest sawmill of that time and that's where he was working and living in the tents.

The British and the white people [in Vancouver] were against the *Komagata Maru* or any Indians being sent here, so they wanted that ship sent back or even everybody killed . . . [My father] thinks the times were very, very wrong [for immigration]. The First World War had already started and the mills were shutting down and jobs were slowing down, so the white people here were against any new immigrants coming. If the conditions hadn't been that bad perhaps the *Komagata Maru* may have stayed and the people allowed to land, but the public outcry was too much.

[As for those Indian workers already in British Columbia], they were a fairly big majority in the mills and they were well liked and had no problem. That's why if it was up to the sawmill people they could have taken [more Indians], it didn't matter how many more.

In Fraser Mills there were about twenty-five Muslims at that time and they prayed regularly. There was a man named Rehmat Ali from the village of Andloo in district Ludhiana who used to lead the prayers at that time. They used to pray five times a day in congregation. They had a place especially reserved—one big room—for prayers . . .

[My father] says that at the same time the Sikhs had established a *gurdwara* [temple] here on Second Avenue in Vancouver, but the Muslims—it didn't seem they were going to live here that long. They wanted to go back to India. During the war in 1914, my dad and a lot of his friends crossed the border and went to California because America was not at war, whereas Canada was at war because of the British government, and so they had better job opportunities [in the States] . . .

Most of them got into business for themselves, like my dad, [who] was a grape farmer himself in northern California. But a lot of people lost money later in the 1920s, whatever money they had made. The Depression came in 1929 and before that there was a market slow-down . . . Some who had made some money went back [home], and others stayed, and by the time things picked up, in the Second World War it was survival of the fittest. Those who had kept any land became multi- multi-millionaires . . . Sacramento cemetery has a large section of Muslim people and a lot of them were from our village, Halwara, and from all over the Punjab . . .

They all came as single men . . . a few went back [to India] a few years after they were here and brought wives and their families . . . People [Muslims] in California, they married Mexican women and had children, and some married American women (very few of them), and they are still settled in California.

Riazat Ali Khan, the son, also conveyed his own memories of the difficulties of living an active Muslim life, involving the education of children and mixed marriages. He said some Muslims had lost touch with their religion, but others had not. Some had gone to India or Pakistan and arranged marriages, just as he and his son had. He joked, "As they say in the Middle East, 'If you're not married to a cousin there must be something wrong with you.'" He, like his father before him, was president of the local Pakistan-Canada Association. He said that currently there were about five hundred Muslims in the greater Vancouver area, and the turning point in the increase of the Muslim population had been the arrival of Fijian Muslims.

During 1979-80 I had interviewed the Fijian president of the British Columbia Muslim Association, Muntaz Ali of Vancouver, a wonderful, quiet man. Unfortunately, the taped interviews with him and his friend

Usman Ali did not survive the arson attack on our house. However, in November 2017, I interviewed Usman Ali again. What is of particular interest is his enduring dynamism and his frankness about the difficulties Muslims often have in keeping their initial communities together before they shake down into comfortable but separate groups.

> I was born in 1936 in Ba, Fiji. I came from a big family, nine boys and two girls, on a sugarcane farm. It was not a huge farm because you had to have the [machines] to farm it. We were of Indian background. My father, Mahbub, came to Fiji in 1913 from around the Lucknow area, and my mother, Sakuran, was born in Fiji. My father came as an indentured labourer [from British India]. That's how the Muslims came to Fiji, as indentured labourers. They came from the late 1800s to the 1920s or so, just like they went to the West Indies and Guyana and all those places. So they went to Fiji because the British Australian company could not find people to work on the sugarcane farms and they found that the Indians were the best farmers. They tried the Chinese and every other kind of islander.
>
> I went to a Methodist school, but I could not finish my high school because of the financial situation of the family, and my brother was going to Australia for his university education at the time because there was no university in Fiji. He had to go to Melbourne for his studies. I was fourth in line so I had to leave and find a job outside the farm. I became an apprentice car mechanic, and then a truck mechanic—so I had experience in farming, as a mechanic, and my spare time was given to the Muslim community who were building the mosque.
>
> I came to Canada because it so happened I had a friend who was working for the British High Commission in Suva, Fiji, and he asked me to come over and I went to see him and he said, "I have an application for you to go to Canada. Do you want to go to Canada?"
>
> I said, "No, I am going to England to attend Bolton College."
>
> He asked, "When is that?" and I said, "Next year," and he said, "Forget it. I'll fill out this application and you'll sign it . . . "
>
> The process took me three months and I got the visa in March of 1964. I said, "Hey man, I still have to work on this mosque," because we were volunteers.

My eldest brother, Ahmed Ali, was the secretary of the organization, so I had to do half of his work because he was a school teacher and a farmer . . . you could not survive on one paycheque. The community depended on us young fellows to do something, so I decided to stay back until June 1964.

Usman Ali delayed his passage until work on the mosque was finished, and he finally arrived by ship in Canada on September 6, 1964. It was the last day before his visa would expire, a Sunday. He was twenty-eight years old. Arriving at the Vancouver immigration office—as he recalled it,

> The immigration officer, knowing me as a farmer from my application, had planned it out, saying, "Since this is Sunday evening, go tomorrow to so-and-so office in New Westminster and they will guide you about how to get to the farm."
>
> Realizing by some correspondence that I [could not farm in Canada] because I didn't know if it was cattle farming or something else, I said, "I am going to change my profession as I still have my mechanic's skills."
>
> So this man said, "You're not going there tomorrow."
>
> I said, "Why?"
>
> He said, "Because we knew you were coming to Canada today, we gave everybody a holiday tomorrow!" I was stunned . . . Then he said, "No, my friend, tomorrow is Labour Day, a holiday, so you can have a rest and then you can go on Tuesday to the office." So this was how I was greeted in Canada, with a day off!
>
> That evening I didn't ask anybody—I had a few friends here— where the mosque was . . . and I was tired. But next day, because it was a holiday, we got together and I said, "Let's go see the mosque."
>
> They looked at me with smiling faces and said, "What did you expect here? Did you expect something like you've been accustomed to all this time?"
>
> I asked, "Isn't there a mosque here?"
>
> They said, "You go and find it." Then they told me there was nothing here, not a community, except for some Turkish people and some Yugoslavians and a few Pakistanis and us five or six Fijians, that's it.

So I said, "What are we going to do here?"

They said, "It's a free country. You can do whatever you want."

I asked, "What do you mean by a free country? I came from a free country."

Everybody has the same idea. It's a free country and you can go and drink or you can go to the night club or do whatever you want. So I said to them, "This is not the way we should live, because we are Muslims and we have to do something."

They said, "There is nobody here. The people have been here for ten or twelve years and they have not done anything, so how are you going to do it?"

I said, "It's not me alone. We have to do it together."

Usman Ali recalled that they had no money and lived in rooming houses in Vancouver's west end, now downtown. They couldn't buy or rent in the area, and they started looking for a place elsewhere to say their prayers.

One day, while I was looking for a job, I came to a bus stop. It was raining and a gentleman came to me with an umbrella and gave me some shelter, so I said thank you. He asked me if I was new in town, and I said yes. Where from? I said, from Fiji. So he said, "You must be a Christian." I said, "No, I am a Muslim." He said "What is that?" I looked at him and I was stunned, shocked, that a person in Canada didn't know who Muslims are. At the same time, the bus arrived and we were boarding, and we went our different ways.

Afterwards, when I came back, I went to the library to see if I could find something on Islam. I went to the religion section and there were books on Christianity, and a few on Judaism, and one on Hinduism, but nothing on any other religion. So I asked the librarian if there were any books on Islam. He said, "I never heard of that religion." So where do you go? Nobody knows Islam, no Muslims here, and those who are here are not interested, so where do you go? That was the question.

He found a job as a mechanic at a gas station. One day a Pakistani immigrant, Mohammed Zainul Khan, came to him. Khan told him that the Pakistan-Canada Cultural Association had bought a place in Vancouver that could be used for Muslim congregational prayers.

The building, at 655 West 8th Avenue, was an old and long-neglected former Ukrainian church, which Usman Ali said was dirty and full of junk. They decided to clean it up and a wonderful Turkish woman, Rabia Dukumaci, and her husband, Mehmet, joined them. The couple were in janitorial work. A week later, Enver Imamovic, a Bosnian, and Gamil Naguib, an Egyptian, augmented their small group. By late December the space was ready to be used. There was a wood stove which had to be kept burning all the time, but little heat was released because the ducts were partially blocked.

On December 26 or 27, 1964 the group invited local Muslims to form a committee. Eleven people turned up. They settled on the name The Islamic Centre of Vancouver for the place. A truly multicultural group of Muslims became the working committee. The chair was Mohammed Zainul Khan; Ann Khan, a Canadian convert married to a West Indian pharmacist, was the vice-chair; Gamil Naguib was secretary; Usman Ali was assistant secretary; and Enver Imamovic was the treasurer. Usman Ali recalled that the newly minted centre's executive decided their role

Fiji-born Usman Ali, founding secretary of the BC Muslim Association, 1964. Photo courtesy of Usman Ali.

was to clean up the building, unite the Muslims, organize prayers, set up Sunday school classes for the children, upgrade the wood-burning system to gas, and prepare for the coming Ramadan.

Another Bosnian couple, Bahriya and Fateema Hamzagic, took over the organization of the centre's social activities. Maintenance was in the hands of Mehmet and Rabia Dukumaci. Ann Khan and M Z Khan's wife, Naseem Khan were the Sunday school teachers. Usman Ali would also work on the school program.

Usman Ali was also in charge of the Ramadan commemoration, including the first taraweeh prayers on record. The first Ramadan was greeted on January 3, 1965. However, because of the poor heating in the building, the nighttime *isha* prayers and the late-night taraweeh prayers had to be cancelled because people wouldn't attend on the cold January nights.

The more "Canadianized" Pakistani community was holding a number of holiday-season events in the building, and that limited the Islamic Centre's activities. However, once the holiday season was over, the Muslim group was able to hold the Eid al-Fitr prayers that marked the end of Ramadan, on February 2, 1965. Usman Ali said that the first juma, or Friday congregational prayer, was held on Good Friday, April 1, 1965.

However, it was not to be clear sailing thereafter, and the Islamic Centre dissolved:

> In the summer of 1965 we were trying to do a lot of things [which included improving the heating] to make people happy to come to this place. We decided to have another meeting to decide how to move forward in a better organized way.
>
> [But] there was a problem [brought up] . . . by some Pakistani brothers . . . regarding the qiblah [or direction to Mecca]. The most important thing we were doing was to find the proper direction from Mecca to Vancouver. They [the Pakistani group] wanted to pray the way they prayed back home . . . There is nothing wrong [with praying in the wrong direction] when you don't know, but when you try to do something right, they started stopping it . . . If you were in Pakistan right now and direct yourself towards Mecca you are facing

southwest, so that's how they wanted to pray here. Another group came along and using a flat map of the world they were going southeast [from Vancouver].

We tried to talk to them and said let's get together and find the proper direction. We went to the University of British Columbia as well but nobody there cared about these things because we were Muslims, and they were not Muslims . . . Finally at the library I saw a globe and I took a string and found that the shortest route [from Vancouver to Mecca] was through the north. Although we were not 100 percent sure, we were very close, so we started praying in the north-northeast direction, and then the trouble started.

They [the Pakistani group] knew we had put in the heating system and everything else without them paying for it. We had collected funds from other people to support this project. It was November and so we decided we should tell people about our accomplishment and see what they wanted to do . . . We could not go on like this . . . But we didn't have anything—the building did not belong to us and we were not a registered organization. We were just volunteers. It was Sunday, November 20, 1965. It was a very important meeting. The time was 1:30 PM . . .

There were about twenty of us there and some people who opposed us were very loud, showing off their authority, saying, "Who are you?" . . . So before the agenda was presented there were lots of questions: Who authorized this meeting in the Pakistan-Canada Cultural Association building? In fact, there was no brotherly feeling. It was so loud, voices could be heard maybe thirty feet away on the street. M Z Khan wanted to say something but he was shouted down . . . Even our treasurer and secretary were abused and told, "You are white Muslims, white Muslims!" Where they got this from I don't know. "I came from Pakistan; I came from here; I came from there," these kinds of words. Shouting. The meeting ended before it started, and that was the end of the Islamic Centre of Vancouver. Everyone walked away . . . except M Z Khan and myself. We looked at ourselves and said that whatever we did, we didn't want our efforts to go to waste, so we should go on with the good things we had. He took me to his house for a cup of tea and I said, "What do we do?" And we agreed we'd come back next

Sunday and see what we could do. Another Ramadan was coming
and what could we do about it?

The Christmas activities of the others set a deadline for the taraweeh
prayers of Ramadan. In the end, Usman Ali and two others held these
late-night prayers and went on to organize a location for their Eid al-Fitr
prayers on January 3, 1966.

After some canvassing, they were given use of a space at the
International House at the University of British Columbia for free. In
May, they started a separate Muslim group. Muntaz Ali had arrived by
then from Fiji; Hamim Harris from South Africa and Farouk Elesseily
from Egypt had joined them, so on July 1 (Dominion Day), with a few
others they organized a Friday prayer and celebration with a light lunch.
This was followed by another event the next day to mark the birthday of
the Prophet Muhammad. Some twenty-eight people attended, and after
a discussion, nine of them formed an ad hoc committee to start what
became the BC Muslim Association. They put together a constitution
and registered the first Muslim organization in the province on November
17, 1966. They still faced opposition and still used the Pakistani building,
because they had no money for a building of their own.

Finally in 1973, the BC Muslim Association bought 4.78 acres of land
in Richmond, at 12300 Blundell Rd, in an agricultural land reserve. They
had to face a lot of hurdles before they could build a mosque. Public
opinion in Richmond deemed them to be a "cult." It was ten years later,
with some support[33] that they finally managed to build the mosque.

> We were very fortunate from the very beginning that we did not
> have a dominant nationality or ethnicity or cultural group. We were
> just Muslims. As I have said, the founding members were from dif-
> ferent countries. It remained that way, and it is still that way today.
> The statement we made that day when the constitution was signed
> said, "For the grace of Allah build the foundation strong and flex-
> ible enough to accommodate the diverse community." Now the BC
> Muslim Association has ten mosques across British Columbia, one
> in Richmond, one in Vancouver, one in Burnaby, two in Surrey, one

in Prince George, one in Victoria, one in Nanaimo, one in Kelowna, one in Abbotsford, and three centres in Chilliwack and smaller places . . . [34]

This is where we are: Muslims from Africa, the Middle East, Europe, Russia, Asia, islanders from the Indian Ocean, West Indies, [and] South Pacific, and locals became brothers and sisters under one banner. Our imams are from different places and so forth. We live like Muslims, and so my daughter is married to an Iranian and my wife's nephew is married to an Afghani girl, and this is how we want the organization to grow. This has been the aim and objective of the Muslims, from the very first day of the BC Muslim Association. Communities [from various places] come in as branches of BCMA and we help them. The new mosques in Prince George, Victoria, and Kelowna [are examples]. We helped them financially, and we go and visit them . . . and when we need their help they help us. This is how the community is. As a CBC reporter once said, "You want to see a bouquet of flowers? Go to Richmond mosque."

Usman Ali married Qamrul Nisa in 1970. They have three children, Farhanah, Razanah, and Zafirah, and one grandchild.

3. Edmonton: The First Mosque

THE FAMOUS EXHORTATION "GO WEST, YOUNG MAN, AND GROW UP with the country" seems to have rung not only in American ears but in those of Arab immigrants from far-off Greater Syria—particularly in the Bekaa Valley, part of present-day Lebanon. Many of these young men, both Muslims and Christians, crossed the Atlantic in the late nineteenth and early twentieth centuries, seeking safety from being drafted into the notoriously severe Ottoman Army and lured by the possibility of riches in the New World. These young men usually came alone, expecting to return home wealthy and marry. Unlike their Christian compatriots, Muslims had no community on this continent that might have welcomed them. It mattered little to the Syrians where they went, as long as it was away from their homeland. The same would hold true in the twentieth-first century, with the important difference that those who left later were not young male entrepreneurs but refugee families.

This story of Muslim Arab immigration differs in several ways from those of the Punjabi and later Fijian immigrants to Vancouver described in the previous chapter. First, the Syrian men landed in North America earlier, starting in the late 1890s. Some of them made their way to Alberta, sometimes via the United States, and took to farming or travelled the roads as peddlers, eventually clustering in the northern city of Edmonton. Some of them headed even further north to set up fur-trading posts before branching out into a wide variety of enterprises.

The achievements of Arab Muslim pioneers in the Canadian West have been described by Richard Asmet Awid of Edmonton in his books *Muslims in Canada: A Century of Achievement* (1999), *Through the Eyes of the Son: A Factual History about Canadian Arabs* (2001), and *Canada's First Mosque:*

Hilwie Jomha Hamdon and Ali Hamdon, possibly soon after their marriage in 1923. Photo courtesy of Richard Asmet Awid.

The Al Rashid (2010). Earle Waugh has published a more thorough study, *Al Rashid Mosque: Building Canadian Muslim Communities* (2018).[35]

Among the most dynamic of the early Muslim pioneers in Alberta was a woman, Hilwie Jomha Hamdon,[36] of Edmonton, who recalled her life for me in 1979:

> I was born in Lala, Lebanon [in 1905].[37] When I was seventeen years old, I married Ali Hamdon[38] and emigrated to Fort Chipewyan in northern Canada [on the border of the Northwest Territories and Alberta, about 500 miles north of Edmonton]. My husband owned a trading post there and four trader boats. He also had a general store and traded mostly with the Indians. They gave him the furs and he gave them groceries and whatever else they needed.
>
> My husband Ali left for Canada when he was seventeen years old, and stayed in Canada for 22 years before returning back to Lebanon in 1922. With my father's permission, we were married that year and left together for Canada in 1923 to begin our lives together there. I was seventeen at the time and Ali was forty-three.

At this time, my brother [Ahmed Jomha] had a trading post at Fort Norman, and my brother-in-law [Jim Darwish] had a store and a trading post. My husband had opened a different store in Stony Rapids which he had someone run for him. My father's cousin also had a post in Black Bay. These were all located in the North. My husband had two Métis clerks at his store who served as his Cree interpreters, and through the two clerks Ali learned to speak Cree.

For the first two years that I was in Fort Chipewyan, I did nothing but cry. I had one daughter, Evelyn, and another, Lavida born one year later. Evelyn was born with a club foot and I needed to get help for her. So Ali, Evelyn, Lavida and I went by dog sled from Fort Chipewyan to Fort McMurray. My husband had two dog sleds with two teams of huskies to pull them, along with two Métis drivers. It took us seven days to travel the 200 miles to Fort Mac. During the trip we sometimes slept in the snow on spruce bows, sometimes in Indian shacks, and I slept in a sleeping bag with my babies beside me. I was pregnant with my third child at the time and a nun from the Catholic Convent told me I could lose my baby, but I said that if it was God's will it would be, but I must do my duty for this child [Evelyn] and I would accept the will of Allah. At that time my second child Lavida was a year old and on the trip with us. I had to hold her in my arms covered in furs to keep her warm during the cold days and nights. After arriving safely in Fort McMurray, we boarded a train to Edmonton to get Evelyn the help she needed.

The mail was very hard to get in Fort Chip because it was so isolated back then. In the fall all of the supplies we needed for the winter were brought to us by train from Edmonton to Fort Mac, and then by steamer up the Athabasca River to Fort Chip. We never saw anyone from the time things froze up in the winter until spring arrived. The mail was brought to us by horse and sleigh. During my first winter in Fort Chip, the locals told me it was safe to walk on the lake, that even the horses could walk on it. I thought they were joking. The first time they took me onto the lake I was very frightened and thought we would sink at any moment. We had a thermometer above the store and one morning when we woke up it was sixty-nine degrees below zero [Fahrenheit]. There was another day after that when it got so cold our thermometer broke.

I felt quite alone for the first couple of years I was in Fort Chip. There was no doctor, no hospital, and I did not know what to do for my daughter Evelyn's club foot. I treated it and massaged it three times a day. The nuns from the nearby Catholic Convent helped me look after my babies as they were born, and they taught me to speak English and about how to live in the North. They were very good to me and I was lucky to have them. Times were still tough but I was one of the lucky ones. I always had a maid and help, and I needed it as I had all six of my children in Fort Chip, the first five within a six year period.

Eventually I grew more comfortable in Fort Chip and I had a wonderful time and I enjoyed our life there. I liked the Indians and they liked me. We visited some of them as I did not see them in the store often. I remember once in my first year there, my husband said to me, "I'm going to ask the Indian chief for supper." I said to him, "What am I supposed to cook?" He said, "Whatever you like. They like meat." So I remember when I went out, he [the chief] was in front of the store—the store wasn't too far from the house—and he looked at me and said to my husband in Cree (as he didn't speak English), "No, I'm not coming for supper." My husband said "Why?" He said, "I think your wife is pretty cranky." My husband said "Why?" and he said "She has very narrow eyebrows, and that means among the Indians that you're not good-natured." But my husband assured them I was very good-natured and he should come. He did, and we became very good friends.

I learned a few Indian words—not too much, because I was so busy. This daughter [she points to Evelyn, who was present] was five when my fifth baby was born, that is five babies in six years. I was very busy with the children and house, and my husband had three men working for him who used to eat lunch and supper with us. Two of the men were Métis and one was the bookkeeper, Mr Rosiceau, who was French.

There was a man named Peter Baker who they called the "Arctic Arab." His Arab name was Ahmed Farah.[39] He was quite a character. He lived like an Indian and was very popular with them. He ran for Member of Parliament in Fort Resolute and won because all the Indians voted for him. He was called a Territorial councillor and represented the North West Territories in Ottawa. This would be about ten years ago [1964–67].[40] He is a Shi'a and comes from a town called Lebatia in South Lebanon.

I stayed in Fort Chip until the children became a little bit older— you know about six—and then my husband said I should go to Edmonton and start them in school. We came here but unfortunately he had a fire back up North and really needed me so I went back with the kids.[41] By that time we had a doctor, Dr Lewis, who had a family of four children (I would later name our sixth child Lewis, after Dr Lewis), a policeman with a family of two children, and Mr Crawley, the minister, who was the school teacher. When I went back North from Edmonton I took a private teacher by the name of Mary Hunter back with me. She stayed for about a year or so, and then an unfortunate thing happened in her life there and she ended up leaving Fort Chip.

After that we came back home [to Edmonton], but I didn't like to stay here while my husband was up North, so I said I wanted to go back up North and take a young teacher named Helen Bathead with us. The doctor and my husband agreed that we would both pay her, but she didn't stay very long because she didn't get along well with the local people and she didn't like the country as there was really nothing for young people to do.

I was always very strict about my religion. There was a Catholic mission in Fort Chip and one of the priests said it was a shame that I should go to the fire [of hell] because I wasn't Catholic and he still liked me so much, [but] he said it was too late for my husband! I asked him if the key to heaven was in the Catholics' hands, and he said to me it was. I told him I was very sorry, and I was brought up in a very strong religious family and I thought heaven was open to everyone who is good, no matter what religion they are. I could never accept any religion except Islam. The other priest at the mission told me to never mind—he liked me as I was. [He said] I was a beautiful person and I would go to heaven in spite of everything.

I was in Canada for five years before I saw a Muslim woman,

[although] I met a lot of Christian women. I heard of a Muslim lady, Mrs Haidar, who owned a restaurant. I belonged to several clubs and when the [Second World] War broke out, we decided we should form an organization to work for the Red Cross alone, although we still worked for the mosque . . .

It was a wonderful life but very lonely. I was young when I had my children, and I enjoyed them and played with them. I loved my children and my husband. Early on my husband built a schooner which he called *Evelyn of the Lake* after our first daughter. It was very sturdy and would carry most anything. We travelled in it up the river from Fort Chip to my husband's other store in Stony Rapids . . . To go into the North Country, as it was then called, people had to have a pioneer spirit.

During our time in Fort Chip, my husband and I came to Edmonton every summer and in 1937 as I already mentioned my husband said to me, "You've got to take the children to school . . . " My husband said the school there [in Chipewyan] wasn't good enough, so we came here [to Edmonton]. In 1937 there were twenty-two Arab[42] people here who organized a group and got together and held a meeting to discuss building a mosque.

Al Rashid Mosque in Edmonton, Canada's first, built in 1938.
Photo courtesy of Noor Al-Henedy.

While she did not explain further (the details are thoroughly covered in Waugh's *Al Rashid Mosque*), what was called the Arabian Muslim Association, founded in 1934, was the fledgling organization that undertook the famous mosque-building enterprise.[43]

> Sheikh Najib had moved there [to Edmonton] from Winnipeg because there wasn't much Islam [there] and he wanted to build a mosque, but he was alone. I attended the meeting, and three [people] wanted a mosque and the rest wanted a hall. I told them if it was a hall they wanted, they could use my house any time for parties—our home was always open. Our president said we were lost but I told him, "No, God is with us." I spoke up and told them I was the youngest there and I was so hungry to hear the words of Allah. I told them, "We have got to know our religion ourselves, to believe in it and know it, and we have got to teach our children."
>
> The motion [to build a mosque] was carried and passed the second time. The president was not convinced the mosque would be built, but I told him that if God wanted us to build the mosque, He would give us a helping hand. I saw the mayor [John Fry] about purchasing a lot for the mosque. There were two lots; one was in a poor district and the other one was $1,110, and all we had in our organization was $50.

Left, some of Al Rashid's founding members, ca 1938; and right, three of them, Kasim Mohamed Awid, Ahmed Ali Awid, aka Ahmed or Ed Awid, and Saaid Amerey. Photo courtesy of Richard Awid.

I convinced the mayor to give us a lot free and told him he would be the first mayor to open a Muslim mosque in North America.[44]

I travelled all over Alberta and Saskatchewan collecting money, and in two years we had our mosque paid in full. Before the mosque was to open, we needed to find someone who could explain Islam. We asked a friend of ours, Espy Shaker, the mayor of Hanna, a Christian and a well-educated man, if we could borrow him as a Muslim for one night. He laughed heartily.

Two days before the mosque was to open, Abdullah Yusuf Ali[45] came, at government expense, to lecture at the University [of Alberta]. I was sent to the hotel where he was staying, with our secretary, Mohammad (Sam) Asiff,[46] to invite him to open the mosque, and he welcomed the chance to open the only Muslim mosque in North America. We asked him if the government would allow him to do so, and he said that no power on earth would stop him from doing this . . .

According to Hilwie's youngest child, Lewis Hamdon, his mother had been "the undisputed leader" of the group, and was envied a bit by the other Lebanese wives because she was able to tell their husbands what to do to facilitate the mosque project, and they did it. Hilwie picked three men and got them to drive her all over the West to raise money for the mosque. She was also involved in other Edmonton organizations. As she said, "I belonged to several clubs and when the [Second World] War broke out, we decided we should form an organization to work for the Red Cross, although we still worked for the mosque."

Lewis Hamdon said his mother was a member of the Order of the Eastern Star, a women's organization attached to the Freemasons, his father being a Mason. She also knew and mixed with "all the influential people in Edmonton." She had arrived in Canada without English but learned to read and write the language of her adopted country.

Hilwie and Ali Hamdon welcomed newly arrived Lebanese relatives and immigrants into their home until they got their feet on the ground and found jobs. The Hamdons always had large houses and "entertained a lot and had a large family." Hilwie also became an accomplished bridge player, Lewis added.

But Hilwie's greatest interest remained the Al Rashid Mosque and Islam—"to her last breath," Lewis said. She became "the face of the Lebanese community in Edmonton," but nothing that she did could have been done without her husband, Ali: "If he wasn't who he was, we would not have had a mosque in those days . . . There's no mosque, no story, without him. He loved and supported her and let her be herself'".

Hilwie Hamdon died in December 1988.

According to Lewis, his father, Ali Hamdon, was born in 1884 in Lala and came to Canada in 1901 when he was seventeen.[47] After making his fortune, he returned to Lebanon in 1922 to find a bride. Hilwie and Ali were married and came back together to "Fort Chip" in 1923. Ali became "extremely successful": his first business with his friend Sine Alley was called Hamdon and Alley Ltd, and it did very well until it was unfortunately destroyed by fire in the 1930s. They rebuilt it, and Ali's son Moneer joined the business in the early 1940s, and shortly thereafter Ali left the store and returned to Edmonton.

Ali then invested in a new importing business called Shaben & King. The company was later renamed Shaben & Hamdon. Ali Hamdon died in 1963, but by then the business was owned evenly by Ed Shaben, and Ali's three sons Moneer, Sidney and Lewis Hamdon. Eventually, Shaben & Hamdon grew to become the largest wholesale toy business in Canada when the Hamdon boys sold out in 1981.

By the late 1980s the Al Rashid Mosque had become too small for the Muslim community, and the development of Edmonton meant that the mosque faced demolition. Dr Lila Fahlman, founder of the Canadian Council of Muslim Women, encouraged the Edmonton chapter to take the lead in fundraising to save the original 1938 building. They raised $75,000 and it was dismantled and carefully reconstructed at the Fort Edmonton Park as part of an historic site. Involved in the group were Karen and Evelyn Hamdon, granddaughters of Hilwie Hamdon, and Mahmuda Ali, granddaughter of Rikia (Mary) Saddy,[48] one of Hilwie's friends, and Soraya Zaki Hafez, then president of CCMW's Edmonton chapter. Also active in this effort was Razia Jaffer, who later became president of the CCMW. It opened on May 28, 1992.

Recent Updates—since the recording of the interviews with Hilwie Hamdon and later her son Lewis, there have been two events that have further reinforced the legacy and importance of Hilwie's life here in Canada:

In 2018, the Edmonton Public School Board built a state of the art K-9 school in the Hudson neighbourhood of Edmonton and named it the Hilwie Hamdon School. The school contains many photos, art work and memorabilia dedicated to Hilwie's life in Canada, and is a tribute to her belief in a proper education for all children. The school's mascot and team name is the "Huskies" which is a fitting symbol of Hilwie and Ali's life in the North.

Also in 2018, Hilwie was nominated by the Federal Government's nominating committee to be featured on Canada's new $100 bill as a Canadian Woman of History who contributed significantly to her community, culture, and country.

One of my favourite stories, detailing a life in Canada from his birth in a sod hut to becoming a Muslim spokesman, is that of Saleem Ameen Ganam, a tall, mustachioed man with a kind, fatherly air and a patriarch of the western Canadian community. Saleem was the older brother of Ameen "King" Ganam, famous Canadian fiddler and entertainer of the 1950s and '60s on CBC-TV's "Country Hoedown." Saleem lived from 1910 to 2003 and is buried in Edmonton as Al Hajj Saleem Ameen Ganam.[49] He was also the brother of Dr Lila Fahlman.[50] The following interview was recorded in 1979.

> My name is Saleem Ameen Ganam, of the family of Al-Qadri. My father [Sied Ganam, also known as Sied Ameen Ganam Kadri] came from Lala, a small town in the Bekaa Valley in [present-day] Lebanon. He came to this country in 1901 on a cattle boat, which took more than a month to come from Beirut to the City of New York. It was a very rough passage . . .
>
> In 1901, my father was over the age limit of eighteen or nineteen, which was the required age for enlistment in the Turkish army. He was much older [and therefore draftable], [however] an uncle was going to South America, so he accompanied him to Beirut. When they got to

Beirut, he decided he wanted to go with his uncle to the New World. He asked his uncle if he could go along with him, and at first his uncle was reluctant. But Dad [was] persuasive and eventually the uncle gave in . . . He managed to get him on the boat . . .

The draft was customary at that time, because Lebanon was then part of Greater Syria and it was under the domination of the Ottoman Empire. Everything was done according to the orders of Turkey. It was a very strict rule, and in many ways the Arabs felt that they were being persecuted by the Turks . . .

Dad of course landed in New York. He didn't know anyone there, but he did meet a few people from Lebanon. Not having any money himself, he wanted to come to London, Ontario, where his friend had arrived about six months earlier—Ahmed (or Ed) Awid, now of Edmonton [Richard Asmet Awid's father].[51] Some good soul in New York started him in business and gave him some small tapestries, needles, thread, and so on, and said, "Here now, take these things and go and sell them and as you go along replace your stock and work your way towards London."

He started out on foot from New York and eventually arrived in London in December 1901. He met Ahmed there and they stayed together. Then in the spring [1902], Ahmed (or Ed) Awid did the same thing as the original friend [in New York]: he gave him a certain amount of stock, put it into a shoulder harness, and set him out to peddle. He would go out of London among the scattered farmers and peddle and then come back for more stock.

Eventually, after a couple of years in London, he decided he wanted to go and see his cousin who had taken up a farm in South Dakota. I believe it was in Sioux Falls. So he started to make his way . . . and eventually got to Sioux Falls and met his cousin there. He worked around there and started peddling in the States. Now he had a few more dollars, so he got himself a buggy and a horse and all of a sudden he was an F W Woolworth! If you had a horse and buggy, this was something very, very big. So he worked his way through into Nebraska to Omaha. There he met my mother, and after a very short whirlwind courtship, I imagine, they went back to South Dakota and were married at a cousin's place by a JP [justice of the peace].

My mother [Chelsea Pritchard] was British. Her mother was Welsh and her father, I believe, was Irish. They were a very religious family, and the Methodists at that time were a very religious sect, and probably still are.

Meanwhile, after four or five years, Ahmed (or Ed) Awid had moved from London, Ontario, to Winnipeg, and all of a sudden my father had word from him that he had gone to Brandon, Manitoba, and was going to open up a wholesale business. So my father said to his new bride, "My friend Ahmed Awid is in Brandon, Manitoba. Let's go see him." They got on their horse and buggy, took their merchandise and started peddling along the road and worked their way north until they came to Brandon.

Sied Ameen Ganam and Chelsea Ganam, 1936.
Photo courtesy of Richard Asmet Awid.

When they got there, they found Ahmed (or Ed) Awid and his store. It was a small place on a side street. He went in and introduced his bride in the old Arab tradition. Ahmed Awid looked at her and said, "Sister," and he reached in his pocket and pulled out a set of keys and said, "Here are the keys and there is your house." He pointed to the house, which meant "Make yourself at home." She did, and they stayed there about six months.

After that, Dad felt the urge to wander again, and they started out from Brandon, working their way into Saskatchewan. In 1910, they went into the northern part of Saskatchewan and landed at a small town which was later called Sheho. It's just a short way west of Yorkton, on the main line out of Winnipeg. He went about twenty miles out of town to take up what we called in those days a home-stead. You paid ten dollars and laid it down on a quarter section of land.

The first thing they had to do, of course, was to provide a place to live in. Dad got himself a team of horses and a breaker plough. They ploughed the field and took the sod and built a house out of it. This was the first house that Dad built in the West. They then cut a few trees that were there and put them on top to make a roof and put sod on top of that again. It was the type of abode that I was born in, in 1911.[52] It was some house!

This didn't last long. It lasted about one year, and then my father got word that his sister had gotten married and had come to Regina. They left the farm to go to Regina and visit his sister and brother-in-law, but they intended to return to the farm.

Dr Naiyer Habib and Mahlaqa Naushaba Habib published in 2015 their compendious 645-page *History of the Muslims of Regina, Saskatchewan, and Their Organizations*. It includes some pages on the early pioneers in Regina,[53] some of whom would have been Saleem Ganam's relations. Saleem continued:

When they [his parents]arrived in Regina, the street railways were being built, and someone said to my father, "Why go back to farm-ing when you can get a job here on the street railways, making cash money daily?" . . . So he started working on the railway as a labourer, laying ties. Because of the language barrier and not having any particular training in anything, you had to take what you could get. He worked there for maybe a year or a year and a half.

Then the call of the plains came to him again, but this time, instead of going back to the original place, he had heard that there was a community of Lebanese in Swift Current [Saskatchewan], and so he and his wife headed out west to Swift Current and again repeated the process of taking out a homestead and starting all over again.

In Swift Current it was different. There were no trees and they had to find other ways of getting lumber, and this time they built a half-sod and half-lumber house, which later became all lumber. The sod was for the walls and it had a wooden frame, wooden windows and doors. For the inside they mixed straw with clay and made plaster and whitewashed it with lime. They made their own lime with charcoal from burnt wood mixed with water. It turns white and you mix it with soil and straw . . . My mother became quite adept at it.

There were two purposes for whitewashing. One was for colour and cleanliness, and the other was to prevent bugs and insects from coming through the sod walls. The lime retards the insects. There was only one colour, and that was white. No tints.

Dad remained in Swift Current until 1918. At that time there were maybe ten families in the area. There were Christians as well as Muslims. I don't recall too much because I was quite young at the time. There wasn't much socializing, but we did visit back and forth. All I was concerned about was going over to the Kazeils' [another Syrian-Lebanese family][54] and going horseback riding with the boys, and so on.

In the country it is not quite like the city. Your socialization is not quite the same. In the country, everybody goes. You enjoy the great outdoors, riding, and people are working, everybody is busy. Even the adults don't waste too much time sitting down and reminiscing because they don't have the time. You have to get up early in the morning, tend to your livestock, cattle, and so on, go out in the fields and do the necessary chores. The only time you have to sit around is in the winter months when you are not actually working outside . . . It was a hard life but I think they enjoyed it . . .

It seems that Dad was always on the move. I don't know if he was never particularly happy, or maybe it was something in the farming enterprise. It was hard. We raised horses. I spent much of my time either chasing horses or chasing sheep around, one or the other. I pretty well lived in the saddle.

Schooling wasn't what you have today. It was very limited, but nevertheless we went to school. I had to go about four and a half miles to school, and you can imagine what that was like in the wintertime. Dad used to drive us there in the horse and buggy, or sometimes others would go with us and another neighbour would pick us up and bring us back in the evening. In the summer months we would walk. At that time to walk four or five miles didn't seem to be difficult at all. My brother found it very difficult—he never liked to walk and wanted to play hooky, but I used to walk and I really enjoyed it. After getting up early in the morning and looking after the livestock, helping milk the cows, we'd have a little bite to eat and we would head out, not walking but running, four or five miles, and think nothing of it. Now I don't even want to walk two blocks.

Our religious education was very, very limited. The old timers [among the Syrian-Lebanese]—they weren't old but in my eyes they were old because I was young—would sit down and they would be discussing Qur'an and *hadith* [sayings of the Prophet Muhammad] and so on. They never taught us in the [same way] that we are trying to teach the children today . . . They would just have a discussion among themselves. Someone would discuss something from the Qur'an or some *hadith* or some story with an Islamic content to it. That is, when they had the time . . . If you listened, you picked up the knowledge, and if you didn't, well that's about the score. Nobody insisted that you learn it . . .

My mother was of the Pritchard family, and she became a Muslim before she married my father. I suppose my dad was able to persuade her. She was formerly a strong Methodist, and religion was a way of life with them. It was practised . . . and they were very active in the church, so the result is that when it was explained to her what Islam was, she was convinced and she accepted it. She always practised it very, very properly, you might say. As a matter of fact, she would even correct my dad on many things in the years to come.

For example, we later moved from Swift Current to another farm in the town of Admiral. One Lebanese peddler came by, and, of course when you go to any home, but a Muslim home particularly, you are welcome, and you are going to have dinner and stay there. He had a buggy with a canopy on it and a lot of merchandise in it. He took his horse and put it in the barn and watered it. Mother was preparing the meal and all of a sudden he went out to the wagon and took out a little parcel and went by the house out to a stone pile . . . and he put his parcel in it. Mother said to herself, "Now what is this man doing? What did he put in that stone pile?"

Later on, when they were busy talking, curiosity got to her and she went out to look in the stone pile, and she found maybe a half dozen bottles of beer. She took each bottle nicely and cracked them on the stones. When the peddler went back to get his beer, he found the bottles broken and he knew who had done it. He came back and said, "Chelsea, I'm sorry, but why did you do it?" She said, "Don't ask me why I did it! Why did you do it in the first place?" He felt badly and knew there was no use denying it because he knew that she knew he had put it there.

That was an example of the fact that she was very, very firm. Liquor was absolutely prohibited. All the way through, I can never remember any time liquor or pork products came near the home. Mother was very strict on that. In other words, she accepted Islam. It wasn't a nominal thing with her. She accepted it, studied it, learned it, and practised it.

We didn't say prayers as such. Dad had a bath, which would be once a week on the farm because the water was cold, especially in winter. Every time he had his bath he would always go to the bedroom and make his prayers and I used to watch him. I was a little guy, you see. At no time were we taught what to do . . .

In the early days . . . around 1914 or 1915 . . . these prairie fires developed, and they would range over vast areas, covering ten or fifteen miles. In one particular incident a prairie fire was coming and there was the Kazeil farm and then our farm. Dad saw the smoke coming, and the farmers were hitching up their breaker ploughs to make four or five furrows to break the spread of the fire. Everyone was very concerned, and a Norwegian neighbour to the south of the Kazeils came over and he said to Dad, "What's the matter? Everybody is fighting the fire, and you're not fighting the fire, you're not preparing for it."

"No problem," Dad said. He was not concerned at all. The fire was within range then and he went up on a little haystack and offered his prayers, and the wind turned and the fire's out! I wasn't old enough to remember the actual fire, but I've been told this by the Kazeil family themselves. You see, our family is descended directly from Shaikh Abdul Qadir Gilani, the Persian Sufi saint of the eleventh century Baghdad,[55] so we belong to the Qadiriyya sect . . .

When I was going to school in those years, the teacher would probably teach one year and the second year there would be a new teacher. In the country nobody wanted to stay too long. At this particular time, the new teacher came and she wanted to know all about her students. "Your name, and your name?" she asked, and when she came to me I answered "Saleem."

"Saleem? Oh, that's an odd name. What's your nationality?"

"Syrian," I answered.

She said, "What's your religion?"

At that time we didn't say "Islam," but we said "Mohammedan," because that was the common term used. I didn't know any better. She didn't ask any of the other students this question. Today, of course, I wouldn't have said "Mohammedan."

All of a sudden, she looked frightened. She took her hand and drew her finger across her throat and said "Turk," and as she said that her face reddened and a boy who was sitting on one side of me and a girl on the other side both got up and moved out of their seats and moved away quickly.

I often think of that today and the changes that have taken place. At that time they were so frightened of the Ottoman Empire that anything that referred to the Turks was frightening, and they became frightened of me. It took some time before my chums in the school would come back and sit beside me. [To them] I was one of those wild

Turks that at any moment could draw out a scimitar from my pocket or someplace and slice their throats! What a change it is between then and now!

Eventually, Saleem Ganam's father moved his family to Regina, where a Muslim organization had been founded in 1931 by Abdul Qadir Haymore. Later, in the 1970s, it became the Islamic Association of Saskatchewan.[56] In Regina, Saleem Ganam's father went into the grocery business in a store situated between an Imperial Oil building and a General Motors plant. His father used to let his customers buy goods on credit and pay him back at the end of the week. When the Great Depression came, they ceased paying their bills, and Saleem's father was unable to get any more credit from his wholesalers and went bankrupt. He had to go on relief and later worked for the city parks department.

Sied Ameen Ganam probably at Al Rashid Mosque, where he taught Islam later in life. Photo courtesy of Richard Asmet Awid.

He was also the *muezzin* of Edmonton's Al Rashid mosque for many years, calling the faithful to prayers.

> Then we went through the Great Depression that we called the "Dirty Thirties" in Saskatchewan. You couldn't even buy a job. I couldn't afford to go on in school. I finished grade 10 and if we had been successful in business I probably would have gone on to do law . . . I couldn't get a job, so I started to read. I read books I think on every religion there was. I spent months in the libraries, maybe years. All of a sudden there was a set of books called *Literatures of the East*, or something of that nature—I remember the purple-coloured binding on a whole set of books. I was looking at this and I opened one particular book and here was a part of the translation of the Qur'an in English. This was the first time I had ever known that the Qur'an had been translated into English! I would be about twenty or twenty-one when I saw that, and it was like finding a diamond. I got permission and took it home and started to write in a scribbler each and every line out of that book. This was the start!
>
> I had read books on Buddhism, Taoism, Shintoism, and Judaism. I read the Torah. I read the Book of Mormon. I think I read everything, and in spite of the fact that I had read them all, when I found this gem of the Qur'an, my faith then became very strong because I saw its beauty . . . It was not the best translation in the world, but to me it was the most beautiful thing in the world. From then on I became very dedicated to discovering more and more and trying to find literature on Islam.
>
> This discovery of the partial translation of the Qur'an was a turning point in my life, in a way, and I suppose in my brother's and sister's [lives] too. Up till then, we had never seen any writings on Islam in the English language, and not speaking the Arabic language, of course, was a handicap. When I got that book and started to copy it and write down all the chapters of the Qur'an, it was like a gold mine. I studied it and so did my mother, brother, and sister . . . We started to ask our dad questions on Islam, and he would start to come out of his shell and to relate to us stories behind it [the Qur'an], and *hadith*, because we didn't have any book on *hadith*. We were never before exposed to

Islam in lectures or anything else. We lived an Islamic life, our diet was Islamic—you might call it a straight halal kitchen because we raised our own livestock and slaughtered it . . .

[As a result of this education], beginning back in the 1930s, news releases would be sent to the *Regina Leader Post* when Ramadan would come up. We would send greetings to the Muslims, usually from my father and myself as leaders of the Muslim community. Actually, there scarcely was a Muslim community as far as Regina was concerned, but we knew there were Muslims in Radville and Lashburn, and there were some up in the north. We knew the paper would reach them.

During the Depression, my father and I took odd jobs that we could find at that time. Jobs weren't too plentiful. I worked for a while for a Lebanese Christian auto-wrecker. That paid the great sum of one dollar a day. We had to work in the sun wrecking cars, and it was a pretty hard job.

Nevertheless, I saved up a few dollars and a couple of years later I managed to buy an old car—I paid twenty-five dollars for the car and ten dollars for the licence. You didn't worry about insurance in those days. I then went to a local wholesaler, persuaded him to advance me some fruits, whatever fruit was in season, and I started going out into the country peddling this fruit. Along the way I picked up some brass, horse hair, eggs, butter, and anything you could trade, and brought it back to the city and sold it there. I did that for a few years . . .

I don't know whether peddling is a tradition with the Lebanese and with the Arabs, but I suppose we go back as far as the Prophet Muhammad, peace be upon him, and the early caliphs—Abu Bakr, Omar, Othman and all those. As I recall in reading, they were all hawkers and peddlers . . .

I would say that the Arab Muslims, generally, have done very well in the West, some exceptionally well. We have the Hamdons, the Shabens, the Awids, the Jomhas, the Shawars—these people are all very successful. Most of them are in very big operations in the whole-sale trade. These operations cover not only the provinces of Alberta and British Columbia but Saskatchewan and all the way north into the vast territories, and they have salespeople on the road representing the wholesale firms. The ones who were not so concerned about making money earned the necessities and this was sufficient for them. Maybe I fall into that category. I think I could probably have been successful if I really wanted to, but I was always concerned [with] just enough for making a living, and the rest of the time I devoted to Islamic work.

According to Earle H Waugh's book, *Al Rashid Mosque: Building Canadian Muslim Communities*, and other sources, the Ganam family members have played a variety of roles in developing the Edmonton Muslim community. The old patron, Sied Ameen Ganam, is reported to have moved from Swift Current to Edmonton in the 1940s, where he helped build the community and also participated in its religious services (see photo, where he appears wearing a fez). His eldest son, Saleem Ganam, is said to have moved to Edmonton in the later 1940s, partly because the community wanted to benefit from his knowledge of Islam. He became president of the mosque, or the Canadian Islamic Centre, and was also a founder and vice-chair of the Council of Muslim Communities of Canada (CMCC). In 1987 he started the Canadian Council Islamic Awareness Foundation. Saleem Ganam conducted Muslim marriages, wrote several books on Islam, and served western Muslims for many decades. Earle Waugh's book on Al Rashid includes a photo of him with the famous boxer Mohammed Ali. Saleem Ganam also became cofounder of the Call to Islam in Canada and was the first Muslim chaplain in Canada, at the University of Alberta.

Saleem's wife, Marie, also had Syrian-Lebanese roots. She was the daughter of Ahmed Hussain Moussa (the name having been changed somewhat more appropriately than, as usual, to Moses by immigration officials), who landed in Halifax in 1904 and married Sarah Elizabeth Plavel in 1909.

Saleem Ganam died in 2003, and is buried in Edmonton, as are others of his family.

His brother, Ameen Ganam, was born in 1915, had a lot of musical talent, and became known as "King" Ganam, the famous Canadian fiddler. He was inducted into the Canadian Country Music Hall of Fame in 1989. Back in the late 1930s he had taught Islam at the Al Rashid.[57] In 1976, Saleem published a fifty-page monograph, *Islam, The Universal*

Ahmed and Sara Moussa, parents of Saleem Ganam's wife, Marie. Photo courtesy of Richard Asmet Awid.

Religion, and several other books.

Sied Ameen Ganam's third child, Lila, was born in 1924. She became a schoolteacher, earned a doctorate in educational psychology, and in 1982 was the founder of the Canadian Council of Muslim Women. Dr Lila Fahlman (née Ganam) is also now deceased, but she told me her story in 1979:[58]

> I was born in 1924 on a farm in Limerick, Saskatchewan. It was a good-sized farm, about five quarter-sections. We left the farm when I was four and a half and moved to Regina . . . We were a family of three children. My mother[59] was born in the States and was of Welsh origin. She married my father around 1910 [or probably earlier] and they came to Canada. She became a Muslim from the outset. Both our parents were keen on education. My mother was a teacher when they were married—at that time you could teach with a grade eight education. Her family was well educated and religious. One of her brothers, a Methodist minister, has a church named after him in Seoul, Korea . . .
>
> Our dad was always talking religion and as the boys got older they were always talking religion and we became quite a vocal family. It

was either politics or religion in those days. When we were growing up, there were no schools or classes for Muslims because there were very few Muslims. In Regina, at that time, there was one other family that were our cousins—my father's sister and her family—and there were one or two others, one or two single men. We were the Muslim community . . . We knew nothing of my mother's conversion. She never talked about it to me.

We did everything we were supposed to do. I remember fasting and praying when I was very young, but we didn't have any formal prayers, you just prayed on your own. I didn't know the *rakas* [verses of the Qur'an] at that time. I knew the *Bismillah* [probably the key opening Qur'anic verse *Al-Fatiha*] and I knew a few other verses from the Qur'an that I had memorized, and I made up my own prayers incorporating these. I didn't learn the formal prayers until I came to

Lila Ganam and her brothers, Saleem, left, and musician Ameen "King" Ganam, right. Photo courtesy of Richard Asmet Awid.

the mosque here [in Edmonton, built in 1938]. There was some teaching here. My brother Ameen was here and then Saleem came . . .

I don't remember any specific incidents at school on the part of teachers, but I always had a feeling of inferiority. I was raised in a part of Regina that was predominantly Catholic, and in fact we lived right across the street from a Catholic church, which didn't help, and all the young people around me were Catholic.

Unfortunately, the rest of this taped interview was destroyed in the fire mentioned previously. However, Dr Lila Fahlman tells her story in *At My Mother's Feet: Stories of Muslim Women*, edited by Sadia Zaman.[60] In it, she provides more details about her childhood, education, developing interests, the conversion of her future husband Al Fahlman, their wartime marriage, and her teaching career. She also speaks about her role in

Educator and CCMW founder Dr Lila Fahlman later in life, probably the 1990s. Photo courtesy of Richard Asmet Awid.

developing the CCMW, her doctorate in educational psychology, and the saving of Edmonton's pioneer Al Rashid Mosque from demolition and its restoration in a historic park. In the 1990s she became the vice-chair of Vision TV and founding chair of the World Council of Muslim Women Foundation. In 1998 she travelled on its behalf to China to meet Muslim women.[61]

Lila Fahlman died in 2006 and is buried in Edmonton.

Another Edmonton Muslim, retired judge Edward Saddy (pronounced "Sadie," close to his Arabic name, Saidi), was born in 1931. He became the first Muslim lawyer and judge in Canada and is the brother-in-law of Larry Shaben, the first Muslim provincial cabinet member in Alberta.[62] Edward Saddy[63] had this to say about his father's arrival in Canada in 1900:

> My father, Said Abu-Laban [then Mahmoud Saddy],[64] came from a small town called Jib Janine[65] in the Bekaa Valley, in what is now called Lebanon. Jib Janine means "burning bush". My father was probably one of the original draft dodgers. The Turkish Empire was controlling the area he lived in and when he was seventeen years old the recruiters came in and took all the seventeen-year-olds into the army for two to four years. The Ottomans did not have a very good reputation when it came to the local boys and so they were not anxious to go into the army. My father left the village from one end as the recruiters were coming into the village from the other end. He had only fifty dollars in his pocket, but he walked over the mountains to Beirut and caught a boat to America, not really knowing where America was. It was just somewhere everybody was going.
>
> My father landed in New York and worked his way across the United States to Iowa. He spent two or three years in the States, and then he heard about the land being given away in Canada, so he came to Canada and worked and purchased some land. His homestead was near Kedleston, Saskatchewan. My eldest brother was born in Saskatchewan and the rest of the family were born in Dilk, Alberta. We had land in Dilk until the Second World War and we owned land

and ranched in southern Alberta until 1966.

My father and mother [Rikia Haidar][66] were married in 1920, and I was born in 1931. We were a large family, four boys and three girls.[67]

My mother came to this country with my grandmother [Amina Shaben Haidar] to visit a granduncle, my grandmother's brother, who resided near Edmonton . . . The boat she came on landed [first] in Vera Cruz, Mexico, before coming to America. Simultaneously, upon their arrival [in 1910], the Mexican Revolution broke out and they couldn't transit Mexico, so they stayed in Mexico City for four or five years until the revolution was over and they could travel. My mother took some formal schooling there and she still sings Mexican songs from time to time. She then came to Edmonton and met and married my father in 1920 . . .

Richard Asmet Awid confirmed that Said Abu-Laban (later Mahmoud Saddy) was called "Big Sam" or "The Turk" by his neighbours, and he and his wife Rikia successfully farmed near Dilk, Saskatchewan. In 1922 they moved to Wardlow, Alberta, raising cattle, horses, and grain. In 1934 they moved with their family to Cold Lake, Alberta and, retaining the farm, moved on to Edmonton in 1936 where they built a family home and became involved in the development of the Al Rashid Mosque (1938). Mahmoud Saddy continued to farm at Wardlow in the summers, until he passed away at age sixty-eight in 1951.

Rikia remained involved with the mosque and its activities, including its move to the Fort Edmonton Heritage Park. She was also active in women's organizations, the Women's Canadian Club and the Symphony Orchestra. She travelled to the Middle East, South Asia, and the Far East and died in 1990.[68]

Edward Saddy recounted stories that he'd heard about the pioneer Muslim traders and farmers:

They used to travel across the country, even if it was a treacherous trip, to visit one another. If they heard of a friend in Winnipeg and they were in Edmonton they would try to get together in groups and help one another and, of course, there was the common language bond. I don't think religion was specifically in mind when they congregated. It was more cultural then, but somehow the religion held them together too.

It was amazing that people who come from a warm and sometimes even desert climate should choose Edmonton and northern Canada as their home. There were a number of Muslim fur traders in this area and Edmonton was the southern point in their travels. They would stock up with goods and would go well into the North, as far as a thousand miles or more, trading for furs. They would go as far as they could by boat, portage overland by wagon, and when the snow fell they would use dog sleighs. They would move up into the Indian country and the Indians would be waiting for them with beaver pelts and fox pelts. They would trade various products, such as clothing and knickknacks, for fur pelts. They slept out in the open against their sleighs with their dogs.

I recall a story about hardships that we couldn't even imagine. There was a group of farmers up in the Peace River country, and in those days there was very little highway after fifty miles north of Edmonton. Peace River is almost four hundred miles north of that . . . Sam Jamha [also Esmeil Jamha],[69] an early fur trader who came out in 1908 or 1909, tells a story of going to help the farmers move the grain and wheat that they had threshed in the fall to a railhead or grain elevator. The snow came early. They loaded up the grain and wheat onto sleighs about twelve or fifteen feet long and three or four feet wide, hitched up a team of horses and then went out in a convoy . . .

He would tell us about approaching these hills in Peace River country and when he would approach the bottom of the hill he would unhitch the horses from all the sleighs, put them all on one sleigh and take that sleigh to the top of the hill and then come back down and hitch [them onto] another sleigh and take it to the top. When they managed to get the six sleighs to the top of the hill, going down the other side caused another problem. He had to put the horses at the other end of the sleigh to keep the sleigh from running down the hill. They would do this with the six sleighs, one at a time, with the horses holding them back. Today, a truck could carry it all in one load with room to spare. To move the sleighs eighty miles to the railhead would take them a week in winter weather. They slept against the wagons or in whatever shelter they could find . . .

Peter Baker[70] stayed his whole life in Fort Smith and Yellowknife. He never came back down. He was a part of the community up there and such a beloved character that they built a monument to him in Yellowknife. He was a Muslim and the subject of the book *The Arctic Arab*. There were also black cowboys in the area where we ranched in southern Alberta. They were basic, independent, well-liked guys, very much integrated into the community. Ranching was so hard and you relied on your neighbour, and this was a great equalizer.

After graduating in economics and law from the University of Alberta in 1959, Edward Saddy toured much of the Muslim world. He was then called to the bar and went on to practise law for some twenty-five years before becoming a provincial court judge in 1990, retiring in 2001. He was very active with the Arabian Muslim Association, which founded the mosque, and was president for a dozen years and board member for twenty-five years.[71]

Edward Saddy's family connections and the varying Muslim tradition in the west have been described in his nephew Guy Saddy's article, "The First Little Mosque on the Prairies: A Canadianized Version of Islam Once Flourished Out West. Can It Take Root Again?" in the October-November 2008 issue of *Walrus*. Guy Saddy talks with some nostalgia about the gradual assimilation of some members of the earlier generations and the contrast with later, more religiously oriented immigrants like Zarqa Nawaz. Born in England in a Pakistani family that later emigrated to Canada, she is the author of the popular CBC-TV series *Little Mosque on the Prairie* and the memoir, *Laughing All the Way to the Mosque* (2014).

As mentioned above, another old Muslim name in Alberta is that of Awid, after founding father Ahmed Ali Awid Amerey, later Ahmed or Ed Awid (1882-1979). Ed Awid came from Lala, Lebanon, in 1901 with his friend Ali Tarrabain, according to one of his sons, author Richard Asmet Awid. Ed peddled goods from Ontario to Manitoba, where he opened a series of stores in various cities. He married Mary, of Ukrainian background, and they had sixteen children, two of whom died young. They moved to Edmonton in 1928. Ed Awid continued in the clothing business until he retired in 1952. He then returned to Lebanon, made the pilgrimage to Mecca, and came back to Edmonton, where he died in 1979 at the age of ninety-six.[72]

His story was related to me in 1979 by Mickey Awid, one of the sons of Ed Awid and a brother of Richard.

> My English name is Mickey or Michael Awid, but I was born and registered as Awid Ahmed Ali Amiri[73] in 1929, in Brandon, Manitoba . . . I got the name Mickey from a housekeeper. My mother was quite prolific [bearing fourteen children] and was unable to take me to school to register me and the housekeeper took me. She thought Mickey Rooney was quite a guy and my names were all Arabic so when the registrar asked "What's his name?" she said "Mickey," and that stuck with me ever since. [He laughs] My first name is Awid—we came from a family called Awid Amiri, and one son of a family usually gets the name of the grandfather—my father's father—who was Awid and I got that name so my first name is Awid and my surname is really Awid Amiri . . .
>
> My father [Ahmed Awid or Ed Awid] had come to Canada in 1901 from Lebanon. It was part of the Turkish Empire at that time, and the Turks were conscripting all the youths into the army, so many of them fled the country to places like Canada and many to South America.
>
> My father landed in London, Ontario, in 1901, and became what is known as a peddler, selling lace for edgings and cushion tops and items like that in the northern part of Ontario, and this was all by foot. Gradually he built up the business and was able to buy a horse and buggy and kept travelling around until he and a number of other Lebanese Muslim people made a trek to Winnipeg, Manitoba, where they settled for a number of years, and then on to Brandon, Manitoba. From Brandon in 1929 the bulk of them moved further west to Edmonton and Calgary where there is a very substantial community. The Lebanese Muslim community in Edmonton and Calgary—and other Arabs [and other ethnicities]—would be in the vicinity of 7,000 to 8,000 at this present time [1979].

In Edmonton, my father with eleven other people in 1938 formed the first mosque [Al Rashid] which we believe is the first mosque in North America and certainly the first mosque in Canada. They struggled and put in whatever they could from time to time and they built up a place where they could go for prayers as well as for community work.

My father was nineteen when he arrived in Canada and he got married at roughly the age of thirty-five. My mother was born in what was called Austria-Hungary [until its dissolution after the First World War] and came to Canada at the age of one and they met and married in Brandon.

A good number of the Lebanese Muslims were single at the time, but as they moved further west, a good number of them married Canadian ladies and many brought wives over from Lebanon. Most of them ended up—and I'm talking about back in the 1930s—either as merchants in the cities or as traders up in the North West Territories. An interesting point is that most of the free traders at one time were of Lebanese descent. Many of them had wives, and many were bachelors, and Edmonton became a focal point for these people and they participated financially in starting the mosque. Basically, the Muslims became recognized in Edmonton and perhaps Alberta around the time the mosque was built.

My mother was converted to the Muslim faith many years ago, but our family, as many other families, has been brought up with mixed marriages in the Muslim Arabic tradition. In our household we ate Canadian food of course but basically we were brought up on Arabic foods, and our home was, and still is, a gathering place for many of the Muslim Lebanese. They tended to be very close back in 1935 and even later because the size of the community was so small. But as the community grew and the youngsters grew up and the city became so much larger we just didn't have the time to get together, but the older people, because of my father's age, tended to congregate at my father's home . . .

Getting back to the reason my father left Lebanon, at that time the Arab kids were being conscripted into the Turkish army at the age of eighteen and the parents would falsify the birth records to show that they were years younger to save them going into the army and allowing them to emigrate from the country, so dad could be one hundred or he could be five years older than he says now. This is not only with my father but with Saleem Ganam's father who I'm sure was many years older than he claimed to be . . . That's the reason we had no definite birth dates.

They were very kind, kind people. I was just a kid but at the age of six or seven I can remember these people. They would shower you with affection and attention, especially people like Jim Darwish, whom I admire, the Skakers[74] and Hamdons. They would come down from the territories, and we were really favourite pets. They spun such fascinating stories, which I'm sure at a later stage I would take with many grains of salt, but they were so fascinating you could almost live them . . .

I come from a large family—eight brothers and six sisters. Going back, I can remember the days when lipstick and nail polish were absolutely taboo, low-cut dresses were taboo, and skimpy bathing suits were out of the question. As far as dress goes, it wasn't Arabic but it was simple, not to be in complete *purdah* but to dress like the people of the country. Anything ornate was not allowable.

I remember when radios came out widely, in the early 1930s, my mother said to my father, "I'm going to buy a radio," and he said, "You try to bring the radio in and I'll throw it out of the house!" It was something that just wasn't allowable. But she bought a radio—I wish I had it now, it'd be a real antique—and it turned out that the person who used it the most was my father!

Our entertainment in those days was strictly a hand-operated gramophone because of the type of records—they were Arabic records and other types, but none of jazz music because it wasn't Arabic. My job was to wind the gramophone . . . I remember getting so fed up of winding it that [one day] I took the winder and hid it under the porch. No one could find it so Dad promised if I could find it, I wouldn't be punished, and I went and got it and from then on my brothers had to take turns [winding it] . . .

[When peddling lace] Dad would go to these farmhouses and he'd be offered ham and potatoes for supper and lodgings. They brought pork onto the table and he would politely say he was off a meat diet. He wouldn't make an issue of it, unless somebody asked him what his religion was, and then he'd tell them and show them that there was no difference between Christianity and the Muslim faith because we all believe in one God. We don't accept some of the philosophy of the Christian world, and they don't accept some of our philosophy, but it was never an issue. But don't forget there were only a handful [of Muslims] at that time and they were more of a rarity or an oddity than today when the word "Muslim" is quite well known. He was well received . . .

I think my father basically used to tell me stories from the Qur'an and the heroes of the Muslim world. [From then on we learned] mostly by example until we got to the mosque [in Edmonton, in 1938] . . . My dad spoke Arabic at home but only with the people who would congregate there, but not with the children. Although you understood a fair amount, when you got into Qur'anic Arabic you're talking about another kind of Arabic and none of the youngsters who went there at that time understood.

We started going to the mosque about the age of fourteen and then quite frankly because of not following the [Arabic] language—I'm only speaking for myself—but because I didn't know what was being said and there were no books in English in those days to tell you about your religion—so I guess I gradually dropped out, except for the holidays, but I seemed to have lost something from when I was younger. Quite frankly I enjoyed going to other churches to see what other religions were like. All of a sudden, it struck me one day that I was going to all these other churches when my first religion has got them all beat, so I started going back to the mosque when I was about twenty-five and I haven't stopped since then.

I can remember very clearly one time [during the Depression] that my dad had a fifty-dollar bill and a two-dollar bill in his pocket, and a fifty-dollar bill in those days wasn't something you got very often. I don't know how many children there were [in the family] at that time but I was with him at the mosque and they were asking, "Do you have any more money because we have to pay this contractor and we need contributions?" What was a person to do in these circumstances?

He had a big family to feed at home, but he gave them the fifty-dollar bill. And not only my dad but others would keep less than they would give, which I thought was very commendable. When you consider twelve people in those days putting up a mosque of that size it's remarkable . . .

Of the Muslim men who married Canadian [non-Muslim] women, I would say the biggest bulk of them by far, of those that had children, the children did not go into the Muslim faith. Unfortunately, those people are some of the best type—professors and people in good positions.

Mickey Awid, while he wavered for a time, did return to the faith of his forefathers. However, being Muslim had not been a real problem for him at school:

It was just that we were oddities because there were so few of us. When I'd say to my teachers, "I won't be here tomorrow because it's our holiday," they would be very kind. It was just that the people of Canada didn't know what a Muslim was and we'd explain it. I can remember one time when I was thirteen years old and I had told this teacher, Mr Barton, and he took me aside and asked me what it was all about. He found it extremely interesting and he told the class about it. I was a little embarrassed—but not much embarrassed—because I didn't know how to explain it. However, since that time we became very, very good friends and when we meet we discuss the religion.

Mind you, it's only been in the last twenty-five years at the most [before 1980] that Muslims have become known as something other than the daredevil Arab on a horse riding across the desert with a fair damsel in his arms. They're becoming known as [followers of] one of the major religions of the world. As time went on—and I was very active in service organizations and civic groups—once it became known I didn't eat pork, I was never served pork even though everyone else was. When I was president of our Kiwanis Club here, they made a point of it—no pork for me—and I'd be brought a steak, and this has gone on in many other places. I think people have grown to respect Muslims.

According to Richard Asmet Awid, his brother Mickey started several family businesses with another brother, Alex Awid, and also organized the Annual Klondike Parade for some years. He died in 1998.

In May 2018, the Edmonton Public School Board announced the opening of the Soraya Hafez Public School, named after Richard Awid's wife. This was the third school named after a Muslim woman in Alberta, the others being the Hilwie Hamdon School and the Dr Lila Fahlman School.

4. Lac La Biche: The Northerners

IN AN ERA OF LETTER-WRITING AND WITH LIMITED OR NO telephone facilities, the early Syrian Lebanese immigrants still managed to keep close ties with each other, even visiting their friends or relations regardless of the large distances involved in the sprawling foreign land. While a number of them settled in the Edmonton area, some made lives for themselves doing business in the far North, trading in furs. Meanwhile they maintained connections in Edmonton and their homeland.

One trading-post location that eventually became a very Syrian Lebanese town is Lac La Biche, originally established in 1798 by fur trader David Thompson, who wintered there while portaging from Beaver Lake to Lac La Biche. Two young Syrian/Lebanese men settled there in 1905. One of them, Alex Hamilton, originally Ali Ahmed Asiff Abouchadi,[75] came from Lala in the Bekaa. (The other was Hussain Ali Abougoush, or Sine Alley, whose story comes below.) The Lebanese community of Lac La Biche has a photo of his two-storey shop with a sign in large letters: Alex Hamilton. Groceries. Dry goods.[76] Eighty-eight years old when I interviewed him in 1979, he had been in Canada for seventy-five years.

> I left the old country when I was twelve years old [in 1905]. My uncle [Hussein Abouchadi] was coming to America along with fourteen others. At the time I was herding cattle about two miles out of town [Lala] and we heard about Canada having a lot of gold, the Yukon gold. So I left the cattle with a friend to go and say goodbye to my uncle and I said look after them because I wouldn't be long. I went running and running and when I caught up with him it was almost

a mile and I asked him if I could go with him to see Beirut. I hadn't seen Beirut, and he said OK . . . I heard them talking about Canada and saw the ocean from the top of the mountain [in Beirut] and asked if I could come along. He said yes [but] I had no passport, clothes, or anything . . .

We went to Marseille and at that time the British [government immigration agents] were hard on the Arabs, the Muslims, the Christians too, and the Jews, because we're a business people . . . They [would inspect] our eyes and say, "No, good, no good, no good" . . . they picked my uncle and when they came to me they said "That's his nephew," so they took three of us out of fifteen and said, "You [other] boys can go home because your eyes are no good to go to Canada." The rest were told they could either go to South America or go back home.

[After landing in Montreal] we come to Winnipeg. There were some people there who had been there four or five years like old man Awid [Ahmed or Ed Awid] and Mr [Ali] Hamdon and Tarabine [Tarrabain][77] and all those people and they were already in business. Our people are business people, they're not farmers. So anyway my uncle borrowed money and went out and bought me clothes so I'd be presentable . . .

I started out selling fans that I bought for sixty cents a dozen and sold them for $1.20, ten cents apiece . . .

We were there for about a month in Winnipeg, and all of a sudden someone said, "Young man, go west." They weren't saying it to me but they were saying it to everybody . . . So we come to Edmonton and my uncle bought a couple of horses, *cayuses* we called them, and an old wagon, and I started peddling stock again . . . We kept going and going until we got to Lac La Biche, me and my uncle [in 1906].

At that time there were only Indians there, except for the Hudson Bay man and his wife. It was an old house and we rented a small warehouse and built shelves in it to hold our things. At that time it took eight days to go back to Edmonton . . . Some days you would make only eight or ten miles a day . . .

I got the name [Alexander] Hamilton [in 1909] because I couldn't spell my name, Ali Ahmed Asiff Abouchadi. They said "How do you spell it?" and I said, "I don't know," and one of the other fellows said, "Say Hamilton, then everybody can spell your name."

My uncle stayed with me for three and a half years. He went back home in 1909, with five hundred dollars. At that time I was about sixteen years old and kept going with the business . . . We used to close the store in the summertime because the Indians had nothing and they lived on fish and other things . . . so I thought I'd take a homestead at Edam, Saskatchewan, northwest of Battleford . . . You had to break ten acres a year every year for three years before they would give you title to the place. Finally I shipped a carload of wheat to Fort William at thirty-two cents a bushel, but out of that I had to pay all the bills, the freight and everything else, and I said never mind. I sold the land for $1,000 [in 1912], and then I went back to my business again and my business had grown . . .

When the railroad came [in 1916] people bought homesteads for ten dollars for 160 acres. We had no [grain] elevator so I built an elevator. I had a saw mill already. I had the Ford agency later on. I had the International Harvester agency and about twenty-five or thirty people working for me outside the store. I was taking a contract from the railroad for making ties for the NAR [Northern Alberta Railways] . . .

The Hudson Bay had been there for 270 years but a fire in 1919 burned down the whole town except for the church, a station, and the [NAR] hotel on the lakeshore.

After the fire, I built a new store, much bigger than I had before— 32 by 130 feet, in 1919. With the Ford agency [1915] and Imperial Oil filling station, I was the largest businessman there at that time. We were also suppliers for a lot of the surrounding country stores . . . Leaving my stores with a manager called Frank Fisher, I started my floating store business. I had a store on a boat and travelled all the way from Fort McMurray to the Arctic . . . In 1926, I took two hundred head of cattle to Fort Smith and sold them to Bill Mahoney. In 1927, I started a saw mill in Lac La Biche at Moccasin Flats . . .

In 1937, we started a mink ranch with Frank Nashman [another Lebanese] by the slaughterhouse—which I owned. Later, I went on my own and moved my ranch to the site by the lakeshore. We bought a quarter section of land there from a man from Slave Lake, in the name of Sine Hamilton [his oldest son], Sam Asiff, and Andy Hamdon.

After the Depression, when business picked up during the Second World War, Hamilton built a new department store, which opened in 1943.

> Hudson Bay left [after the 1919 fire] and came back after twenty-seven years [in 1946]. At that time I was about ready to retire and sold out to Hudson Bay. I was fifty-four in 1946. They made an agreement with me that I couldn't build a store or business within thirty-five [or fifty] miles of Lac La Biche.

Hamilton and his wife, Josie, moved to Edmonton, where he built several houses and bought and sold property and a hotel.

> After I retired, my wife and I travelled to Scotland, England, India, South America and through all the States except Alaska. She was Ukrainian and she became a Muslim [in 1950]. We went to the hajj twice, the first time in 1958 . . .
>
> I learned a little bit in Lebanon about religion. I got the Qur'an and practised it and read it [through] six times a year. Saleem [presumably Ganam]'s grandfather taught me. I prayed, fasted and kept Islam and kept contact with the community. We got together to pray, four or five families . . .

Alex Hamilton and his wife Josie had five children—Sine, the eldest son; William, the second, who served four years in the RCAF; Marie, Selma, and Lila. By 1980 they had twenty grandchildren. Josie died suddenly in April 1974, and Alex Hamilton died in December 1985.

Another early northerner was Mohammed Mustapha Fyith, also known as Mike Fyith, or Fayath.[78] He was born sometime in the 1890s. The following interview is from 1979-80.

> I came to Canada from Kherbet Rouha, Lebanon, in 1927. My father [Mustapha Fyith] came to Canada in 1901, stayed one and a half

years and went home [to Lebanon]. He came back the second time with two brothers to Nova Scotia, stayed three years and returned home. The third time he came to Minnesota and stayed for about eight years. He went home to stay in 1919 and took with him $25,000. He wanted me to go to Canada and so I did. I came with a friend from Nova Scotia and we went on to Edmonton to work.

When I was coming to Canada, I went to the immigration office in France and the immigration official said I couldn't come to Canada unless I could read. I said "God help me." He gave me a sign to read that said "Open the door." I didn't even know how to read it, [but] he was a good man.

Fyith recalled how he'd grown up poor in Lebanon, when his father was in America, and when he came to Canada he knew or remembered little about Islam and he couldn't read or write in Arabic. In Canada he worked on a farm during his first year here in order to earn his naturalization:

I worked long hours. I used to milk twenty-five cows morning and night and all the farmer gave me was one egg for dinner and one egg for supper with bread—I used to drink milk when I was in the barn. This was during the Depression . . . I heard there was big money in furs. You could get $300 or $400 for one fox. I wished I could find a fox, kill it, and go [back] home because the language [in Canada] was too hard and I didn't want to work anymore. One fox would do it!

One day I was stooking hay in the field and I saw something black and white walking in the grass. I thought, "Now the time has come for me to go home." It was close to me, didn't see me, and it [the skunk's spray] got on my face. I was blinded. I yelled and ran away thinking it was following me. I was scared. I thought the farmer would see me and fire me for not working. I ran a little way and found a stook and put it on my face and turned back to see if [the animal] was following me. I wanted to get [it] and go home.

I went home to the farmer and he laughed because he knew it was a skunk. I changed my clothes and he washed me . . .

When I came here I was alone and had to work to send things

home to my family. If I had had someone to help me maybe I could have gone to school . . .

While the time sequence in the original interview seems somewhat inconsistent (I have tried to correct it), it seems that Fyith soon followed in his father's footsteps and starting peddling goods in the countryside:

I peddled goods that I bought from Jewish wholesalers for about eleven months. I travelled on foot with a suitcase on my back even when it was sixty degrees [Fahrenheit] below zero. Sometimes I would have to sleep in a school house and it was so freezing cold I put fourteen pairs of socks on my feet. Sometimes I would put on extra socks and keep walking all night.

I couldn't speak English and most people said they didn't have room but sometimes they would say yes. One place I went they said yes, I could stay. I ate supper and she told me there was no extra room but I could sleep with the hired hand. I thought she was telling me to get out and I left and walked all night. Another time I stopped at a small shack. There was a woman and four or five children. She motioned for me to go, that she had no room. I put some spit on my eyes as though I was crying and so she said to one of the children to put my suitcase on a sleigh, take a flashlight and take me to the uncle's place. When I got there, he put me outside on the verandah to sleep, and this was in the winter.

I had it easy compared to some others. After a while I bought a car and [went peddling in the car]. I used to sleep in the car and I would sleep on my arm. I would sleep so long because I was so tired and my arm was stiff sometimes. It got worse and I saw a doctor in Edmonton and he gave me a treatment for my arm for a month . . . Finally a friend got me some medicine and even today I can't throw anything with that arm. My car was a Model T Ford and I drove it for about four or five years.

After I learned to speak a little English I opened a dry goods store on Slave Lake. One man who bought goods from me couldn't pay so he gave me five mink from his mink ranch. I had a dog and the fishermen used my dog on the lake and in return they gave me food for the mink. I bred the mink and had twenty-five pups. I started the first mink farm in Slave Lake in 1939 . . . Then I sent for my wife and three children . . . I stayed in Slave Lake for two years and then moved to Lac La Biche and have been in mink farming ever since.

I brought over my brothers, cousins, and nephews and started them in mink ranching too. Today in Canada there are 172 Fyiths, mostly in Lac La Biche . . .

There were [almost] no Muslims in the North. We were very isolated and to be honest with you, we didn't fast or say our prayers very much. In 1939 we brought a minister [or imam] from Winnipeg and he taught us . . .

During the winter [as the community grew], there was not much work, no radio or television, so we would sit around and discuss our religion, the history of all the prophets. We also got books from home in Arabic . . . Then when I came here [to Edmonton] I couldn't even read the letters from home that were written in Arabic. I would have to wait until some of the old folks came from the north and they would read it to me. Later my brother came over and got some books and helped me. I can read now, the Qur'an. I pray five times daily and read the Qur'an all day long. I was lucky.

In recalling his life, Mohammed Fyith mentioned his role in the widely remembered founding of the Al Rashid Mosque in Edmonton in 1938:

We were very limited [in number] in Edmonton, thirteen or fourteen members. We had a man come from Montreal to teach us but he was not very educated. We wanted to build a mosque so Mrs [Hilwie] Hamdon and I went all over collecting money. We travelled by car and went to many of the wholesalers her husband knew. She was well respected and could get in any place and people would give her anything. She was the best woman in the country. I sold my car for $250, kept $100 and gave the rest to the mosque.

When we went to Lac La Biche my relatives gave a lot and everyone agreed we should build a mosque. We even brought a minister [an imam] from the old country [for the Edmonton mosque] . . .

Mohammed Mustapha Fyith died in 1989.

A third western Muslim pioneer family from Lebanon that traded in furs with the Indigenous people was that of Sine Alley Abougoush. He was born in Lala in 1891 and arrived in Halifax in 1908 at the age of seventeen. There the immigration officials turned his name into Sine Alley. In Halifax, Ahmed Farrhat welcomed new immigrants like him and took him home and fed him. Farrhat put Sine Alley on a train for Edmonton, from where he headed north to Lac La Biche to meet his cousin Ali [Alex] Hamilton and went on to become a great trapper. Sine Alley met his friend Ali Hamdon (who later married Hilwie) in Edmonton, and the two of them travelled to Fort Chipewyan where they opened a fur-trading post, Hamdon and Alley Ltd.[79] Later, in the 1920s, Sine Alley and his Canadian wife settled in Lac La Biche, Alberta, with their four children.

Sine Alley's son, Ameen Abougoush, also known as Ameen Sine Abougoush, was born in Fort Chipewyan in 1927. He became a noted mink rancher in Lac La Biche and president of the Lac La Biche Muslim Association. His story (1979) follows:

> I was born in Canada in 1927 as were my brother and two sisters.[80] My mother [Rose Albina Mercredi] was Canadian, part French, part Irish and part Cree, and my father was Lebanese, from a village called Lala. They were married in the early 1920s and my oldest sister was born in 1924. My mother adopted Islam and was able to express herself in Arabic . . .
>
> In 1930, we all went back to Lala, where my father built us a house. In Lebanon in our times there were no teachers like now, only a *sheikh imam* to teach us the Qur'an and when we finished learning to read that, he would teach us how to read and write. Later, the government of Lebanon sent us a teacher from Beirut who taught us to read and write the proper way. We were taking some French at the same time.
>
> I lived next door to the mosque and my grandfather was a very religious man. He taught us all kinds of lessons and the history of Islam, how Allah and Islam became known, etc . . .
>
> The [Second World] War started and we stayed in Lebanon until 1948. I came back with my sister [Malaki] to Lac La Biche to our relative, Alex Hamilton. We stayed with him for a while and I helped his

son who had a mink farm down by the lake. Later my sister married a Lebanese man, Sam Asiff, and he was a mink rancher also . . .

In 1948 I peddled dry goods with horses, no cars at that time, and didn't like that very much, so I have been here [in Lac La Biche] since 1949 . . .

When I came back to Canada I had relatives here, my sister and brother-in-law, and I [brought over some other relatives]. Some farmed mink and others are in the city working . . . The Muslims in Lac La Biche own mostly grocery stores, barber shops, men's wear stores, auto parts, service stations, a theatre—the only one in town. The Crescent IDA [supermarket] is owned by my nephew.

I married my wife [Zakia] in 1955. I had known her in Lala and sent for her. We have eight children, seven girls and one boy, all healthy, all Muslim—we hope. We have two daughters married to Muslim boys and we hope the rest will follow. We are trying our best . . .

Most of my friends are my own people. You can't make friends with Christian guys, I don't know why. If you want to make a good friend with them, then you have to drink. If you don't drink, you are no good. Ourselves, we don't drink because it's against our religion, and we don't enjoy it, so we stay away from them. We have difficulty making close friends. We know everybody by name but when it comes to sincere friends it is very hard, not just for me but with everybody . . .

In 1955 we decided we should have our own organization. Mr Mike Fyith[81] and Mohammad (Sam) Asiff, my brother-in-law, started an organization called the Arab Muslim Organization. We started to meet once a week in my house and once every month in a different house. We liked it. We talked together, talked over problems, had coffee and had a good time. We got bigger, so we hired a carpenter, bought material and built a small mosque. All of us worked [on it] in our spare time and began to pray. This would be in 1958.

This was the second mosque in Alberta. In 1966 the local school board needed the site for a high school, therefore by an agreement the organization bought some other land for a larger two-storey community centre and mosque, which expanded in 1986 and became the Al Kareem Mosque.[82]

Ameen Abougoush:

> Later on, we sent for an imam from Lebanon to teach our children. My daughter learned to read and write Arabic from him. When she began school, she didn't know one word in English, just Arabic. He [the imam] is Mohammed Chebli and he is in Calgary now. He was not really an imam, only a teacher, but he studied Islam and started leading prayers. He worked on mink too. He later sent for his family [from] Lebanon.
>
> The imam we have now came in 1976. He is the third one. Before him we had Mohammed Sharkawi, who stayed in Lac La Biche for five years. He didn't go home after his four-year term. He is now in Vancouver, BC. The present one is Mohammed Kasaby . . .

Ameen Abougoush returned to Lebanon to visit his aged parents in 1972 and 1977 and died in 1981. He was noted for his kindness and sense of humour.

The first mosque in Lac La Biche, built in 1958, the second in Alberta after Edmonton. Photo courtesy of Mariam Abougouche.

5. Saskatchewan: Swift Current and Regina

SWIFT CURRENT (POPULATION IN 2000: 16,600) MAY OR MAY NOT BE an inspiration for Zarqa Nawaz's very successful television series *Little Mosque on the Prairie* on CBC. Its Muslim community consists mainly of the descendants of Syrian Lebanese pioneers who had turned from trade to farming and newly arrived South Asian professionals. After decades of inaction, the community was finally inspired in 1982 to build a mosque.

In 1950, the farmer Mohamed Hattum was born somewhere south of Swift Current. His father, Sine or Sam Hattum, was also born in the area, in 1925. Sam Hattum's father, Ali or Alex Hattum, had arrived in Canada from Syria via the United States in about 1909; he later returned to Lebanon and came back with a wife in about 1924.

The following is Mohamed Hattum's account of his family, recorded in January 2019:

> I was born in 1950 in Vanguard, Saskatchewan, a small village beside the farm, about forty kilometres south of Swift Current. We have a house here too [in Swift Current]. My dad was Sam Hattum, called Sine in Arabic, but they called him Sam, and my mother's name was Mary Abdullah. My father was born in 1925 and he passed away in 1987. My mother was born in 1928 and she's still living.
>
> My grandfather, Ali Hattum, [stowed away on a ship] in Lebanon. He had a sister in Detroit, Michigan, and so he and his brother found this ship that was going to America and they stowed away on it because they didn't have any money to go anywhere. Part way on their journey the captain caught them, and what do you do? So he put them to work. It was a steam ship so he put them to work shovelling coal into the boilers 'til they got to their destination. That would have

Alex Hattum and Karia Zanidean Hattum, aged eighteen when they were married, ca 1938. Photo courtesy of Richard Asmet Awid.

been probably in 1901 or 1902.

His name was Ali Hattum but they called him "Alex" on the papers. He landed in the US, and he went to Detroit, Michigan, where he peddled around for a while and then he got a job with the Ford Motor Company. Then he heard the Canadian government was giving land for $20 more or less per quarter section, so he came to Canada probably in 1909. He wound up with a homestead south of Swift Current, beside [what is now] our farm, probably near Governor, the smallest town. He farmed, and probably cattle came in in small amounts shortly after. He had to break a certain amount of land every year to keep the homestead. In 1924, he went back to Lebanon and he married Karia Zanidean. [Next interviewee] Zakia Zanidean's grandfather was a brother to my grandmother. They had, I think, nine children, including my father.

Speaking of his exposure to Islam, Mohamed said there was no formal religious education in the Swift Current area in those early years. Parents taught their children, but much was lost. Some married Christians. They also experienced racism in the local community:

I faced that when I went to school. It was difficult, especially for my sister and me. We didn't know a word of English and the school happened to be in a convent. The nuns would teach us and they hired others as teachers. We took grade one, two, and three in there. The English wasn't hard to learn. We learned that quick, but the religious festivals and stuff like that we had to stay away from, and were looked upon as outsiders [he laughs]. One of the nuns told my sister something about Jesus Christ and my sister said, "We don't believe in Jesus Christ." Well, she [the nun] took her over her knee and paddled her, because we weren't supposed to say that. After a couple of years . . . they understood [about Islam] and our parents talked to the teachers and got it through to them that we were not Christians. It was traumatic, oh yeah, but after we got older it didn't bother us anymore, but when you're a kid, it's different, I'll tell you. You get worried . . . My sister was a year older than I was so she went through everything before I did.

We read the Qur'an and we did the fasting, but the regular prayers, our parents never did teach us that. But when we got the masjid [in 1982] then we learned it all, how to do it. But growing up, there was no association here. There was nothing. We formed an association probably in 1980–81, and we bought a mosque in '82, a [former] Church of God church. Mohammad Afsar [who arrived in Swift Current in 1980] was the one who set up the association and everything, and he did all the letter-writing to foreign countries for money. He was an engineer working here and he felt there was a need for a mosque. He got people together and made an association and had a board of directors—I've been on it all [the time] . . . Nobody else wants that job.

We had to hire an imam years ago, but there weren't enough people around to keep an imam so we let him go. We just get different guys from the community to lead the prayers. Our biggest number right now is fifteen or twenty people for juma, but prior to that if we had ten, that was a big [number]. There might be thirty or forty Muslims here at the most. It's a struggle all the time. [He laughs.]

But if we keep it going, someday more people will keep coming. Through all the years that I've been on the board, people come and they use Swift Current as a stepping stone, and [then] they get into something and they move on after. Nobody wants to stay here. There's no airport, so it's a struggle to keep people to stay. And if there's no university in the city nobody wants to be there. Regina's got a big university and Saskatoon's got one. We have a college here, and they teach a few things. It's limited but you can take a few courses . . .

My mother [Mary Abdullah] came from North Dakota. There was a big Lebanese community there. They [his parents] had connections somehow. It's a good five-hour drive away. His [his father's] cousins were doing custom [grain] combining in that area and that's how he got to meet them. One of his cousins is married to one of mum's sisters too.

I did grade nine and then I dropped out. I was missing too many classes helping my dad at the farm . . .

We have three children, Jamal, Mary, and Nadia, and my wife is Fatima [Zanidean]. She's from Lebanon. We met through letters. She's a second cousin to my dad [and] a first cousin to Zakia [Zanidean]. When they grew up we took them to the mosque all the time. We drove them the seventy kilometres each way every weekend. One daughter is still involved a bit, but the other two, they shy away from it now, but what do you do?

I think the future [of the Swift Current Muslim community] will be OK. We have immigrants coming in. There are four [recent] Syrian families here now. One family has eleven kids and another has five or six, and they're learning English and so in time hopefully they will stick around and take it over, insha'allah. They all say their prayers five times a day. You have to hope for the best.

Zakia Zanidean is one of the more recent arrivals from Lebanon, but her family connection to the Swift Current area goes a long way back. Zakia and her husband, Ali Zanidean, still live on a farm about ten kilometres west of Swift Current. She explained the complex story of the family she married into, who were also relatives. Her husband Ali's father, Husni Zanidean, had been brought to Canada at thirty-three by his sister, Karia Hattum. Karia was the wife of the original family arrival, Ali Hattum, who was also grandfather of Mohamed Hattum, whose account just precedes this one.

My father-in-law Husni Zanidean worked for four years before he brought his wife and his four children here in the year 1957 [including Zakia's future husband Ali Zanidean, born in 1952]. He [Husni] worked very hard on the CPR to provide for his growing family, and his wife Ishei worked alongside him to raise a family of nine children. They also bought a quarter-section of land. Between his job on the CPR and farming it left him a tired man. They had it tough but they were survivors. They never forgot their culture or their beliefs.

. . . There were the Zanideans, the Hattums, the Saddens, the Hendous, and the Gaders, probably in 1920 or something like that. They talked [later] about the "Dirty Thirties" around here so they had been here for a long time. They were mostly farmers and they bought a lot of land and they were successful that way. They didn't know the language at all but they got jobs . . . My father-in-law retired at the age of 60 from the CPR—the Canadian Pacific Railway. His brother worked in the city right away and the other brother too, they both worked for the city . . . The other ones, most of them became peddlers. They bought some stuff and they went to sell it and they made some money and they would buy land. It is amazing.

They worked hard and from working hard they all succeeded and [so] they tried to get together to make a mosque for worship. They were the Zanidean family, the Hattum family, the Gaders, the Himour family, the Hendous family, and the Sadden family. But they were always trying but they didn't succeed until the early '80s when Mohammad Afsar and Zia came here [from Hamilton, Ontario]. Then we started talking with each other and we said we have to do something. Mohammad was an engineer for the city at the time and he had connections and he knew how to write letters. Yes, they were a big factor in the building of the mosque here in Swift Current, the Masjid Al-Khair [also called the Islamic Centre of Swift Current].

It's a huge mosque. It was a Church of God before that and we converted it to the mosque and we worked really hard to do that. Abdou Himour led the renovation. My father-in-law went out of the country to collect money, he and Saleem Ganam, to Libya and they got money from there. We also wrote our story and sent it to Saudi Arabia. One lady heard of our story—it is a small city and we are trying to build a big mosque in here—and she went from door to door, she said, and she collected $15,000 to send to Swift Current [from Saudi Arabia]. During those years and until today a lot of people want to come to Swift Current for work but they ask if there is a mosque there first, and so it's a continuing effort. The newcomers they do their work too. They volunteer and they donate.

We made really good friends with Zia and Mohammad because we both wanted the same thing for us and our children. She was a leader and I was a follower [she laughs]. My mother-in-law Ishei Zanidean was my idol and then Zia was the number two. My mother-in-law had to bring [her first] four kids here and she had another five boys to raise pretty much on her own because her husband was busy working and farming. She didn't know the language and she was an amazing human being. Zia was my idol because she opened my eyes more to the world and educated me a little bit more about Islam. I taught the Arabic language for thirteen years and she taught the religion at the mosque for thirteen years. The accomplishment was teaching our kids their cultures and most importantly their faith. As a result, the children in Swift Current had done very well in Islamic quiz competitions between the kids from Regina and Saskatoon. We are proud of what we accomplished. Life is a struggle and battle and I hope we leave this world in a better place for the next generation.

The grand opening of the mosque was in 1982, and it was attended by over two hundred people. The mayor came to the opening and all the ladies were there because they contributed so much of their time and their effort and everything. We put them on the front line to cut the ribbon. The high-ranked people came from Edmonton, like Shaikh Yusuf Chebli and Ali Tarrabine's son, Mahmud Tarrabine.

I would like to mention a few families which were a big part of keeping the mosque going with their help—it doesn't matter if it was money or volunteering or anything else. Those families are the Shukoor family, the Abougundia family, the Mohamad Jadi family and the Hussein Khalaff family and many more. I should add that in 2001 the Jadi family, the Khalaff family and the Moola family took it upon themselves to talk to the city about getting a partition in the Hillcrest Cemetery. Now we have a small place in a beautiful new cemetery.

By 1982, the children of the old settlers had adapted to the life of the Canadians so when we went from door to door to collect money they knew they were Muslims but they didn't know much about it. They used to come and listen and then their children again were straying away from the mosque, but that's how it goes in every city. We got quite a few of them back into the mosque, and some of them we didn't. For example, my eldest son Fadi's wife converted as well. She and my son met in university and then she converted and they got married, but my other son Rayath's wife didn't convert, but that's fine too. I couldn't ask for better human beings and mothers to my grandchildren.

All the long-term Swift Current Muslims were of Syrian-Lebanese origins, but starting in the 1960s, Muslim professionals from South Asia—doctors, business people, etc—began arriving. Mohammad Afsar and his wife, Zia Afsar, from Pakistan were among the more recent arrivals and they played a major role in the establishment of an association and a mosque in the city in the early 1980s. Mohammad had arrived in Hamilton in 1964 at McMaster University, as a Pakistani graduate student of engineering, and later he worked for the city. He was one of a handful of really active Muslims in Hamilton, he formed an association and built a mosque there. But in 1980 he moved to Swift Current with his family. In December 2018, Mohammad, by then retired in Vancouver, told me:

> I had started my engineering career with the City of Hamilton in 1967, and I played a significant role in Hamilton's downtown redevelopment and in the preparation of the Hamilton-Wentworth Regional Development plan. In 1980 we moved to Swift Current, Saskatchewan, with our three children. This was a career-enhancing move and I became the head of combined planning, engineering, building, and public works functions of the city.
>
> In Swift Current, the Muslim community was of Lebanese descent. In early 1900s, Saskatchewan was offering land for ten dollars a quarter section, so people could buy and become owners, with the requirement that they develop the land and grow crops and so on. Some

of them had come to the United States [first] and become peddlers before moving to Swift Current. They established farms in the Swift Current area and settled there. In 1980, they were into their third generation. They always had at the back of their minds that they were Muslims and they had a desire to have a Jamia, a big mosque, but they didn't know how to go about it. So in 1980 we organized and formed the Muslim Association of Swift Current. We also started a weekend Islamic school for children in a facility provided by the United Church of Swift Current, where the community also held Friday prayers and Eid prayers. Zia also prepared a few Muslim funerals of some female members of the community.

In terms of relationships, you hear people talk about "Islamophobia" and this and that, but here was [an example of] the "Islamophobia" that we experienced in Swift Current: The priest of the United Church gave my wife and me a tour of their church facility in downtown and showed us what classrooms we could use for our children and the meeting room, and so on. As he was going around— and to show you the height of acceptance that people had for Muslims at that time, and you know how in churches they have these pictures hung of Jesus and Mother Mary and so on—I still remember, and I could never thank that priest and community enough, when he said, "I know Muslims do not allow pictures in their places of worship and where they gather and if when you gather in our church and that is not compatible to you, if you wish we can cover them up."

I was so moved, with tears in my eyes, I said, "Listen, if our faith is that weak then we cannot call ourselves faithful. There is no need of that. We are thankful for your generosity and the use of the facility would be enough." We used that church for three years.

The community worked hard under my guidance and raised the required funds to buy an existing unused church, and in 1983 we established the Islamic Centre of Swift, also known as Masjid Al-Khair.

In 1991, I got a job with the City of Regina as director of planning, building, and social development, so we moved there. We became part of the Muslim community of Regina, which was an established community and [already] had a mosque. Zia started teaching in weekend

Islamic school and I got involved in the mosque. Zia also assumed the chairperson's role of the local chapter of the Canadian Council of Muslim Women (CCMW) . . . and developed close working relationships with other local women's groups concerned with women's rights issues.

During the war in Bosnia [in the early 1990s], Zia approached different faith groups and an organization called "Women United" was formed. This group organized a rally to raise awareness of the atrocities happening in Bosnia. It was -40° Celsius weather when about 250 women and men walked in downtown Regina to protest violence against women. CCMW's Regina chapter received an award from YWCA Regina for their fight on violence against women. In 2007, she also received "Women Who Inspire Award" from the Canadian Council of Muslim Women.

After five years in Regina, I got a job with the District Municipality of Squamish, British Columbia as director of public works, and we moved there in 1996. The reason for my moves to different provinces was that from the beginning I wanted to work and live in all the provinces of this beautiful country which we call home. I retired in 2000 but we are still involved in the local Muslim community. I also initiated a multifaith group in Squamish and worked closely with the Sikh community there.

Now retired in BC, the Afsars have three children, Khalid, Erum and Aamna.

The Muslims of Saskatchewan also owe a great debt of gratitude to Dr Naiyer Habib and his wife Mahlaqa Naushaba Habib for publishing their magnum opus, *History of the Muslims of Regina, Saskatchewan, and Their Organizations*.[83] Indeed this holds true of much for the province's scattered Muslim population, including that of Swift Current, Saskatoon, and other smaller settlements.

In the opening pages of their compendium, the Regina-based Habibs cited both the late Dr Anwarul Haque[84] and Dr F M W Al-Katib[85] of Davidson on Muhammad Ali Ta Haynee (also known as Michel Alley Haynee), the first known Muslim in Regina. Al-Katib mentioned speaking with Haynee, who was born in what became Lebanon in 1864. He served as a captain in the Ottoman army, was wounded in 1885, and reached North Dakota in 1889. With a friend, Sied Ganam, the father of Saleem Ganam, he moved northward to Regina in 1903. There, Haynee established Alley's Fancy Wholesale and Retail Dry Goods at Winnipeg Street and Twelfth Avenue, which sold various products to peddlers in southern Saskatchewan, presumably including to fellow Syrian-Lebanese. He apparently returned to Lebanon in 1911 and married Ganam's sister. They had seventeen children, one of whom, presumably Zackary Haynee, becoming a founding member of the Regina associa-tion. Muhammad Ali Ta Haynee died in 1982 at the age of one hundred and eight. His wife died the same year at ninety.[86]

The Habibs noted the arrivals of a further handful of Middle Eastern immigrants, including Abdul Qadir Haymore, aged sixteen, in 1912. Haymore reportedly took a variety of jobs and then qualified at night school to become a teacher in the Regina public school system. In 1931, Haymore, Haynee, and some others founded the first Islamic Association of Regina, with Haymore serving as president and imam and Saleem Ganam as secretary, until the latter moved to Edmonton in 1941. The association lasted until 1967 when Haymore died.[87] It was revived by Haque, Al-Katib, and others in 1970–71. The Regina community bought a business building in 1982 and opened it in 1984 when Abdul Qayyum was president.[88]

6. Winnipeg and North: Town and Country

WORKING MY WAY EAST FROM ALBERTA AND SASKATCHEWAN, I met communities in Manitoba that exemplified the Muslim multiculturalism of the Canadian ummah. They were a mix of early twentieth-century Syrian Lebanese farmers, Trinidadians, and Syrians who had come in the 1950s and 1960s as graduate students and stayed on.

My first meeting in the Winnipeg area was with Canadian-born Ernest Abas, of Syrian Lebanese origin, who lived on an isolated farmstead in Hodgson. His family's story follows:

> I was born on December 6, 1926, in Hodgson, and my father's name was Alec or Ali, and my mother's name was Jemily or Jenny. Ali was the most commonly used name. The neighbours called them Mr Abas and Mrs Abas, as was customary at that time. My father came from a small town, Kherbet Rouha, near Beirut, Lebanon, and my mother came from Homs, a city in Syria . . .
>
> My parents were married before they came to North America in 1912. They [wanted to come] by steamship on the *Titanic*, but it got so popular that the tickets got sold out. It hit the ice and went down so it was quite by chance [that they lived] or we wouldn't have been around. They came right after, on the Cunard Steamship Line.
>
> Prior to coming to Canada, my father had been in the United States when he was fifteen or sixteen and then returned to Lebanon. While in the States he worked at Thief River Falls and Crookston, Minnesota and also in North Dakota. My father had worked as a farmhand and on the railroad after the turn of the century.
>
> My parents lived in Minnesota for a year and a half but decided to leave the States to get away from the people and to be on their

own, so they went north to Winnipeg [in 1914]. They went to the homestead office and leased a farm for a modest cost of five or ten dollars. My father was allotted a location, sight unseen, and took it from there . . . Since then, my brothers and I have farmed two to three sections here . . .

My parents came to Arborg by train. This was their first trip to their homestead . . . I believe they were picked up by John Ross, the mail driver, stayed overnight at his place and then went on to see this unknown land, which he had acquired through the homestead deal. It was solid bush! They cleared a little spot and put up a shack. They stayed in the shack and as time went on they improved it. It was quite an experience and a difficult way of life . . .

[They] had very kind neighbours. As I understand it, there were several families that were very helpful to my mother and dad when they first came out. [Among them were] the Peter Sinclair family, the John Ross family, and the Hyslop family who were helpful, especially to my mother, in adjusting her to life in this area when things were very difficult. The land was virgin land, a lot of water, no roads to speak of, just wagon trails, with lots of moose. For quite a while they were quite isolated from a Syrian or Lebanese community.

We didn't know the English language very well when we were growing up. We were eight children ranging from age one to eighteen. I found school was lots of fun and we soon learned to speak English properly. The other children were from a variety of ethnic groups, and they didn't know English initially either. There was one boy, of Ukrainian descent, Ben Hanischuk, who didn't know a word of English and later became the minister of education for the Province of Manitoba. We went to school together for a number of years and he now lives in Winnipeg.

The children in the school were mainly Christians. It seemed they knew we were Muslims but it was not taken too seriously. At that time, people were more friendly, and they didn't seem to inquire into personal things. There were no pressures on us as far as religion was concerned. Our parents did what they could to teach us about Islam. Neither parent could read or write but they did teach us prayers and stories. In later years we ordered in books and literature [on Islam].

The Kadri family soon arrived and lived close but didn't stay too long and moved out to the States—this would be in the 1920s. Then the Ferris family, two brothers Ed and Alec, both bachelors, came to live close by. Ed Ferris moved to Saskatchewan after some years and Alex Ferris passed away in 1978. They came from the same town my father did. Ed married a girl of Syrian descent and Alex married a Canadian girl. Their children became Canadianized [suggesting not remaining Muslim] from what I could see . . . Other than these two families we [remained] quite isolated.

When I look back, I believe that maybe my mother and father were in some way instrumental in having so many come to Winnipeg in the last few years. I think it is a chain reaction through marriage and through relatives. There were several families named Tasse and then the chain reaction started from there. There are now twenty or thirty Tasse families in this group.

My oldest brother was named Joe. His Arabic name was Yusuf but they called him Joe. He got married and his wife's name was Hilda Kenny. The next one was my oldest sister Freda, she was married to Albert Austin. Next there was my sister Lily, she was married to Clint Norton. The next one to her was Annie, she was married to Abraham Hager, from Michigan, North Dakota. The next one was Dora, and she was married to Zeno Scaletta. Next to Dora was my brother Omer, he only passed away less than a month ago. He lived right next door to where I live. His wife's name was Rushdie Tassi.

Next to Omer was myself, I'm married to Anne or Amine Abraham. My wife was also from Kherbet Rouha, and many other people were. My sister Irene was next, she was married to Andrew Gulay. I have three kids, and we are now great-grandparents. My kids' names are Austin Abas, Lillian Ahmed, and Alec Abas. Austin married a woman named Seeham Hagar. Lillian married Imtiaz Ahmed, and Alec married Amine Swide. [His son] Austin is an accountant, Lillian is a housewife, and Alec lives in Calgary and works at Fort McMurray in the oil sands . . .

I was never involved much in the Winnipeg mosque, but I've gone there many times . . . There were ups and downs but all in all, I've had a quite reasonable life.

In a 2015 interview with Tasneem Vali, office manager of the Manitoba Islamic Association, Ernest Abas recalled his early life:

> There was no electricity in Hodgson then and we had to heat our homes using wood. Most people were farmers; we milked cows and grew our own vegetables. I cut wood to earn some money. Later, times became even more difficult in the 1930s and [later] when the Second World War started. I had two brothers who were old enough to join the Canadian forces during the war, but they were not accepted due to medical reasons . . .
>
> . . . We were thankful for what we had and it was enough but not much. Nowadays everybody is into the latest gadget and that makes for poor citizens. Our one-room school [three miles away] taught us discipline and honesty. Parents today do not know how to discipline their children and that is a shame.[89]

The pioneer Abas and Tasse families are mentioned in the website of the Manitoba Islamic Association, founded in 1969. One panel on the website reminds us that there were "tens of Muslims in Manitoba around the turn of the twentieth century." It adds that most of their stories have been lost, and the end of restrictions on "Asian" immigrants had added to Muslim numbers. "Larger waves of immigration started after 1967, when a point-based immigration system relaxed many of the discriminatory restrictions placed on immigration. Most [of these post-1967] migrants came from the Caribbean, Lebanon and the Indian subcontinent."

This acknowledgment of the early twentieth century's dearth of Muslim immigration and the reference to the post-1967 "larger waves," including people from the Caribbean, leads nicely to the story of a Trinidadian student named Khaleel Baksh, who arrived in Winnipeg in 1962 and went on to become a founding figure of the first Manitoba mosque in 1976:

> I was born in Trinidad in 1928 in an agricultural village. My father Ibrahim Baksh was also born in Trinidad, but his father, my grandfather, was from India. My grandfather's brother, who came before him, was also from India, from Burrabaksh Barabunki, close to Lucknow in

northeast India, but I don't know the details of it. My father was given to [his] uncle—in fact the first two children were two boys and both of them, my father Ibrahim and my uncle Asghar Baksh, were given to his uncle . . .

My grandfather had a cocoa and coffee estate and two shops, and one was given to my father and one to my uncle Asghar. My grandfather used to do the supervising of the estate. In those days cocoa was a great thing and the quality was excellent . . .

I grew up with my other grandfather and we lived upstairs, and downstairs was the warehouse . . . My father, and my mother, Aisha Ali, had eleven children. I went to elementary school at age four— my father told them I was five—and I finished at eleven. One day I noticed that three of these students were going to San Fernando where the high school was to do some exams to get into the school and I asked about this. I told my father about this and he went to the school. The principal was a Canadian and he told my dad to bring me. I didn't have to do the exams but my father got money from the estate to pay for my education. But before going to the school the principal wanted me to wait until I was fourteen so I could learn how to teach the students in the elementary school. But my father said no.

The year before, one of the teachers started a private school and so I left the first school and went to that place, and there I passed my final exams that year, so I got a job teaching in the same school I went to! I was nineteen, at the end of high school, and I started teaching the five-year-olds to read and write. Then the supervisor of this Presbyterian school, another Canadian guy, talked to me and he wanted me to become a Christian and he gave me all the nice things that will happen to me, so I said to him, "I'm not a really good Muslim. You think you want to make me a worse Christian?" He didn't like that [Baksh laughed] so next year he moved me from there to another school in the same area but that was far away, so I had to ride my bicycle. I think it was a punishment.

I went there for a year, and then I told my father I am going to move from here to San Fernando because the children go to high school there. We didn't have a high school in the village where we were. I went to the Trinidadian guy who had this private school and

I said to him, "You need somebody to teach here." He said "Sure," and so he paid me the same amount. We were not getting a lot of money anyhow. So we worked together [and moved] from where he was which was from a small place to a larger building. He wanted to move out of the school business and go up to teach in another school where he was getting a principal's job. So I said OK, I'll take it over, so I paid him for the school and I took it over. I moved the school, Kenley College, from a few people to three hundred. I developed the high school and it became very popular and I had quite a few people teaching. We had people taking their exams and everything.

Khaleel Baksh eventually left high school and went on to take an agricultural degree at the University of the West Indies in Jamaica and at St Augustine, Trinidad. He married Salima Edoo, on May 4, 1952 and they had several children. They sailed to England to try university there but didn't stay long, instead following the lead of a friend who had gone to Winnipeg. He arrived in Winnipeg in March 1962 and worked for the railway on the trains. His family followed in September, in time for the children's school fall term:

> Things were different here [in terms of racism when looking for advertised lodgings]. In London they'd look at me and say, "We have people coming already." I came here and the people told me to come in and look at the place. It was completely different.

Baksh completed a science degree at the University of Manitoba in the mid-1960s and then took one year of teacher-training before starting to teach middle-school in Winnipeg. After two years he moved on to a provincial school teaching adults and then went on to become the school's principal. Later, he joined the Department of Indian Affairs and became responsible for a large section of northern native schooling based in The Pas as superintendent of Adult Education Northern Manitoba.

> I went up there for five years . . . I had asked my boss if he could move me down, because I wanted my kids to come to school in Winnipeg . . . but I still had a northern area, so I would fly there and

Khaleel Baksh with wife Salima and children at his graduation, Winnipeg, 1964.
Photo courtesy of Khaled Baksh.

come back home after a few days. Basically what they tried to do was to provide education for adults, this time in the Interlake Region.

In Winnipeg we [had] started a Muslim group when I was at the university and there were nine of us. One of the guys wasn't at the university. He was a graduate and he was working outside. We didn't have a particular place [to meet] so the owner of the building [where I was staying] had a room downstairs that he used as an office but he wasn't using it then. So I asked him and he said, "Use it any time you want." So we got a room where we could meet, especially on a Sunday when we could do *salat* [prayers] and things like that together. We grew from there. Most of us were university students, but it grew and later we began to get people who came to work in Winnipeg.

Later there was a Christian religious organization, Anglican or United Church, and they would allow us to use their basement on a Sunday. When I went up north [for five years] I wasn't so up on what was happening with the guys who were still there [in Winnipeg], but when I came back I organized the group a little better. We used the International Centre downtown for Sunday meetings and school. The group was developing and I wanted to get it registered as a MSA [Muslim Students Association of the United States and Canada] branch and we did that.

Then myself and Jameel Ali said, "Let's get some kind of a build-ing," and we did. We got a piece of property on Hazelwood, in the St Vital area of Winnipeg, and we said we would put up a building there . . . We started collecting money from everybody. At the time there were at least thirty people. We got somebody [a contractor] to start the building but once he was paid some money he left. So I started getting people who could do individual things, like carpentry and trades, and I got them to do what I wanted them to do and we got the building going. I was on the board of trustees which was respon-sible for construction and maintenance. I became the president . . .

As president of the Manitoba Islamic Association, Khaleel Baksh would have been involved with the CMCC (the Council of Muslim Communities of Canada) and I first met him there and visited the Hazelwood Avenue mosque with him, which was opened in September 1976. It was the first mosque in Manitoba, but now the modern Manitoba Islamic Association runs the Manitoba Grand Mosque and Community Centre at 2445 Waverley Street in Winnipeg, which opened in 2004.

Khaleel Baksh:

Later I wanted to move away from Indian Affairs so I didn't have to go up north all the time. When I saw an advertisement from the Correctional Service, [I applied] and got the job as the principal of the school at the Stoney Mountain federal prison, just outside of Winnipeg. I was there for a few years and then they wanted somebody for an office in the department in Ottawa in 1978, and I got it. In Ottawa I was responsible for all the prisons in Canada with National Technical Training schools. I spent five years there with the federal government and then I asked them to move me to Kingston to run the school at the Prison for Women. The salary was the same and I didn't have a lot to do until I retired at sixty-five.

After retiring in 1992, Khaleel Baksh remained in Kingston with his wife and children, Salima, Imran (Rayhana Bhabha), Khalid, and Ashan (Leanne Kilpatrick), and started a bicycle shop, Cyclepath, with Ashan.

Khaleel lived in Kingston until 2012, when his wife Salima died and then
he moved in with Imran, a dentist in Kanata, where he died in 2014.

Dr Farouk Chebib and his wife, Laila Chebib, New Year's Eve, 1956,
Damascus. Photo courtesy of Laila Chebib.

Among the earliest Muslims in Manitoba were Dr Farouk Chebib and his
wife Laila Chebib from Syria who arrived first for a year in 1958, when
he was a graduate student at the University of Manitoba. They returned
permanently in 1965, when they saw their lives in danger at home, and
because she had loved Winnipeg so much. They were among the founders of the Manitoba Islamic Association and the Pioneer Mosque on
Hazelwood Avenue.

In what follows, Laila's 2019 recollections have been enhanced by a few paragraphs from her own shorter biographical sketch:

> I was born in Damascus, Syria, in 1938. I lived in Syria for eight years. My father had a business in France, so at the end of the war we went to France. I was with my mother, Fatima Chebib, my father, Fouad Chebib, and my younger sister. My uncle was there [in France, where] he had a business too. His wife was French, and he had children, three girls. I lived in France for eight years, and I got my primary and secondary education there.
>
> In 1954, my father went to Syria close to the death of his father. He and his brothers, who had come for the funeral, decided that I, Laila Chebib, should get to meet my cousin, Farouk Chebib, and marry him. In 1953 he had just graduated from the University of California, Berkeley, and gone back to Syria. They thought it was an appropriate time for him and me to get married. I could have said no, but I met him and thought he was good, he was nice, and I approved. There were many other contenders . . . but I liked him and I accepted and so we were to be married on New Year's Eve, 1954 in Damascus. We had got engaged in September [after which] he left for India for a course. He came back just a few days before our wedding!
>
> Farouk was working as a civil servant in the ministry of agricultural in Damascus, Syria. A consultant from FAO [UN Food and Agriculture Organization] came to Damascus and saw what Farouk was working on and he said the FAO would sponsor him to study in Canada. The consultant, Mr Harrington, was a Canadian from Saskatchewan. Farouk was to get his master's in plant breeding from the University of Manitoba. So in 1958 we left. He went ahead of me in May. I stayed in France with my mother for a couple of months, and then I followed him to Winnipeg. I had with me our son Louay, who was about a year old.
>
> We found a place in the attic of a couple, who were living in the main floor. Their son and daughter-in-law lived on the second floor, and we were on the third floor with one bedroom and a tiny kitchen. The bathroom was shared on the second floor. The people were extremely nice. They were the Tremblay family, and they treated me

like a daughter . . . I spoke very little English, only what I took in high school in Lyon, France. And so at one point I went to English classes to learn English, because everybody in our immediate family spoke English.

It was Winnipeg and it was very cold and very snowy. I had no idea what a Fahrenheit degree meant! Thirty-two degrees for me was beautiful weather, but in Canada it was otherwise! During our stay we met only one Muslim family, Omar Ibrahim, who turned out to be related to the Tasse family who immigrated to Canada at a later date. Winnipeg at that time was still a very small city.

In '58, when Farouk came to Canada, they had installed a computer at the University of Manitoba . . . it took up a huge space and he was the first one to program it . . . He spent his evenings, his days, and weekends doing this while I was alone with our son. Farouk got his master's degree in one year and we went back to Syria in May 1959.

We stayed in Syria. He had to do his military service. It was supposed to be for two years, but he had it good and so after the first four or five months at the preliminary service training he was given a job, along with the military service, administrating an experimental farm near Aleppo, so we went there. Then a Ford Foundation representative and several other experts with their families came to Aleppo. Syria was setting up an agricultural university in Aleppo, and Farouk was lecturing there too, outside of his military duties. The Ford Foundation offered to give Farouk a grant to send him anywhere in the world to get his PhD so he could come back as a professor at this university. He asked me and I answered I would like to go to Winnipeg [most,] of anywhere in the world. People think I am crazy for choosing Winnipeg, but I loved Winnipeg, I loved the people, I loved Canada. And for me that was a beautiful choice.

However, before we returned to Canada for Farouk's PhD, there was a coup d'etat in Syria in 1961. Farouk's brother was in the military. He was a colonel. He participated in the coup. A military tribunal had him executed. As we were still at the agricultural farm, one of the workers warned us of a plan by one of the drivers to kill our son, who was being driven to an English school back and forth

from the farm to Aleppo, by throwing him out of the moving car.
So, we really panicked and moved out immediately from the farm,
even though the house and the utilities were free. We found a house
in Aleppo and moved out of the farm. Therefore when the chance of
going to Canada [in 1965 on a Ford Foundation grant] for his PhD
came along, we embraced it.

We returned to Winnipeg in '65, when I was pregnant with my
second son, Oubay . . .

About the beginning of the Muslim Community in Winnipeg, as I
remember it, it was mainly composed of graduate students from Arab
countries such as Egypt. They were mostly engineers, entrepreneurs
from Lebanon, immigrant families from Palestine, and professionals
such as doctors from Pakistan.

As our numbers were increasing, in the late 1960s we decided
to have a place of our own for the [Muslim] community to get
together . . .

We started fundraising. This work was done by women with the
help of their families. Muslims and Arab Christians, women from
Syria, Egypt, Palestine, as well as some American friends who had
lived in the Middle East all worked on the fund-raising in the six-
ties and seventies to build the mosque on Hazelwood. We would get
together in someone's kitchen and bake Arabic sweets to sell at the
Red River Exhibition. We would cook Middle Eastern food, sell tickets to gather funds. We sewed folkloric clothes to show folkloric dances
and [display in] fashion shows . . . Then we started to connect with
Muslims from Pakistan, mostly doctors, who were in England at the
time and they came to Canada.

Farouk had been working on his PhD for two years at the University
of Manitoba when the war between Israel and Syria broke out in
1967. All the experts were kicked out of Syria and his grant was cut
off, so Farouk had to find work to feed his family. He was given a job
as lecturer at the University of Manitoba, and while he was teaching,
he got a job at the dental college as a researcher. The government of
Syria asked him to return, but we did not return. We applied for citizenship [in Canada].

In '68–69 I enrolled in the university as a mature student. In 1969 the Manitoba Islamic Association [MIA] was established, with my husband on the board of trustees. I was [a member of] the Canadian Arab Student Association at the university, so we had two different associations. We were receiving guest speakers to talk about the Palestinian situation and human rights and so forth . . . We were active politically, socially [and in mosque affairs] . . .

In 1974, I received my BA in French and psychology, and after we returned from our 1975–76 sabbatical leave in the Middle East, I continued to study. In 1980 I also started to work full-time teaching civil servants French. I got my master's in French in 1982. [Actually I had] wanted to continue studying psychology, but I was discouraged. [I was told], "You're a woman, and you're too old, thirty-five years old, and by the time you finish your experiments and so on and so forth it's no use in you going into psychology," so I switched to French! I don't regret it. It was the best job I ever got. It was the Cadillac of jobs . . . [laughs]

In 1978, I started teaching French in the City of Winnipeg recreational program for adults in the evenings and for the Public Service Commission, which luckily became a permanent job in 1980. In 1988, I was assigned to the Court of the Queen's Bench to teach French to federal judges.

Meanwhile in September 1976—through the efforts of Khaleel Baksh and others—the Manitoba Islamic Association had opened the Hazelwood Avenue mosque. Laila, who was chair of the MIA Ladies Auxiliary, worked at the Arabic-Islamic Sunday school. On its fortieth anniversary in 2016, the Hazelwood Avenue mosque was recognized as a historical site in Winnipeg and named the Pioneer Mosque:

When the Hazelwood mosque was built, we held many functions there. We set up Sunday school in the basement of the mosque to teach our children Arabic and religion. It was a volunteer, non-formal setup. There were no permanent teachers. However, some of the parents contributed in teaching. Most of the children were of Arabic or Pakistani origin. Arab families wanted their children to learn how to read their language, and non-Arab families wanted to prepare their children to understand the Qur'an. We celebrated weddings and funerals; we had open houses for the neighbours to introduce them to our community. We worked on the landscaping. I decided to plant evergreen trees because they do not lose their leaves and they produce shade. [And] we set up summer Islamic girls and boys mixed camps at West Hawk Lake or Gimli. Wahid Mustapha and his wife Zuleigha were the more prominent family at the camps.

This modest start developed through the years. In 1996, a regular school, Al Hijrah Islamic School that teaches grade K-11 [adding a class year by year], was set up by Abdo Tasse and Wajih Zeid. Another school, Sofia Academy, set up in 1999 by Dr Taib Soufi, teaches French, religion, and Arabic. Plus, weekend schooling of Arabic is given in various school districts under the direction of Mr Dassouki, [in addition to] a respectable Islamic teaching program at the Grand Mosque on Waverley.

However, as has been shown to have happened before in this history of Muslim pioneers in Canada, friction over the meaning of Islam and the methods of practice can divide communities, since immigrants arrive from different places bearing different traditions. This also happened in Winnipeg, as Laila noted:

> In 1985 I distanced myself from the mosque and the MIA [Manitoba Islamic Association] because of the many conflicts [that had arisen]. I did not want to be involved in them. In 1986, as more newcomers settled in Winnipeg they took control of the administration of the Pioneer Mosque. Their retrogressive ideas, such as treating women as second class and separating them from the men, disenchanted many of us, and we withdrew from the MIA.
>
> Then in 1987 my husband took early retirement [and] went to teach at King Faisal University in Saudi Arabia. He supervised theses and consulted on research methodology at the Faculty of Medicine in Saudi Arabia. We visited back and forth. In 1989 a retired senior ex-ARAMCO employee asked him to join him at his new job, working on the space shuttle in Utah. He retired [from there] in 2000 and

became a consultant for some of the larger aerospace corporations in the United States. We both finally retired in our beloved Winnipeg, he in 2005 and I in 2016.

Asked if she thought Muslims were on the right track in Canada, Laila Chebib said:

> I hope so. I think that Canadians are ninety percent wonderful people . . . [but] we Muslims have to become more engaged, more communicative, more connected. The MIA is doing a wonderful job of welcoming people to the mosques by inviting the public to our open houses. We also need to get some of our Muslim brethren to open their minds, we are all one people. There are some narrow-minded Muslims of course and these Muslims need to be hit over the head [she laughs] to become human beings.

But as a further statement of Laila Chebib's views I cite here the somewhat less optimistic last paragraph of the autobiographical essay she sent me:

> I have always believed in a strong community, we need each other. I am ready to defend and promote our religion by countering extremist views on both sides. I had suffered a lot from discrimination while we lived in France and my sons encountered a great deal of discrimination in their schools and our neighbourhood right here in Winnipeg when they arrived. The only way to combat discrimination is by dialogue, getting to know and accepting each other. When we arrived in Winnipeg in 1965, there was not one black person there, French was spoken in a whisper in the stores. We came a long way in the acceptance of different people. It takes all kinds to make the world . . .
>
> We were not involved in the [construction] of the new Waverley Grand mosque [opened in 2004] because we were out of the country. But we came back to the MIA after they finished building and opening it. We got involved again, and to this day, we all are still very active members of MIA.

Dr Farouk Chebib's story runs jointly with that of his wife Laila. However, there were other interesting points and anecdotes about their involvement, indeed leadership, of the Manitoba Muslim community which he described:

> I was born in 1933 in Haifa, Palestine. We had to leave quickly, [without] most of our belongings, after the attack on Deir Yaseen when the Jewish Haggana gang killed all the inhabitants of that town [April 9, 1948]. We were scared. Our parents thought things would get resolved and we would soon be back in our home. My parents were from Damascus, Syria. They packed their belongings and one child (me when I was fifteen) into a truck destined for Damascus . . . The remainder of the family managed to migrate by other means. Our family, Chebib, was one of the well-known families in Damascus. Ours was a large, well-connected family. Since a few years now, I have become the oldest survivor of our family.
>
> After we arrived there, I went to high school, and upon graduation in 1950 I won first place in a government scholarship competition and was sent to the University of California in Berkeley for five years. As soon as I received my BSc degree—in two and a half years—in June 1953 I went to Texas A and M for graduate studies. However, I was ordered to return to Syria to a position in the Ministry of Agriculture in Damascus. I worked there 'til I received a United Nations fellowship to come to the University of Manitoba in Winnipeg, in 1958.
>
> [When we arrived], my wife Laila and I considered ourselves the first Muslims in Manitoba until we found out about the [Ernest] Abas family. I am now considered one of the elders of the Syrian community in Manitoba . . . When we first came to Winnipeg, of course there was no mosque, no nothing whatsoever, even no yogurt. My wife brought a yogurt "starter" from Belgium and has been ever since making her own yogurt . . .
>
> At the first general meeting of the Manitoba Islamic Association in 1969 I was elected first trustee. The trustees were tasked to find a place of worship for the almost one hundred Muslims in Manitoba. The trustees did what they could to get some money to build a humble mosque. Our friends were mostly Christian Arabs from the Middle East, [and] they worked closely with us in fund-raising activities, helping us in organizing and cooking. We held many functions at

community halls, hotels and at the University of Manitoba . . .

A memorable event was a dinner and a fashion show at the Ramada Inn sometime in 1968 or 1969 that was crashed by members of the Winnipeg Blue Bombers football team. Such activities united the diverse Muslim community. Farouk Chebib:

> As I was complaining to some friends about our failure to raise any decent amount of money for the mosque fund, they suggested that I ask the oil-rich countries of the Middle East for help. The following Tuesday, they came to my office at the university and we drafted three letters to King Hussein of Jordan, King Faisal of Saudi Arabia, and President Mohammad Al-Khadhafi of Libya, telling them that we, the Muslims of the God-forsaken land called Canada, have no mosque to pray in. Soon King Faisal sent us a cheque for $20,000 which was eventually used as the seed money to build the Hazelwood Mosque. Meanwhile a new MIA executive were elected. They were considered by many as strict fundamentalists, which caused us and other Muslim families to lose interest and distance ourselves from the Mosque. When the cheque arrived it stayed in the MIA post office box for a couple of months before it was noticed!
>
> Now that the seed money was available at last, [everybody's] interest was renewed. That was when a group of volunteers led by Mr Khaleel Baksh took over the lead and made things happen. Mr Baksh was very creative and took over the contracting and the actual work of building the mosque. For that he should be given credit.

For the record, Farouk Chebib named other Muslim pioneer elders of Winnipeg: Dr Ezzat Ibrahim from Egypt, Mrs Sayeda Inayatulla from India, Abdo El-Tassi from Lebanon, Dr Abdul Malik from Pakistan, Mrs Shahina Siddiqui from Egypt, Wajih Zeid from Palestine, and Wahid Mustapha from Trinidad. He also acknowledged some conflicts regarding matters such as the direction of prayer.

> I organized a Readathon, where the children would memorize suras from the Qur'an and receive donations for the mosque from their

sponsors for each sura they learned. The MIA trustees also contracted Glen Lawn Cemetery and purchased a few burial plots. Some families also purchased plots for themselves, thus creating the current Muslim cemetery in St Vital . . .

For the last few years, we have been closely involved with the Syrian refugees. There are many, many families that we directly supervise and help in getting settled and adapted to the Canadian way of life, helping them with doctors, dentists, and other appointments, accommodations, family relations, paying bills, banking, shopping, etc.

Our friends keep flooding us with donations of clothes, books, toys and furniture which we drive to our families. The excess we give to the CMWI, the Canadian Moslem Women's Institute . . .

We are not very religious. My wife prays, and we are proud of our religion and what we do. We stand and watch to see if anything goes wrong and we try to fix it.

Right now, there is a big issue. Two or three [men, calling] themselves sheikhs or imams are conducting, against the laws of Canada, marriages encouraging polygamy. Many men I know have got another wife without telling the first wife. They have made "religious" marriages and they have made illegal arrangements with these sheikhs. It needs to be stopped. That is our next challenge . . . The Canadian Council of Muslim Women . . . should be encouraged to cause an end to it . . . I myself intend to report such marriages to the police and bring this matter to the attention of Members of Parliament and Provincials Legislators.

[As Muslims in Manitoba] I think we are on the right track. We are very comfortable in Winnipeg and I am very happy about that. As for outreach activities, the mosque has been making open houses on a regular basis. We have had many successful events there, attended by the public. A few politicians are regular attendees of our functions. We have about six Members of Parliament or Provincial Legislators who come regularly, as well as City Councilors. It is becoming very well respected.

7. Windsor, Ontario

ON DECEMBER 11, 1982, DR GORDON JASEY, WHOSE FAMILY HAD moved from Nova Scotia to Windsor in 1947, related to me his father's and his own experiences in Maritime Canada. In Windsor he was a respected specialist in obstetrics and gynecology and continued his practice until December 2018. He died at the age of 90 on July 12, 2019.

Dr Gordon Jasey began by giving me his father's Arabic name, Hamid Said Hejazi:

> In Canada, the Jasey family is known as the Jaseys, in Lebanon as the Hejazis and in Hejaz [Arabia] as the Al-Adawis. A Google search of Al-Adawi shows the name Said bin Zaid Al-Adawi [whose] wife Fatima was the daughter of Al-Kuttab, grandson of the sister of the second Khalif of Islam, Umar.
>
> My father was Said Mohammed Hejazi, later Jasey, born in Kherbet Rouha, Syria, in 1882. Following the First World War, the area became Lebanon. The Jaseys were educated landowners and had a library in their home. Said married Amounie Mazloum [1889-1980] and in 1908 they had a son Naif, and in 1913 a daughter, Audrey. My father had two half-brothers, the older, Najib, and the younger, Ali Al-Kadri. [see photo] During the First World War, Ali immigrated to Minnesota, USA. Several months later, Said followed him. Their stay was short due to Najib's death [in Lebanon]. They [Said and Ali] both returned to Lebanon. Years later, Ali returned to St Paul, Minnesota. [Said followed him.] On passing through immigration he was given a name change—Hejazi to Jasey—by an immigration officer. This was common practice at that time. [There were] a few other people from Lebanon, and of course they were involved in trade, as peddlers.

Front row, left: Dr Gordon Mohammed Jasey's father Said Jasey, brother-in-law Joseph Edwards, Gordon's brother Naif Jasey, holding Gordon in front. Back row, left: Gordon Jasey's sister Audrey Edwards, Amney Jasey, Amounie Jasey, holding Amney Jasey's child Hazel Jasey. Photo courtesy of Dr Gordon Jasey.

In 1922, my father, Said Jasey, travelled to Edmonton, Alberta . . .

They [Arab immigrants] were fairly well accepted at the time . . . except when the [First World] War started, because that area of the country [Syria] was under the control of Turkey. They were referred to as Turks, and in that sense I think they had some problems with getting along with people, but other than that I can't remember any real problems they had.

To become a naturalized Canadian one had to work on a farm for one year. After completing his year on the farm he [Said Jasey] settled in Edmonton, Alberta, where there was a relatively large Lebanese community. Most of them were from the Bekaa Valley in Lebanon. He and a friend, Brahim Jazey, from Karoun in Lebanon, bought a chocolate store where they made and sold chocolates. Subsequently, the store was sold and Said opened a trading post near the Hudson Bay Company in northern Alberta, trading in furs with the natives. In early 1927, my elder brother, Naif, who was nineteen, joined him . . .

In 1928, Said returned to Lebanon to settle affairs . . . They left Lebanon on the *Westernland*, owned by the Red Star Line, arriving in Halifax April 20, 1930. With him was his wife Amounie, daughter Audrey, daughter-in-law Amney [Naif's wife], and myself, Mohamed Said [soon to become Gordon Jasey], aged one. Before proceeding to Alberta, they visited Joseph Edwards (Abdul Kareem Al-Kadri) in Bridgetown in the Annapolis Valley, Nova Scotia.

Joseph Edwards and his brother, Mohammed Abdul Jalil Al-Kadri, had immigrated to Nova Scotia before the First World War. Both had worked in the coal mines in Cape Breton, Nova Scotia, for a year to

Mohammed Abdul Jalil Al-Kadri, left, and Abdul Kareem Al-Kadri, later Joseph Edwards. Photo courtesy of Dr Gordon Jasey.

become naturalized citizens. Mohammed Abdul Jalil Al-Kadri [later] returned to Lebanon during the First World War and was conscripted into the Turkish army and unfortunately killed in action.

After working in the coal mines, Joseph Edwards peddled goods door to door with a friend A R Joseph [Said Al-Rafia, Murray Joseph's father] from Becca, again in Bekaa valley. He eventually established a successful general store business in Bridgetown, Nova Scotia.

After visiting [Joseph Edwards in Bridgetown] for several days, Said and his family journeyed to Edmonton, Alberta. The trading post [in the North] was later sold and a general store was opened in Edmonton. While in Edmonton, my brother Naif and Amney had a daughter Azeze (Hazel). Myself, Mohammed Said, now two years old, had a name addition, "Gordon," given to me by a babysitter from Lebanon.

In 1932, our family moved to Nova Scotia where Audrey married Joseph Edwards. Joseph and Audrey later had four children, Mamie or Fatmy, Dora (Durra), Hammudeh (Moody), and Abdul Jalil. Naif and Amney [also had four children], Albert (Jaffar), Walter (Abdul Rahaim), and later, in Ontario, Sydney (Said) and Gary (Ghazie).

During the years 1932 to 1947, my father, Said Jasey, operated a general store in Granville Ferry, located on the Annapolis River, across from Annapolis Royal [on the north shore]. My brother Naif had a clothing store first in Bridgetown, then in Annapolis Royal.

In Nova Scotia, there was a relatively large number of Lebanese Christians and Muslims. Most of them were living in Halifax, the capital. My father was recognized by the Muslims in the province as their imam. They were scattered and living in many villages and towns, like Liverpool, Mahone Bay, Bridgewater, Halifax, Dartmouth, Truro, Antigonish, Guysburgh, Pictou, and Mulgrave. To serve them he travelled by train or car. On some trips, I, his youngest son, would accompany him. He performed at weddings and funerals, and he helped resolve family conflicts and gave advice on religious matters. In 1938, the Edmonton community invited him to be the imam of the Al Rashid Mosque, the first mosque built in Canada. He, however, was committed to the Nova Scotia community and did not accept the invitation.

In Nova Scotia, the big event was the building of a cemetery there near Truro . . . As you probably know, most of the people that came here from Lebanon originally came over to make their little fortunes and move back again. I think it started to dawn on people in the '30s and '40s that they'd rather stay and live in Canada. They were starting to develop ideas of building a community of their own and of taking on responsibilities they'd never thought of before. A Mr George Harris—[his Arabic name was Hussein Merhi, as explained in the Truro chapter]—it was his idea of starting a cemetery. The families of Nova Scotia were scattered—actually there were maybe one or two families in each town, separated in a few cases by hundreds of miles—but they all visited together now and then and there was a consensus, and they did buy the property outside Truro and now they have a Muslim cemetery . . .

In 1946, Sami Al-Kadri, nephew of my father Said Jasey and the son of his half-brother Ali Al-Kadri, visited [Nova Scotia] from Argentina. After visiting with my father and cousins his plan was to continue his trip to Lincoln Park, Michigan, a suburb of Detroit . . . and my father went along too.

While visiting in Lincoln Park, my father also met his half-brother Ali Al-Kadri, who was living in St Paul, Minnesota. He enjoyed the reunion and was impressed by the large Muslim community in Dearborn, another suburb of Detroit. The majority of this community were Lebanese from the Bekaa Valley. They had formed the American Muslim Society, and in 1937 built the second mosque in the USA. It was located at the corner of Dix Highway and Vernon Road. At this time it was a basement with a roof. When my father returned to Nova Scotia he related his happiness on meeting and renewing relations with his family members. He also said he was greatly impressed by the Dearborn community and their activities.

In the autumn of 1947, he [Gordon's father Said Jasey] required surgery and was admitted to the Victoria General Hospital in Halifax. Postoperatively he developed an infection which was resistant to the only antibiotic of the day, sulfa. After a prolonged struggle he passed away in November 1947. He was buried in the Muslim cemetery in Bible Hill, outside of Truro. The land had been purchased by George

Harris in 1944 for the cemetery.

My father died in Nova Scotia in 1947 and it was soon after that that my brother Naif moved to Windsor and then my sister and her family moved up here and became established in Windsor.

When my brother arrived in Windsor there were nineteen families present. There was no community activity. In Dearborn, Michigan, there was a large population from the Middle East [and] he found an active community organization. My brother joined this organization, the American Muslim Society. He eventually became president of the association in the early 1950s and in a couple of years due to his efforts at raising money from people in Illinois, Ohio, West Virginia and other places—I travelled with him—he was able to complete the construction of the Dearborn Mosque by the mid-1950s.

Dr Jasey had joined Dalhousie University in Halifax in 1946, but when his father died a year later, he took the year 1949–50 off to help move his family to their new home in Windsor, Ontario. He graduated from Dalhousie with a bachelor of science degree in 1951 and joined the school of medicine.

I graduated from medicine in 1956 . . . and returned to Windsor, Ontario. At that time, we had some very social and active young people and because of the activities in Detroit, Michigan, they had the idea of formalizing a youth association.

I think the big event in Windsor was the formation of the Windsor [Muslim] Youth Association . . . It just so happened that in 1956 and '57 there were fifteen or twenty young Muslims that [had] come to Windsor . . . a couple from western Canada and a couple from Ottawa and ourselves from Nova Scotia, [and a few others]—there were ten or fifteen families living here. This group of young people decided that they would like to form their own society or association. At that time I had just graduated from medical school so they—sisters Hilda and Dee Sadaka from Ottawa and Albert and Hazel Jasey—came to me to see what they could do and how to go about it. We spent quite a few weeks discussing why we should even bother—because we were such a small group—and trying to examine what would be accomplished . . . Finally, as a result of these discussions, we formed the Windsor Islamic Youth Association.

In those days—and still in these days—there are divisions between families and communities—even people who are related or come from the same village—over nonsensical things . . . [So] one of the premises of the association was that none of the older people would be allowed to be members, but they would be allowed to come and participate in our social functions and our cultural functions and so on. That way, we thought we would be able to do the job and keep everybody involved. This situation went on for three to four years . . .

I left Windsor in 1958 to do postgraduate work in obstetrics and gynecology and I did not return until 1962. During this time, my brother Naif continued to be very active in the community, as were Albert [Jasey] and his daughter and my sister Audrey. My brother served as president of the Windsor Islamic Association on a couple of occasions, as did Albert, and other members of the community [also] took their turns. The success of the community was based on coop-erative efforts by everybody.

At about this time, the Federation of Islamic Associations of the United States and Canada was in the process of being formed. This was initiated by Charlie Igram from Cedar Rapids, Iowa. He vis-ited Windsor, and as a consequence our community became associ-ated with the federation. In 1959, the federation held its convention in Windsor, and as a result of the money raised within the commu-nity, in 1960 a house located at 379 Wellington Street was bought, which represented our first mosque and community centre. In August 1960, and at this time because the number of youth was increasing, the senior members of the community were invited to join the [Youth Association]. The name was then changed to the Windsor Islamic Association Inc and was operated under Robert's Rules of Order. Prof Razoulhaque wrote the first set of bylaws in 1965, and they have been updated twice.

It was in the 1960s that the community started to grow, due to immigrants from Palestine, Turkey, and what was once Kurdistan. In 1968, the house on Wellington Street was sold, and the lot located at 1320 Northwood was purchased. A mosque was built on this lot and it was completed in the spring of 1970. At this time the community had grown from approximately 100 people to about 1,500 to 1,800.

From a later correspondence in 2016:

> During the 1970s and early 1980s the community kept growing due to immigration from various countries. In April 1984, we bought twenty acres of land with the idea of further expansion, but instead of expanding on that property an addition was made to the present mosque. This addition was done in 1991. In 1993, a school was purchased to house grades kindergarten to grade eight [in an Islamic school setting]. In 2015 this An-Noor Elementary School was named one of the top ten elementary schools in the province. The Amounie Jasey Scholarship Fund, named after my mother in 1981, was well financed for six years. It was discontinued.

From an earlier correspondence in 1982:

> I think we have a great future . . . I think the importance of the Islamic communities of America is that they will eventually be the source of the renaissance, you might say, of Islam worldwide . . . Eventually we will provide the thinkers, maybe, that will challenge the present authorities and make them look at things in a deeper way. [The challenge will be met] because of dialogue, because of interest in religion and the curiosity of those who are born here to develop an identity that they understand and feel comfortable with. They're not going to just accept this and go on. They're constantly being challenged by other values around them and other things, so they're going to have to examine who they are and what they are . . . [As a result] they're going to come up with alternate ideas but maybe not agree with the learned scholars of [earlier] times because I think the terms of reference are changing all the time and we have to learn to change with them.
>
> Regarding issues of religion and differing cultures, I think that we have to distinguish between Islam, for what it is—it should be the same everywhere and anywhere—and the frills that have been attached or associated with it in the different cultures.
>
> People haven't got to the stage of separating the two, one from the

other, and I think that they're not going to do this within their own [native] countries, but [they are going to achieve it] over here . . . We who belong to different cultural groups will have to say "This is Islam, [and] this [other thing] is practised in this country and it's not contrary to Islam, but it's not Islam and you shouldn't accept it as Islam. If you want to do it, it's fine, and if you don't want to, it's fine" . . .

More than thirty years later, in 2016, Dr Jasey was a little less optimistic about the subject:

> Since our community has been overwhelmed by mass immigrations from various Muslim countries due to problems there I now feel there will be a delay in the results I suggested earlier. The new immigrants unfortunately bring with them the various social and cultural problems that they had in their country of origin. I am an optimist! I

Dr Gordon Mohammed Said Jasey's July 2019 obituary card.
Photo courtesy of Fay Jasey.

believe that the next generation or two will eliminate the biases which their parents now have and they will get back to the basic roots of Islam. I believe Islam in this country will be more accepted in future.

For the record, my wife Fay and I met in Grace Hospital [now Hotel-Dieu Grace Healthcare] where she was an operating room nurse. We married in 1965 and have four sons—a dentist, an orthopedic surgeon, an obstetrician-gynecologist, and a high-school teacher. We have one daughter who graduated in dramatic arts and also works in the real estate business. We have ten grandchildren. My wife taught Sunday school at the mosque, and she helped the ladies with special events.

8. London, Ontario: A Magnet for Muslims

MIDWAY BETWEEN WINDSOR AND THE GOLDEN HORSESHOE—
including Niagara Falls, Hamilton and Greater Toronto—lies London. It
is the home of the first mosque in Ontario and the second largest Muslim
population in the province. The two descendants of Muslim pioneers
interviewed here, like those in most of the previous chapters, have Syrian
Lebanese roots. Their interviews were recorded in 2013 and later. They
are American-born Najet Hassan and her Canadian-born husband,
Hanny Hassan, both their families having arrived in North America in
the first decade of the twentieth century.

I will let Najet tell her story first:

> My name is Najet Alia Hassan. My maiden name is Najet Alia Bedra,
> and I was born in Cedar Rapids, Iowa, in 1941. I have three siblings.
> My sisters Nayfee and Sohame were also born in Cedar Rapids. My
> younger brother, Slayman (Jim) Najeeb Bedra, was born in Toledo,
> Ohio. There were two brothers before me. The first died at childbirth
> and [the other when he was] four years old. He was hit by a sixteen-
> wheeler in front of my parents. I was only around three years old
> when that happened.
>
> My mother, Ella (Alia) Kannan, was born in Greenwich Village,
> New York City, in 1908 . . . Back then, everyone's name was changed
> in one way or another. My maternal grandfather, Milhem Hassan
> Kanaan, and my grandmother, Nayfee Howie, came to New York
> City in the early 1900s. His family name was dropped and he ended
> up as Hassan on my mother's birth certificate. I believe they returned
> to Lebanon in 1910 or 1911, before the First World War. My mother,
> and her older sister and younger brother, who were also born in New

York City, [also] returned and were raised in what is now Lebanon.

My father, Najeeb Slayman Bedra (Jim Bedra), was born in what was then Greater Syria in 1888, and in his very early teens his mother passed away . . . There was no country called Lebanon until much later.

[When] the Turkish Army entered his village, Jadidee Yaboos, my father said it fell under the rule of the Ottoman Empire. [To escape getting drafted in the Turkish Army] . . . he and his brother Sam, who was a year or so younger, hopped on the first ship they could to get away. He was thirteen so that must have been around 1901. [They landed in Argentina, where] they worked as labourers . . .

They entered the US through Ellis Island in 1914. I found my uncle's name listed but could not find my father's name. I know he was in the First World War in France. We have his American army

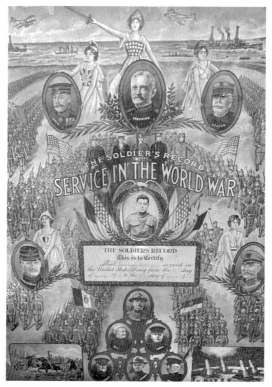

Najet Hassan's father, Pte James (Najeeb) Bedra, in US Army demobilization poster, 1919. Photo courtesy of Najet Hassan.

pictures and discharge papers. It is quite a large picture of him with his platoon. We also have a picture of him in his army uniform, which has circulated on the Arab America website telling the history of the US Arabs in the early 1900s.

They ended up in Cedar Rapids, Iowa. There is a photo of my father as one of the early founders of the Cedar Rapids mosque hanging in the mosque today. The mosque was completed in 1934. There were about fifteen to twenty Muslim families there. We never asked our father, "How did you get there? Why did you go there?" but I do recall they had a cousin who lived in Cedar Rapids, and it is possible they knew that. He was considerably older than my dad. I remember that his name was Dave Abrahim and his wife's name was Minnie. They were still alive when I was a child, but we only saw them once a year after we moved to Ohio. I have a few pieces of Minnie's jewelry [given to me] after she passed. It's unfortunate that we did not ask questions about our heritage back in the '40s and '50s. By the time *Roots* [the book by Alex Haley, 1976, and the subsequent TV series] came along and I started questioning my roots, my parents had passed.

Like many of his friends, my father had been married prior to his marriage to my mother. We know they had no children. He was divorced before he returned to Lebanon in the late 1930s to see his siblings . . . His father had also remarried and he had several new siblings. He married my mother in Lebanon in 1938 [and] returned to the US and my mother followed in 1938 to Cedar Rapids, Iowa. She came, of course, as a US citizen. I remember we had a white house near many of their friends. My father worked for the Quaker Oats Company as a miller after his discharge from the army. [When he retired] . . . at the age of sixty-five he received seventeen dollars a month pension. Unfortunately, there were no unions when he began work . . .

We lived in a very tight-knit community in Cedar Rapids. In those days we called the mosque a *nadey*, [which] could mean "beckoning," "congregational centre," but not the *jamaa*. We used to go to the mosque every Thursday night. Most of the elders owned grocery stores, consequently they were free in the evenings. Their children were older [than me]. Parents and kids all went together. We sat on chairs in a large circle, which today would be considered a *halaqa*. Someone always read from the Qur'an. The kids sat around with the other kids. One of the older fathers would give us bubble gum to keep us quiet, but we always managed to get into trouble blowing big bubbles and getting it in our hair. They always served coffee and sweets and treats for the children. That's where we went every Thursday night. I do recall during Eid time that they used to burn incense. The prayer room was upstairs. After prayers, everyone went to the basement hall. Men and women and children would sit and have traditional sweets. There was no segregation.

We left Cedar Rapids and moved to Toledo, Ohio in 1945. My parents . . . [had] a very close friend who had moved to Toledo and opened a business. They were more like sisters than friends, so my parents decided to follow them. They felt that opening their own business was better than working in a factory. Most of the community members [in Toledo] had neighbourhood bars. Many first generations couldn't read or write [but] there were only two or three kinds of beer, so all they had to do was memorize the different labels. Most of the neighbourhood bars did not sell liquor.

In the late 1940s, people were coming in [to the United States] from Lebanon and Palestine. The families lived upstairs in a one-bedroom apartment in the same building we lived in, until they could find work, save some money and find a place to live. My parents gave them free housing and meals, on condition they would teach their three daughters to read and write Arabic. I was the oldest child so I always had the first lesson.

I was in elementary school during those years, and I knew my only option was to get top marks in all my subjects. My mother always instilled in us the importance of higher education. The fact that she did not get an education haunted her all her life . . . She [would say] that they [she and her husband] would not be in the bar business if they could only read and write.

Toledo built its first mosque in 1954. [It] was our weekend indoor recreation space. There was no room on the property for an outdoor play area. Other kids went to dances on Friday nights, but we, as [Muslim] teenagers, went to the mosque. That's where we had our parties and dances. We had an Islamic Youth Association for boys and girls, who became eligible to join at the age of twelve . . . On Friday nights, we [would] go and clean the mosque. After that we would have a party with western-style dances [and] live bands. Around 11:30 the parents would call and say it's time to come home.

As a teenager, growing up in Toledo, I did not [enjoy] going to high school because my parents were quite strict. They controlled where we went and what we did. Going to activities at the mosque was acceptable, so the social aspect was no longer an issue. Most of our social activities were held at the mosque. We had chaperones who were parents born in the US. We went to school dances and proms, but it had to be with a Muslim boy. The norm in those days was girls asking a boy to school dances . . . I [went out] in my sophomore, junior and senior years at high school, but only with a Muslim boy.

The big hammer over our heads was that we had to go to university—we had to get an education—no ifs, ands, or buts! My mother insisted everyone had to go to university. She also understood the inequities that women faced. Her famous line was "If I was a man, I'd show them!" She was a good business person for somebody who didn't have an education. She had started to take English [lessons] when they were living in Cedar Rapids. When my brother was struck and killed in front of them, it was the end of everything for her. We never had a bicycle because she was afraid one of us [would] get hit by a car or truck. We were, however, allowed to take the bus every Sunday and go to the movies when we were in sixth grade.

After graduating from high school, I went to the University of Toledo. When I was younger, I dreamed of going to law school. During that era, girls didn't go to law school and definitely could not go out of town to university. They became teachers and nurses. I didn't want to be a teacher, and my father definitely did not want any of us to be a nurse whose "job it was to empty bed pans," so I took business courses. My parents thought it was a good choice because they felt I should know how to run my own business, so that's what I did. My mother was impressed with beauty salons, and thought that would be a good investment after I finished university. I could hire people to work for me and I could stay home and raise my children when I got married!

Hanny and I met in 1958, at the Federation of Islamic Associations meeting in Cedar Rapids, Iowa. That was the beginning of the Islamic Youth Association of the US and Canada. He was representing the London, Ontario Youth Association, and I was representing Toledo. Teenagers from each city would invite youth to meet several times a year in our respective cities . . . to come and stay in our homes, so we could get better acquainted. The Sunni and Shi'a walls [Sunni-Shi'a separation] did not exist with the kids or their parents. Many marriages came out of these weekend conventions.

Teens from Toledo, London, Detroit, Michigan City, Indiana, and Cedar Rapids, Iowa, would go to a camp on the long Easter weekends from Friday to Sunday. We went to a fully operational YMCA campground. It was in Michigan so we would drive from Toledo. Imam Vehbi Ismail was the Albanian imam from Harper Woods, Michigan . . .

Hanny and I got engaged and planned to marry after we finished university. Long distance relationships were very difficult when you could only communicate by letters and long distance calls. We were one-car families so trips that took four or five hours one way on a weekend were few. So we decided to get married in 1961 after my first year at the University of Toledo. We continued having the Islamic Youth Association meetings. Teens from all the different cities would congregate in one city on a holiday weekend. The imam from Toledo was from Yugoslavia. He travelled with youth to the host cities and attended the activities with the kids.

In London, an old house was purchased and turned into a mosque. All social functions were held there. The youth held western[-style] dances and dinners, as well as educational lectures . . . The whole weekend was a great party. That kind of openness is gone. I have difficulty with the attitudes of people today. [Back then among us] were many illiterate, uneducated immigrants who knew the importance of education and of their kids associating with one another, giving them an option to going to a Friday-night dance at high school or local community centres. Even during my boys' teen years we had the mosque and a youth club . . .

When I started looking for a job, one of the first places I applied to

Najet and Hanny Hassan's wedding 1962. Photo courtesy of Najet Hassan.

was an insurance company and the first question was "Are you married, and are you having any children?" I said, "My husband is at university and we are not planning on it." Today you can't ask these questions. I ended up getting a job at Kelvinator in their accounting department. I worked there for a very short time and then I got pregnant and then I got very sick. Our eldest son Ali arrived, while Hanny was still at school. We had Ali and Najeeb by the time Hanny graduated.

I was on the board of directors of the London mosque. In the 1970s, there was no problem with me being on the board. It was no big deal. We would have Eid parties for the kids at the mosque and we rented movies and had all kinds of functions for them. Then, in Toledo from 1966 to 1974, I taught Sunday school for the kids and I was on the women's auxiliary.

From my freshman year to my senior year, I belonged to some service clubs, like the Junior Council on World Affairs, the Periclean

Literary Society, YWCA organization, plus half a dozen different ones . . . I had a column on the school newspaper.

I was also involved in the elementary schools . . . Hanny was president of the Parent Teachers Association and I was president of the elementary school Mothers Club in Toledo. [We were also involved in] local civic and political issues in Toledo. When we moved to London, Ontario we just continued our volunteer work. I joined the London Youth Orchestra Women's Committee . . . [and] was president for two years; I remained a member for twenty-five years, helping with fundraising . . . I [also] sat on the London Symphony Orchestra Board of Directors.

In 1982, Lila Fahlman [of Alberta] called and said they were having an organizational meeting of the CCMW, the Canadian Council of

Original house which became London Muslim Mosque in 1957, second in Canada, above; and below, the purpose-built London Muslim Mosque of 1964. Photos courtesy of Hanny Hassan.

Muslim Women . . . Hanny was on the board of the CMCC [the Council of Muslim Communities of Canada] . . . And so I started a CCMW group here in London in 1982. Not everybody was happy about it. Some of the women didn't think we needed another organization. I was president at the time of the London Muslim Mosque Women's Auxiliary and I brought their attention to the fact that there was a national organization. There were a handful of people who thought the idea was good, but the bulk of them were immigrants and their attitudes were very narrow . . . [And so] I got them to give me a letter indicating I could represent them . . .

I have been there ever since. I was the treasurer and served on the board for about ten years . . . I was on the nominating committee the year Alia [Hogben] and Razia [Jaffer] came on . . . I had met Alia and Razia and I thought, these people can take the organization in another direction. Talat [Muinuddin] was doing a good job for Toronto, but it needed to go beyond Toronto. A good thing back then was that board meetings were held in different cities. We had to pay our own way to attend . . . When I started working, I could afford to pay for my transportation. The board used to stay at Talat Muinuddin's house so there was no expense for hotels or meals. CCMW finally received funding to cover board meetings across Canada.

I am still an active part of CCMW in London. I volunteer in the London community at large and I am on the London Health Sciences Foundation Country Classic Auction Committee. I am still doing volunteer work for our community as well as civic activities. That's part of our life. I am a founding member of the Islamic Centre of Southwest Ontario.

Asked about the future direction of Muslims in Canada, Najet said:

I guess I am very concerned that children identify with their Islam in North America. As North Americans, they need to be comfortable with their place in North America and their Islam. Even though my mother was born in New York and went back to Lebanon at a very young age, the difference between her and some of the newcomers today is very great. The town that she came from had Catholics and

Orthodox Christians and Muslims living together. She came with a totally different attitude than people who are coming from more fundamentalist villages today. They seemed to have a great deal of respect for one another. Acceptance and respect are necessary.

This is a story that my kids get a charge out of: my mother was baptized! My maternal grandmother had lost a child due to illness. [She had a dream that she should take her remaining children and get them baptized.] So she went to a family friend. He was a Syrian Orthodox priest and she told him about her dream. He prayed over my mother and her siblings. I recall that when my mother was in the hospital, she always appreciated the nuns. Nuns could always be found in the hospitals. They would come and say a prayer over her. She respected them and believed in their prayers.

I guess I'm coming from the perspective that we should always have respect for people of the cloth, if you will, whether they be priests or nuns. My father never went by a nun without tipping his hat—that was in an era where men wore hats . . . That's how we grew up. Today, I'm frustrated with poor behaviour towards people who are perceived to be different.

I had a culture shock when I came to Canada [as a young married woman from the US]. I was surprised at the attitude of some people who were born here. They hadn't contributed or volunteered in the mainstream community. I was accustomed to Muslims participating outside of their mosque community. In London, it wasn't that way for the majority of the people. My mother-in-law was the other side of the story. She came to Canada from Lebanon, but was out there pounding the sidewalks enumerating and meeting politicians, supporting issues she believed in. She spent many years working with immigrants from all over the world, helping them with orientation and surviving in their new country. She was an exception in the Muslim community.

The only time my mother covered her head was for cooking . . . so her hair wouldn't get in. Even in the mosque, the imam never ever told us to cover our hair. We knew to cover our heads for prayer. We only wore a scarf and a long-sleeved shirt when we went to pray. When the prayer was finished, everyone uncovered their heads.

Hanny Hassan's story follows:

> My name is Hanny Assaf Hassan. I was born in London, Ontario, in
> July, 1940. I am the son of Hussein Ali Assaf and Ayshi Shousher. I
> believe that I was the second Muslim born in London. My late cousin,
> Norma Hassan, who preceded me, was born in April 1940. She was
> my father's niece, his brother's daughter.
>
> According to my father's records, he arrived in Canada from Syria
> in 1913. The Ellis Island [New York] records indicate that he might
> have arrived in 1911. My father's name was anglicized to Alex Assaf
> Hassan when he immigrated to Canada. Because of the intimidation
> of immigration authorities and the fact that he had planned to bring
> his siblings, whose last names had been registered as Hassan . . . he
> never corrected the record. Our last name became Hassan rather
> than our family name, Assaf.
>
> My father was in his late teens when he came to Canada, just before
> the start of the First World War. He settled in London, Ontario, where
> an older brother and other young men from Baaloul, his hometown in
> Syria (before it became Lebanon), had come a few years earlier. My
> father, and many other Syrian immigrants to Canada, worked initially
> as peddlers in the countryside and small towns. He settled in London
> for reasons unknown to us but probably because there were some set-
> tlers from near his hometown in Syria.
>
> Most of the Syrian immigrants worked as labourers after settling, as
> they had little education or skills. There was also a nucleus of Syrian
> Christians in London, some of whom brought their spouses with
> them. None of the Muslims in London had brought wives from back
> home in the early years. I can just speculate that the Christians under-
> stood that there would be a religious home for them in the churches
> in Canada. However, many of them joined other denominations than
> their own, particularly the Orthodox Christians. The Catholics, of
> course, found a place within the Canadian Catholic community.
>
> Among the Muslims, there was a reluctance to allow their women
> to come to an unknown place until the men had settled. Many of the
> immigrants thought that it would be temporary and that they would
> soon return to Syria well off . . . They didn't really see Canada as

an ultimate destination. However, when the men got to Canada, they found that it wasn't as easy as they thought. That was certainly the case with my dad early on . . .

[During the First World War, because they came from Ottoman territory and their passports described them as "Syrian Turk," they were considered enemy aliens in Canada.]

When they arrived, they didn't speak the language and they had virtually no skills. Many of them could not even read or write Arabic . . . My father started out as a peddler, basically going to farms selling dry goods out of a suitcase. He got his supplies from a Syrian wholesaler in Montreal, who tagged each of the items in English and Arabic, so customers could see the prices in English and he would read the costs in Arabic. Later on, he worked in a tanning factory and in the former McCormick's Biscuits plant in London. He and his friends worked hard and had long hours. [They] roomed together and skimped by. Even though everything was cheap, pay was very low. He made three or four dollars a week, which was not considered too bad. However, even if he saved most of his pay, it would take a long time to accumulate significant funds.

Ultimately he operated a concession stand selling hamburgers in the summer in a park in London and at Port Stanley, on Lake Erie, during the heyday of the big bands. The big bands used to come to the Stork Club in Port Stanley in the summers and play in the arenas during the winter time. From this small business, he was able to save enough to buy a grocery store, with a partner. Ultimately they expanded that into three grocery stores in key locations in London.

With the onset of the Great Depression, many of their customers could not pay for their groceries. My dad would give away groceries or allow customers to pay later. His partner was not very happy about that . . . he moved to Dearborn, Michigan . . . and my dad stayed in London. He bought a small apartment building, which he later converted into a hotel.

From the beginning of the First World War until the end of the Second World War, there were virtually no Muslim newcomers to Canada, because Canada had shut down immigration from Asia and Africa. Of course, with the First World War and the Depression, it was not easy for most of those who had come before the war. It was a sort of subsistence living. My dad was among the more fortunate.

During that period, the Muslims and the Christians from what is now the southern part of Lebanon, mainly from villages on the Litani River, formed the Syrian-Lebanese Benevolent Association. It was primarily a social club. With the meager funds they had they rented space on the second floor of a store in downtown London.

. . . [T]here were several Muslim men who had come to London, and they were relatively young. While most had worked as labourers, some of them [later] set up businesses. One had a restaurant, another had a clothing store, and the third had a confectionery store where he made candies and chocolates. When I was a child, the owner of the confectionery store was a jolly old guy. We called him Uncle Sam, even though we were not related. He never married. In Canada he was known as Sam Fine, but his real name was Hussain Tijan.

The Second World War was coming, and by this time my dad had accumulated a bit of wealth and he had an older brother, Hassan Assaf (known as Harry Hassan), who had come to Canada a few years before him. He had gone back to Lebanon and married. He had three sons, who remained in Baaloul, the Assaf family village. Uncle Hassan returned to Canada [when] his wife was expecting their third son. [This would have been in the mid 1930s.] He died shortly after of appendicitis. He is buried in a cemetery in London.

Another of my dad's brothers, Ahmad Assaf (known as Albert Hassan) came to Canada in 1923. My dad set him up in a pool hall business in Glencoe, a small Scottish Presbyterian and United Church town about thirty kilometres west of London. Uncle Albert was somewhat fluent in English [and very sociable]. He fitted well into the town and made a lot of friends. Through his friendships, he was asked to teach Sunday school at the United Church. Because of this experience, he later began interfaith outreach to the Christian community in the formative years of the Muslim community in London. He stayed in Glencoe for several years. He then returned to London to work with my dad at his hotel. Later the two brothers, with several Muslim and Christian Lebanese investors, bought a steel factory in London, which became Hassan Steel.

By the late 1930s, my dad and Uncle Albert were doing well . . . [and] decided to go back to Lebanon to marry. They left Canada in 1938 . . . Their partners were from Karoun, a town near their village. My dad married Ayshi Shousher, who was born in 1922, . . . and Uncle Albert married Suhyla Fadel. My uncle and his new wife honeymooned through Egypt and came back to Canada soon after they married. My father and mother decided to stay a little longer in Lebanon. They arrived in Canada in 1939 on the cruise liner the Empress of Britain, just as the Second World War was breaking out. My mother told me that the ship was torpedoed on its return voyage to Europe.

After his return in 1939, my dad continued with his hotel business. Both families lived in the hotel together until they had saved enough to buy homes. Uncle Albert bought a home in about 1942 and my dad in 1944. Both families were well on their way by then, with three children each. Norma, Mary and Ali (Alec) were my cousins. In addition to me, my parents had two daughters, Jessie and Helen (Hilwi).

In 1940, when I was born, our two families plus about ten or fifteen single men made up the Muslim community in London—less than

Hanny Hassan's parents at their wedding, Lebanon, 1938.
Photo courtesy of Hanny Hassan.

Hanny Hassan's mother, Ayshi Hassan, in Lebanon, 1939.
Photo courtesy of Hanny Hassan.

two dozen people. My mum and my aunt, my uncle's wife, immediately applied to have their siblings come to Canada.

My father's oldest brother, Uncle Hassan, who had gone back to Lebanon in the early 1920s, was there long enough to have three sons, Omar, Abdo and Kassim, [before returning to London, where he died]. By virtue of his having Canadian citizenship, [his three sons]my Lebanese cousins were able to claim Canadian citizenship . . . They arrived in London in 1948. The oldest would have been about eighteen and the youngest maybe ten or twelve.

My mother was also finally successful in getting her mother and siblings permission to come Canada. She experienced racism and obstacles in making the application, . . . and it took about ten years to get approval . . . My sister, Jamelie, has done artwork around this subject, around the immigration barriers and the racist letters from the authorities. The letters basically said that people from that part of the world were not suitable for immigration to Canada. The correspondence was sent to my parents. Finally, my mother was able to bring my grandmother, Fatima Sallah, and her three brothers, Yehia, Hanny, and Hussein Shousher, in 1949. Her married sister, Jessie, and family came to London a few years later.

In the meantime, three other Lebanese Muslim families came to London from within Canada. Yusuf Hijazi, who was known as Joe Jasey, came from Watertown, Nova Scotia, with his wife, Ayshi Hassan . . . I believe she was probably the first or second Muslim woman born in Canada—unless you consider the Love family of Daood Hamdani's early 1871 census statistics research. Uncle Joe, as we knew him, was a shoemaker. When he moved to London he opened a shoe repair shop. In addition to doing shoe repairs he also custom-made shoes and orthotics.

Another family, Ahmad and Addie Seede and their children, Annesa, Kamel, and Silvia, had come to London from Saskatchewan via Kirkland Lake, in Northern Ontario. Addie had also been born in Canada. She was about the same age as Ayshi Jasey . . . There was a fifth family, the Burketts (originally Barakat)—Kassim and Khowlah (née Wahab, sister of Eva Wahab of Ottawa), with their daughter Shirley. The husband's family was from up near Barrie, on Georgian Bay, and Khowlah had been born in Ottawa. During the same period,

Hanny Hassan's father, Alex Assaf Hassan, 1949.
Photo courtesy of Hanny Hassan.

my Uncle Albert's wife, Suhyla, was successful in arranging to get her family, the Fadels, to emigrate from Lebanon to Canada.

So by the early 1950s there were five Arab Muslim families in London. There were also a few Muslims from Albania and the former Yugoslavia who had arrived in London . . .

There really were no Muslim organizations [in Canada] back then. Edmonton had the only mosque [built in 1938], but there was a thriving Arab Muslim community in Dearborn, Michigan with many from the same area of Lebanon as my parents. We had no car until 1948, but we could go by train and we went often. My mother had a maternal aunt in Melvindale, a suburb of Detroit. My mother also had a brother, who lived in Toledo, Ohio with his family . . .

We would go to Detroit to see Arabic movies at the Detroit Institute of Art. A special treat was to go to the Middle Eastern restaurants in Dearborn. There was a partially completed mosque in Dearborn, with only a basement. It was a multi-purpose facility, used for prayers, dinners, weddings and community gatherings. At that time, there was an imam in Dearborn, Imam Hussein Kharoub, who officiated at weddings and funerals throughout the region. Later, there would be two more imams in the Detroit area, Imam Jawad Chirri, who served the Shi'a community, and Imam Vehbi Ismail, who was of Albanian background. The three imams were very collegial and served the [American] midwest and southern Ontario as best they could.

This was the formative stage of Muslim organizations in the United States. There had been a mosque in Cedar Rapids, Iowa, built in the 1920s [1929]. There was also a very old mosque in Michigan City, Indiana, on Lake Michigan, not far from Chicago, whose age is indeterminate. When I saw people in Michigan City, they said it was the oldest mosque in North America, but they didn't have any documentation. A mosque was built in Toledo, Ohio in 1952.

A large number of Shi'a Muslims from Lebanon settled in Michigan City. Many of them [later] migrated to Dearborn, where there was a very large Shi'a community and the establishment that is now the Islamic Center of America. Imam Chirri, who served that community, was probably the first Shi'a imam in North America. He had been educated in Iran, I think in Qom. He was quite articulate and had a radio program about Islam as far back as 1958.

The majority of the Muslims would have been Sunni, but nobody made a distinction. We were all together. In Toledo, in the early years, there was no Shi'a community that was separate from the others. Later, Imam Chirri began organizing the Shi'a community within the larger American Muslim community. My wife Najet's family is Shi'a. When we met, there had been several marriages within the Muslim community where one partner was Sunni and the other was Shi'a. My parents said, "Don't ask. It doesn't matter. If somebody asks, you just say you're Muslim."

In 1952, the Federation of Islamic Associations of the United States and Canada was established in Cedar Rapids, Iowa. My parents and a few others represented the London Muslim community at the founding convention. Other cities represented included Detroit, Michigan; Toledo, Ohio; New York, New York; Cedar Rapids, Iowa, and possibly Edmonton, Alberta. Most of the initial members were of Lebanese or Syrian origin.

I believe the Federation was the only national Muslim organization then. It met annually in one of the member cities. It grew, and by the end of the 1950s consisted of about forty community organizations. London was a member community from the inception. A black Muslim community from Philadelphia—not the Black Muslims of Elijah Muhammad [the Nation of Islam] or [new] Muslims by conversion—were early members of the Federation, which held its 1961 convention in Philadelphia. They were Muslims who had immigrated to the United States several generations previously and settled in Philadelphia and had retained their Islamic identity.

The formation of the Federation had stimulated the London Muslim community. The Muslim young people who had come to London in the late 1940s and early 1950s said about the Syrian Lebanese Benevolent Society, "What's with this social organization? We need a religious organization." [And so] in 1952, coincident with the founding of the Federation, the Canadian Muslim Benevolent Society of London began.

By then there had been a large increase in the London Muslim community because the immigration rules had changed. Now there could be family reunification. Through marriage, and through the extended family relationships, the community grew. Muslims of different ancestries in other parts of Canada became aware of London's emerging Muslim community and were attracted to the city . . .

An Arabic language [teaching] program was initiated about 1954. Classes were held on Mondays, Wednesdays, and Fridays from 5:00 PM until 6:30 PM at HB Beal High School, near downtown London. The school board provided the classroom space at no cost . . . and the parents paid the cost of the teacher. Our first teacher was Adnan Fadel. That is where I learned my limited Arabic. An Islamic Sunday school was also started, with classes in our homes. Each week the school was held in a different home. There would have been about twenty children in the two programs.

The community kept growing in numbers so that *Milad* [the Prophet's birthday] and Eid celebrations could no longer be accommodated in our homes. It became necessary to rent a facility for the Eid and other community events. In the mid-1950s, Turkish airmen were sent for training, through NATO, to the Canadian Forces airbase in London. The Canadian military officials would arrange for the Turkish trainees to join the London Muslim community for Eid celebrations.

During that period, my uncle [Ahmed or Albert Hassan] would take four or five of us Muslim teenagers by car around the countryside to visit and speak at churches about Islam.

By 1955, London was prominent enough in the Federation to be able to host [its] annual convention. It was held at Hotel London, with six to seven hundred Muslims from all over North America attending. The Federation had become so well known that embassy and consular representatives of Muslim-majority countries would attend. The convention in London also attracted a huge amount of media coverage.

A lot of the young Muslim newcomers [in London] were still labourers. The membership dues for the Canadian Muslim Benevolent Society were five dollars per month but that was a very large amount for guys who were earning between twenty-five and fifty cents an hour. The organization's objective was to raise money to buy land to build a mosque . . . In 1957, the Canadian Muslim Benevolent Society bought a very large residence at 151 Oxford Street West in London and converted it into a mosque.

I married Najet in 1961. We had met in 1958, and the Federation played a large part in our lives. That was our first exposure to large numbers of Muslims . . . We became exposed to the diversity of the Muslim ummah and became acquainted with Muslims who had an educational background in Islam. We learned more about the problems that Muslims were encountering as they acculturated to North American society and tried to retain their religion and culture.

It was a formative period because for many of us there were no Muslim peers who had experienced what we had as Canadian-born Muslims. In my case, my Muslim friends in London were my cousins and a few young people who had moved to London from other places in Canada. Those near my age were all young women . . . [and so] my next three siblings were all sisters and my uncle's two eldest children were girls as well, so I had five big sisters keeping track of me [he laughs]. And like it or not, they looked to the males for leadership so I was kind of thrust into doing translation, being a spokesperson, and doing other things at a very young age, like speaking at churches. I was fluent in English and my uncle was one of the few others who were.

So for me it was tremendous to see role models at the Federation that were my age or older from within the community. None of our parents had much education and so learning the ropes and being able to talk to people was a big thing. It was during that period from 1955 to the end of that decade that the Federation grew . . .

The young people who [went] to the Federation conventions, in addition to meeting other Muslims, were expecting to learn more about Islam, as there were limited Islamic education resources in their own communities. Most of the communities didn't have imams, so the conventions were a wonderful opportunity to bring together the handful of imams . . . in North America to come and talk to the youth and to their parents. The adults had similar expectations as the youth in terms of their learning more about Islam.

[But] the adults tended to monopolize the presentations and workshops, [and] the youth were getting restless. In 1958, with the

Federation convention in Washington DC, the young people rebelled, threatening to form their own organization. However, a compromise was reached . . . the Islamic Youth Association of the United States and Canada (IYA) was formed, with subsidies from the Federation and linked to the Federation. The IYA's president would automatically be a vice-president of the Federation. The IYA would also have two representatives on the board of directors of the Federation. The IYA would be autonomous, with its own programming, and it was agreed that when the Federation had a program, there would be a youth component to it.

The founding meeting of the IYA was held in Cedar Rapids, Iowa, in 1958. I was chosen to be the delegate from London and Najet was one of three or four chosen to be delegates from Toledo. Even though both Najet and I were at the Washington Federation convention, we did not meet each other until the IYA founding meeting in Cedar Rapids . . . I became the vice-president coming out of that meeting and Najet was secretary. The president, Joe Aossey, who was a young man from Cedar Rapids, promptly got a job that took him to the Philippines, where he worked for Air Products Corporation when he completed his conscription in the US army. So I ended up, by default, as the president until after Najet and I married in 1961 . . .

In the early years of the IYA, we had many activities. We had the youth program, the camp program and several conferences. We even published a newsletter and several short Islamic essays. One of the conferences was held in London at the University of Western Ontario in 1962. We had invited Dr Isma'il al-Faruqi, a visiting fellow in the Faculty of Divinity at McGill University in Montreal. Professor al-Faruqi was the keynote speaker at the conference and also addressed the philosophy department at Western. Those were the kinds of things we were doing initially, as a youth organization. Later, IYA took a different direction and became more social.

When Najet and I met through the IYA and married in 1961, I was a student in engineering at Western University. We remained active in London in the local Muslim community. We lived not far from the London Muslim Mosque on Oxford Street. The mosque was an older, large house that had been converted for use as a mosque.

In about 1961, a fire seriously damaged the mosque. The mosque had been purchased with funds provided by the Canadian Muslim Benevolent Society, which at the time was a registered charity. The title of the property was in the name of the society. After the fire there was a serious division in the community around two issues. There were those who felt that the mosque should not be in the name of a corporate entity—that it should be an association, if you will, without any corporate structure—and there were others who said that while the mosque was open to everybody, somebody should be held accountable financially. The Canadian Muslim Benevolent Society had said there should be no restrictions on programming and use of the mosque, but the Society was financially accountable. In the end, there was the threat of a lawsuit and so the Canadian Muslim Benevolent Society walked away, saying, in effect, "If it is the wish of the community to take over the mosque from the society, they can take it."

. . . [The community took it over.] The key change was that people who were not donors or members could participate in the decisions about the mosque, financial and otherwise, in the new arrangement . . . [As a consequence, in the new arrangement it was decided to tear down the surviving building and build a new mosque on the same spot.] It was poorly executed, requiring ongoing maintenance because it was built on a shoestring . . . It wasn't finished when I graduated in 1964. Over the years there have been several upgrades and expansions, including the construction of an Islamic School. A major renovation was completed in 2012.

I couldn't get a job locally after graduation, so we went to Halifax, Nova Scotia, where I had been offered a position with Public Works Canada working in their Harbours and Rivers Engineering Branch. The Nova Scotia Muslim community was loosely knit, mainly through familial relationships. They had a cemetery, but there were no mosques. We arrived in Halifax in May 1964, in time to participate in the first Eid prayers in the province. We became acquainted with Muslims in Nova Scotia who had relatives back in Ohio. We made friends in Pictou, Bridgetown, and Halifax, Nova Scotia. We weren't actively involved in the community, but we attended events.

My job with the government required me to travel regularly from

Halifax along the south shore of Nova Scotia, up the Bay of Fundy coast and across the Annapolis Valley back to Halifax. It was a monthly tour during which I inspected fisheries harbours. The whole province was sprinkled with Lebanese and Muslims. I had an opportunity during those trips to meet people and made some friendships with people, particularly the Jaseys, in Bridgetown, whose shoemaker brother had settled in London.

While he was in Nova Scotia, Hanny was encouraged to enrol in the master of engineering program at Nova Scotia Technical College and so took a year off work. Afterwards, in 1966, when his employer wouldn't give him credit for his MA, he looked for and found a post in Toledo, Ohio, where he and Najet both had relatives. He settled and became very comfortable there, and his career in engineering advanced. He also became a fixture in the local Muslim community. But in 1973 his father became ill and so he and Najet moved back to London. Here he became involved with the CMCC [the Council of Muslim Communities of Canada] and came to know Dr Fuad Şahin, Muin Muinuddin, Hamid Shaikh, Ebrahim Sayed, Murray Hogben, and Haroon Salamat and Ishrak Ali.

The CMCC was founded in 1972 and published a quarterly news magazine, *Islam Canada*, from 1973 to at least 1979, edited by M Salman Qaadri. He had arrived in the United States from Pakistan on a government scholarship to study nuclear engineering and then moved to Toronto in 1966, where he went into the radiation sciences business. He became heavily involved in Islamic activities and represented the community to government and to the Rabitat al-Alam al-Islam in Mecca. His wife, Dr Mussarrat Qaadri, like many of the highly educated 1960s immigrants, was a gynecologist.

Hanny Hassan became a counsellor at one of the several CMCC camps run by Qasem Mahmud. He became very concerned about safety and other issues and the CMCC leaders said it was his job to make it better. This led him to become more involved and build on his IYA and Boy Scout camp experience and as director he set up counsellor training and lifeguards, etc. He worked on this project for ten years, roughly from 1978 to 1988.

Salman Qaadri, editor of CMCC's magazine, Islam Canada, presenting a
copy to Prime Minister Pierre Trudeau in the later 1970s.
Photo courtesy of Dr Shafiq Qaadri.

The week-long boys and girls camps were held at a variety of camp-
grounds near Ottawa and elsewhere in Ontario funded by the CMCC.
They were first named year-by-year after the first four *khalifas*, or successors of the Prophet Mohammed, and then Camp Al-Mu-Mee-Neen,
(Camp of the Believers). They were held mainly northwest of Westport,
at the Long Bay Campground on Bob's Lake and in 2013 it was renamed
and re-organized as Camp Deen (Camp of Faith) and later moved to a
better site.

Hanny Hassan:

> I was very much involved in the [London] mosque . . . we had some
> very rigid people who virtually took over the mosque and there was a
> great conflict. Some of it was instigated by the Iran-Iraq War, as there
> were partisans on both sides. It wasn't a Sunni-Shi'a thing, it wasn't
> that. It was ideological, . . . and following a strict line on the issues. We
> had come to a point where we banned the distribution of literature
> from either side inside the mosque. We said that . . . we shouldn't be
> taking sides in that war and urged compromise.

Then the issue of the women's place in the mosque also came to a head because in London there was comingling [of the sexes] at all mosque activities except *salat*. We didn't have separate entrances in London. Families sat together, and then this new edict came down that women had to come in the back door . . . women had to be separated, and families couldn't sit together. They [the mosque administration] put up a barrier separating the men from the women in the prayer area—a high one, ceiling height. There was great conflict over all of that stuff. It wasn't about one issue; it was everything.

I was the secretary of the board in the midst of the Iran-Iraq War[1980-88] and the board had [announced] that if you wanted to hand out flyers then do it out on the sidewalk . . . Everything was going well [after that until] one day after juma [the Friday midday congregational prayer] this guy was standing in the lobby of the mosque handing out hate literature. I don't even know what side he was on, but my job as secretary was to enforce the rule.

So I came out and confronted him, asked him who had given him the authority to distribute the flyers . . . and before I got half way through my spiel I was attacked. I was beaten up, my glasses were broken, and the police came. But I didn't see who did it. I was protected by Hassan Kajan, who was an old-time Yugoslav member of our community. His arm was cut when he put his arm up to protect me from being hit on the head, so there must have been a knife. But nobody would identify the assailants, even my relatives, who knew who the perpetrators were. So I left. I quit the mosque board in about 1980.

Then others started leaving the mosque for various reasons. About a year later I had a call from a fellow I considered relatively strict and orthodox, an Egyptian acquaintance, and he said, "There are a lot of us who have left and we feel we should have something that is reasonable." So we started meeting in a community room at the mall in town. Ten or fifteen of the dissidents met to say, "Look, we are not going to challenge the mosque. If that's the way they want to interpret Islam and behave, that's fine. We're not going to raise a challenge to them . . . but we can create another space." So we met probably for a year in a room in the mall at night. They weren't religious meetings, they were strategy meetings about what we were about, and then we started renting space at Fanshawe Community College on Sundays for khutbas and prayers.

After the Sunday programs, we stayed on and tried to create a vision for our identity as Canadian Muslims. The group expanded. There were probably a hundred of us [including] family members. We had had quite large gatherings, and we would talk about contemporary issues that we were facing, not about the mosque but what our place was and how to deal with our children and stuff like that. We had a different speaker every Sunday, and then we would stay on and have a potluck snack—it wasn't a meal—and held consultations with the various sectors of the group. So we had the kids in one group, seniors in one group, women in one group on one Sunday to talk about, maybe, how do we deal with youth. We might have a mixed group the next time to talk about vision [for the future] . . .

We did that for about a year and then wrote up a statement of values about who we were and what kind of community we wanted to have. We [agreed] that programming was more important than building, and identified the programs that we wanted to do. Some people were thinking ahead about finding a place, and my focus was on programing and that the place would have to fit the programs, not the other way.

Then a strange thing happened in the early '90s. GM Diesel had a big factory here in town [London], they also had a training building, and they had decided they weren't going to do training [there] anymore . . . They hadn't been able to sell it, so one of the members of the community, who was a real-estate agent [suggested we approach GM for a donation of a significant part of the cost of purchasing it.]

They were originally looking for a million bucks for it, but . . . we ended up getting it for $300,000. So now our focus was not programming but "we've got a place and have to pay for it." It was probably twenty years ago now [in 2013] . . . I and about thirty others each contributed $10,000 as loans to buy it. Ultimately we got paid back and the thing just took off. It was called the Islamic Centre of Southwest Ontario.

There was a lot of tension between the Centre and the other mosque. They continued in their stiff ways and we tried to be more open, but over the years they have come together. They have become more open and the Islamic Centre has moved closer to them . . . Both mosques are struggling to meet the pastoral, social, and other needs of the community, especially the young people. There are also another couple more mosques in London now that I don't know much about. There is a small Shi'a mosque and the Bosnians have built a place, and the Ismailis have a jamatkhana.

The London Muslim Mosque now has a full-time school attached to [it]. Interestingly, . . . both mosques are doing the same things. But there are still gaps in meeting the community needs and [the] narrow focus that doesn't attract many of the educated and professional people in the community. They do get them for juma prayers, and they do get them for Eid and fund-raising dinners, but in terms of their involvement in decision-making and programming, it's not happening. We have a seniors group that Najet and I attend at the Islamic Centre once a month, including a potluck dinner followed by a secular speaker on some subject, such as retirement investments.

I was away from London, in Toronto, for ten years, from 1995 to 2005, and during that period I [was involved] with the Noor Centre and did a lot of interfaith work independently and by conscripting people like Imam Patel and others from within the Muslim community. I took over the role that [Muin] Muinuddin had in the National Muslim-Christian Liaison Committee, after his untimely passing [in 1998]. That continues on. I also got involved with St Michael's University College [of the University of Toronto] assisting in their Islamic and three-faiths programs by identifying Muslim academics and other resources. I have also been involved with Roshan Jamal of the Canadian Dawn Foundation [regarding the activities] at Emmanuel College at the University of Toronto . . . in reaching out to the diverse Muslim community . . .

My mother, Ayshi Hassan died in February of 2014, the mother of eleven, grandmother of twenty, and great-grandmother of eighteen. She was recognized as a mother to a host of new immigrants to Canada. Since the 1950s she had been involved in building and supporting Arab and Muslim community organizations . . . and helped to build the oldest mosque in Ontario, founded by the Canadian Muslim Benevolent Society in London . . .

Throughout her life she was a strong advocate for multiculturalism and human rights. For example, for fifteen years she was night manager at the Cross Cultural Learner Centre in London and guided refugees through their difficult periods of transition, helping them navigate through government bureaucracy, shop for groceries, use public transit, and so on. Ayshi Hassan retired from that role in 2002 at the age of eighty. She was on the Mayor's New Year's Honours List in 2004 and was recognized for her contributions to humanitarianism in the city. The Islamic Centre of Southwestern Ontario also recognized her contributions to the community and she was further recognized as an ideal "Global Citizen" in 2006 on the sixtieth anniversary of the United Nations.

My mother died at the age of ninety-two in February 2014.

9. *Hamilton, Home of Big Ideas*

UNLIKE MOST OF MY PREVIOUS INTERVIEWEES, THOSE I MET IN Hamilton were all South Asians who had come to Canada as graduate students, teachers, or librarians. They made Hamilton a centre of Islamic activity that included the development of the Council of Muslim Communities of Canada (CMCC).

Arriving in Canada in 1964, Mohammad Afsar was one of a handful of early active Muslims in Hamilton who helped organize the community, build an association, and purchase a succession of potential mosque sites in the late 1960s and early 1970s. He told me in December 2018:

> I was born in 1939 in Dakhan Paiser, in Pakistan. It was a very remote village in the North West Frontier Province—now named Khyber Pakhtun Khawah. My parents were agriculturalists basically, but my father was able to establish a bakery business in Karachi so he was able to come out of that.
>
> Fortunately I was able to obtain a degree in civil engineering from Peshawar University in 1962. Following that I was a lecturer in the same department there for two years before coming to Canada. McMaster University had offered me a scholarship and after completing my master's degree, I joined the City of Hamilton's Department of Engineering in 1967.

While at McMaster, Mohammad met his future wife, Zia. According to her:

> My real name is Fakhr-Un-Nisa, and Zia is my nickname. I was born in 1941 in Balrampur, India and migrated to Pakistan with my family

as a child. When I was a teenager, I wanted to become an engineer. At that time women were not allowed to go to engineering universities in Pakistan. I applied to three or four different universities and got rejected because of my gender. So I initiated a struggle against gender discrimination, for which I received support from women's organizations and the media.

The issue went before [the courts in Pakistan who deemed the discrimination] contrary to the constitutional provision of equal opportunity for men and women. After that, women could go to engineering universities. However, I could not wait for this change to happen, so I continued to study the sciences and received my master's degree in physics from Punjab University, Lahore.

I then worked as a lecturer at Kinnaird College in Lahore for two years, after which I received a Commonwealth Scholarship and came to McMaster University in Hamilton [and earned] a master's in nuclear physics in 1966. After completing my education in Canada, I went back to my family in Pakistan. I returned to Canada in 1972 after marrying Mohammad.

Mohammad:

At the time, when we were students at McMaster University, our acceptance and relationship with the local community was probably the highest. There were very few Muslim students at the university and we would [obtain] university facilities for our religious and cultural activities, [including Friday prayers]. In general, the environment was very welcoming and friendly. There were very few other Muslims around Hamilton and they were also very well connected within the community.

At that time mostly very highly qualified people—engineers, doctors and PhDs—were able to come to Canada. For us who came in the '60s we had no cultural issues to deal with. Because most of us were educated, forward-looking, and open to learning new ways, we forged cordial relationships with many social and religious groups . . . My best friends were of the Catholic faith who offered us the use of their church facilities to hold dinners and celebrate the Eid at the end of Ramadan . . .

When we were in Hamilton, we worked together . . . Every year when it came to a multicultural day in the park, the Muslim group, even though we were few would set up our exhibits showing our cultural artifacts, including Arabic writing and copies of Qur'an, and all those sorts of things, to expose Muslim religious dimensions to the local community.

However, we also felt a need to develop Muslim community organizational structures [such as] religious and educational institutions, community centres, and mosques . . . basically where Muslims coming to Canada could feel at home and their children's religious needs were met.

So the Muslims bought a small house and converted it into the first mosque in Hamilton. Later, in the '70s, when funds were raised, including contributions from outside Canada, a church with land was bought in the Hamilton mountain neighbourhood and a larger mosque was built.

I had started my engineering career with the City of Hamilton in 1967 and I played a significant role in Hamilton's downtown redevelopment and in the preparation of the Hamilton-Wentworth Regional Development plan.

Mohammad and Zia left Hamilton in 1980 and went on to play major roles in the subsequent development of the Muslim community of Swift Current, Saskatchewan, where they helped to raise a mosque. Later they were active in the Muslim community of Regina.

Mohamed Bhabha, a South African teacher, arrived in Canada in 1965, a year after Mohammad Afsar. I interviewed him in 2019.

I was born on Valentine's Day 1942 in the Transvaal, South Africa. My father had a general store in a holiday resort, Badplaas, where natural hot mineral springs were the attraction. I was born in the nearest town with [the assistance of] a doctor, Carolina.

All my grandparents were born in the village of Kholvad, in the Surat district of Gujerat, India, in the nineteenth century. My maternal grandparents, Ismail Mohamed Kajee and Rasool Tickley, emigrated to the island of Reunion, which is an overseas *departement* of France. My mother, being born in Reunion, was French [by citizenship].

My paternal grandfather, Ahmed Yusuf Bhabha, emigrated in 1888 to the Zuid Afrikaanse Republiek [ZAR, the South African Republic] which had been established by Dutch-speaking settlers unhappy with British rule in the Cape Colony of southern Africa. I don't know whether his wife, Rasool Pahad, travelled with him or joined him later but they made their home in Middelburg, and their nine children were born there. My father, Abdul Samad, was the youngest.

My grandfather [Ahmed Yusuf Bhabha] had a general store and during the Boer War, when most of the cities of the ZAR had fallen to the British, ZAR President Paul Kruger commandeered saddles from his store to wage guerilla warfare on horseback. After the Boer War my grandfather marched with Mahatma Gandhi to protest unjust laws against Indians in the Union of South Africa and was briefly imprisoned.

I attended school in Roodepoort near Johannesburg and did two years of teacher's training in Johannesburg itself. I went into teaching because there were no other educational opportunities available to me in Apartheid South Africa. I taught for four years then came to Canada in 1965 because I wanted a university education. My first order of business when I arrived in Toronto was to enrol in three evening courses in the arts faculty at York University. During the day I worked for a while as a supply teacher, because when I arrived in late August 1965 there were no teaching jobs in the Toronto area, and I needed to stay here to attend night school. Later I worked in a bookstore for a while.

In 1966 I got a job [in Toronto]with the Canadian government, and I stayed there for the next thirty years. My first government job was as an admissions officer in the immigration department, interviewing people who wanted to live permanently in Canada. Then I worked as an immigration judge. Finally I moved up into senior management and worked in various responsibility areas in Toronto until I retired in February, 1997.

I [became] involved in volunteer work from the start. I was with the labour union at work and served as vice-president of our local branch of the Public Service Alliance of Canada. I was also editor of the local's monthly newsletter. My union involvement ended with my move into management.

My connection with Hamilton was [due to] my volunteer work. My cousin, Ahmed Bhabha, had started a weekend Islamic school at the Hamilton Multicultural Council. The small Muslim community met there on Sundays for prayers and socializing. In the late 1970s the Muslim Association of Hamilton got permission from the board of education to conduct heritage language classes at the John A Macdonald Secondary School. They had applied on the grounds that Arabic was part of the cultural heritage of Muslims. By this time the weekend Islamic school had doubled from the original three teachers to six and there was a need for an additional teacher. I was approached and I accepted. I was living in Oakville at the time so for the next decade or so I travelled to Hamilton every Saturday to teach from nine AM to noon.

Hamilton in those days was interesting because for some strange reason it became an incubating hub for spawning Muslim organizations at a time when Canada lacked Muslim institutions. One of the residents, Qasem Mahmud, had great entrepreneurial energy which he directed to helping the community. He started an investment company with a group of community members and built a townhouse complex. Qasem Mahmud, together with people like Muin Muinuddin, a teacher from Toronto, and Dr Fuad Şahin, a urologist from Niagara-on-the-Lake, established the Council of Muslim Communities of Canada [CMCC] and held their first national conference in Hamilton . . . Some of the organizations that grew from the CMCC were Camp Al-Mu-Me-Neen, the Islamic School Teachers Association, the Canadian Council of Muslim Women [CCMW], and the International Development and Refugee Foundation [IDRF]. There was also a national publication, *Islam Canada*, and a weekly TV program broadcast by CMCC.

One of the first major national endeavours undertaken by CMCC was the nationwide celebration of the beginning of the fifteenth century of the hijri era in 1979. CMCC had applied for and received federal government funding for this project. Muin Muinuddin and Hameed Shaikh, secretary of CMCC, were in charge of developing plans for the celebration. I was asked to become a member of the committee and was mainly responsible for public relations. The year-long celebrations were kicked off in Vancouver with a workshop on Islam and a huge banquet. It was attended by federal, provincial, and municipal politicians as well as by local Muslim leaders and a delegation of CMCC officials, including myself, from Ontario. The keynote speaker was Warith Deen Muhammad, the leader of the Nation of Islam, the NOI, who had by this time brought the NOI into the mainstream of Sunni Islam. The banquet was also a celebration of successful lobbying by CMCC that had resulted in the BC Muslim Association receiving a permit to build the first mosque in BC, and we conducted a public sod-turning ceremony for the proposed mosque. The building permit had initially been denied because of BC's "green" policy, in effect at the time to protect agricultural lands. Programs to commemorate the fifteenth century of the hijri calendar were also held in Toronto, Montreal, and the Maritimes. No Muslim organization had done anything like this on a national scale in Canada so it was a great triumph for CMCC.

Another lasting initiative of CMCC that began in Hamilton was the formation of the IDRF. There had been much talk of establishing a national charitable organization and several unsuccessful attempts were made until it was recognized that in order to successfully establish such an organization a full-time employee would be needed. Hameed Shaikh agreed to take up the challenge. He took a one-year leave of absence from his job as a librarian with the City of Hamilton. An inaugural meeting of about a dozen people was held in 1983 at Dr Şahin's home in Niagara-on-the-Lake. I was invited but I informed Hamid that for personal reasons I wouldn't be able to take any official role, but I would help in whatever other capacity I could.

At that meeting an organization called International Refugee and Relief Program or IRRP, was formed. The name suggested that one of its priorities was to help with the growing international problem of refugees. Hameed worked eighteen- to twenty-hour days, seven days a week, to get the organization established. He consulted with refugee groups in Toronto, and a couple of church organizations were very helpful. They advised him . . . and as a result a decision was made to incorporate IRRP as the IDRF, the International Development and Refugee Foundation, in 1984, with refugees still a key focus. Hameed remained as executive director after the Hamilton Library refused to grant more extensions of his leave of absence and lengthy searches for a replacement ED were unsuccessful. Sometime in 1995 or '96 Hameed resigned as executive director, and the IDRF was shut down. In 1997 it was revived through the initiative of a former board member, Dr Cassim Bhabha and his friend, Zeib Jeeva. Shortly thereafter there was another name change, this time to International Development and Relief Foundation, to reflect the changing priorities in the international aid field.

In June 1971, I married Marie-Carolle Rossignol, whose French-Canadian family's roots in Canada go back over 250 years. I met her at an anti-apartheid event in Toronto. She was Catholic but a few years after we were married she converted to Islam and adopted the name Mariam. She was also active in community work from the beginning of our marriage . . . She served as president of the local NDP Constituency Association and was a member of the board of directors of the Halton Children's Aid Society and served as its secretary; she also served on the board of the Halton Muslim Association as its treasurer and was the founding president of the Federation of Muslim Women.

During the Serbian-Bosnian War Mariam was president of the Bosnian Canadian Relief Association and was instrumental in raising funds and supplies nationally for Bosnian refugees. She visited refugee camps in the war ravaged area several times, including one visit through an underground tunnel to the besieged city of Sarajevo. In 2002 she joined the fledgling British-based International Women's Peace Service that was formed to recruit international volunteers to act as witnesses to the persecution and harassment of Palestinian civilians at flashpoints in the West Bank such as checkpoints and olive harvests. She was with the first four-member team deployed to the West Bank to establish a permanent base in one of the villages. During her four-month stay there she and a colleague were involved in an incident with Israeli soldiers who were shooting randomly and without cause into the village. As a result they were arrested, detained for several hours, and deported by military order from the West Bank.

In 2003 Mariam and I were recruited by a Quebec-based international humanitarian organization as volunteers to serve in Israel/ Palestine. Working out of its Jerusalem office Mariam would be coordinating projects in refugee camps in Jordan and Lebanon. I was assigned to work on a project with an NGO in Ramallah that specialized in providing in-service training to teachers. On our arrival at Ben Gurion Airport we were detained for several hours and interrogated by Israeli intelligence apparently because of Mariam's previous year's encounter with the Israeli military. I was eventually admitted into Israel but Mariam was jailed overnight at the airport. At a court hearing the next morning, that she was not permitted to attend, she was declared to be a threat to the national security of Israel and deported from Israel that day.

I stayed on in Ramallah for two years to conduct research on how well the recently introduced civic education curriculum was being applied and to identify any shortcomings. I also developed workshops for Palestinian teachers and facilitated several workshops in the Jerusalem and West Bank school districts. The study, "Cultivating Civic Sensibilities—An Approach to Enhancing Civic Education in Palestine," was published in English and Arabic in 2005. Resource material developed by me on classroom management was included in a book published at the same time in Arabic and English in which a Palestinian academic contributed an article.

What was beautiful about those days in the late '60s and '70s with the mosque in Toronto and in the community in Hamilton was that while the community was small it was very diverse and we accepted everybody. In Hamilton we had a Shi'a family of Bohras, the Fivers instead of the Twelvers, and they would attend our Islamic school and they would attend the mosque. Nothing was made of it. We knew they were Shi'a and it was accepted, just like in Toronto where there was a Shi'a schoolteacher teaching at Toronto's first mosque on the weekend. He was a top man from Iraq. He couldn't go to Iraq at that time under Saddam Hussein, but after Saddam he went back to Iraq and became a member of the government. He was Hussein Shahristani . . .

So that was the kind of society we had here, and it's captured in that TV series *Little Mosque on the Prairie*, and that was the kind of mosque we had in Hamilton and in Toronto and that was the kind of mosque we lost when the Muslim Brotherhood-inspired people came in, like in Hamilton at the university. We had lots of trouble with them. They were very extreme. And they influenced some of the community members also and it became really bad. I know I attended meetings where people were saying what ISIS is saying now, and I couldn't believe it.

The thing to learn from all of that is that while we have grown in numbers, we have divided up into different ethnic groups and we have become very doctrinaire in our beliefs and rituals and we are less willing to accept differences. The other point, in conjunction with what you mention in terms of the future, is that there is hope for the future in our youth because the youth are Canadian and they are getting away from the sectarianism of their parents. It will take a while, but I think there is going to be a difference there. I see it with my children's friends and I see it with the newer generations that are coming up. That's the hope.

Another Muslim arrival in Hamilton in the 1960s, was Hameed Shaikh (who has been mentioned previously). I interviewed him in January 2019.

I was born on July 12, 1939, in a socially active lower middle-class family in the district of Jalgaon, Maharashtra, India. I finished my secondary school education in my home town and moved to Bombay and enrolled in Ismail Yusuf College. After completing my BA in 1961, my master's degree from St Xavier College in 1963, and my diploma in librarianship from the University of Bombay in 1965, I worked for a few months at the university library.

Some of my close friends applied to go to the UK so I decided to join them and find a job and begin a new life. In 1965, I went to the UK on an Employment Voucher and worked in a public library for over two years near Cardiff, South Wales. My plan was to continue my postgraduate education at a British university and then return to India. However, the British library system was different from the Indian, and so my library qualification was not recognized.

He followed the advice of friends and came to Canada with his wife, sending their young daughter back to India to be cared for by his family.

I clearly remember that we left Britain for Toronto on Good Friday, 1968. When we arrived, we found a rental room in downtown Toronto . . . I decided to work as a night-time security guard and continue my search for a library position. Shortly thereafter, I couldn't believe my luck! I received two job offers! One was as a teacher, with a condition that I acquire a teaching certificate within the next three years. The other offer was from the Hamilton Public Library, on a six-month probationary contract period. I accepted the library job in Hamilton.

Within a short time, the probationary condition was removed, and I accepted a full-time permanent position with them. I applied and was accepted in the University of Western Ontario's Master of Library Science program. After graduation, I returned to the Hamilton Public. It was at this time that my wife and I returned to India to bring our children to live with us. I lived in Hamilton for eighteen years and it was one of the most enjoyable times of my life. It was a brand-new beginning for us with a new home and a new community. It was a period of challenges for me to achieve economic stability, establish a more responsible life.

Within a short time, I met Mohammad Afsar and he took me to the McMaster Student Centre. Every Sunday afternoon, a few young families and mostly single graduate students would meet for zuhr prayers followed by a social get-together. Reflecting back, I guess this was an initial step towards the establishment of a Muslim community in Hamilton. Within a short period of time, this small group grew and was able to begin congregational prayers, religious classes for children, and social gatherings.

In the initial stages, the group consisted of a few dedicated and committed individuals consisting of the late Qasem Mahmud, Ahmad Bhabha, Mohamed Bhabha, Ebrahim Sayed, Noor Khan, Mehdi Hashemi, and Mohammad Afsar. We would get together and plan for the formation of the Muslim community. This also was the beginning of lifelong relationships with these individuals and their families.

Hameed recalled that the topics at social gatherings included the politics of Pakistan, the lack of halal meat locally and the difficulty of securing loans and mortgages so that Muslim families could move out of their rental properties into their own homes. Also,

> Interaction with local non-Muslims was rare, and involvement in civic affairs was almost none. Many new immigrants considered Canada an anti-Muslim country. They chose to come here to pursue professional opportunities as this was difficult in their countries of origin. A small number had fled either religious or political persecution.
>
> Despite this, the community members were eager to show solidarity with the less fortunate people. They became involved in the rehabilitation and settlement of Kurdish and Ugandan refugees. They were welcomed to the mosque and a lot of assistance was provided to them towards settlement in Canada.
>
> The Hamilton Muslim Association was established in 1966 or 1967, under the leadership of Qasem Mahmud. He was an electrical engineer from Palestine. President of the association was Dr Taqdir Husain, a prominent mathematician who worked at McMaster University. Dr Abdul Waheed, a postdoctoral fellow, became the first secretary. The association began holding Sunday get-togethers and plans were formulated for arranging more and bigger gatherings, beginning with children's religious classes and finally establishing an Islamic Centre. Eid prayers followed by Eid dinners were arranged to attract Muslims within the city as well as from the neighbouring towns.
>
> In 1969–70, a small house was purchased in an industrial area . . . and renovated by volunteers as our first place to congregate. As the place quickly became too small, in 1971 or '72 a large parcel of land approximately fifteen minutes' drive from the city was purchased

to accommodate the rapidly growing Muslim population. With this came new professionals who were interested in volunteering their skills and had more disposable income. A grander plan was developed to include a mosque, community centre, cemetery, and housing complex. We were hoping to access funds from the oil-rich Muslim countries of the Middle East and Far East. The key people involved in this project were Mohammad Afsar, Hashim Ali, Liaqat Sidiqui, and myself. We quickly realized that this new location was impractical for many to drive five times a day for prayers. This was abandoned in favour of a more convenient location within the city. Another drawback of this location was the sulphuric-smelling water from the property's well . . . Eventually the farm property was sold and a property with a large house was purchased on the Hamilton mountain.

The Muslim community began to explore different venues to share our socio-religious values and varied cultures with the larger community. A local folk festival was an excellent opening for them to participate and establish their presence. Volunteers such as Hamida Din and Salma Ali organized the Muslim pavilion, which highlighted artifacts and food and set up exhibitions to share Muslim values and cultural practices. Participation in this event continued for several years until the community focused their attention on other matters.

Initially, given the size of the community, there was very limited interaction that took place with other faith groups, primarily the churches. Occasionally someone from the community would be asked to speak to a church congregation. Once, Christ the King Cathedral offered us space to hold an Eid dinner. The association gladly accepted, and the dinner was held on a Saturday night. Unfortunately, the smell of the spicy food was still present during the Sunday morning service, and this was very embarrassing for the priest who had kindly reached out to the association. This was one of many growing pains experienced by the community in the beginning.

Hamilton was the second largest city in Ontario, so it attracted many new immigrant Muslims and gradually became a breeding ground for Islamic activists. A history of Hamilton would be incomplete without the mention of some of its key players who went on to make a bigger contribution to Muslims in other parts of Canada.

A noted Muslim resident of Hamilton, with a lifetime of successes to his credit, was Qasem Mahmud, of Palestinian origin. Unfortunately, although we had set up an interview, he died before we could meet. This was some time in 2018. Of him, Hameed Shaikh said:

> He was a visionary whom I consider to be one of the architects and builders of the Canadian Muslim Community. He played a prominent role in the formation of the Muslim Association of Hamilton, CMCC, Youth Islamic Camps, and the Ahram Construction Company—a nonprofit housing society for Muslims in Hamilton. In the early 1970s, Ahram Construction built townhouses for eighteen Muslim families, to my knowledge, [the only venture of its kind] in Canada. He was instrumental in the purchase and development of the Long Bay Camp site, which was to encourage Muslim community members to invest in a property that would provide year-round facilities for youth camps and family camping. He authored and published a series of eight books for children, called My Book of Islam. Qasem Mahmud moved to Ottawa and focused his attention on the establishment of the Ottawa Arabic School and the development and operation of the Long Bay campsite north of Kingston [and west of Westport].

Hameed Shaikh mentioned two other eminent Muslims in the region. Ahmad Bhabha was a teacher who was instrumental in the establishment of the Islamic weekend school as well as the Association of the Islamic School Teachers of Ontario. Ebrahim Sayed was involved in the affairs of the Muslim Association of Hamilton; since he was working in Brantford, he was cofounder of the Brantford Muslim Association. He was also the first treasurer of CMCC, was on the board of the charity IDRF, and was a founding member of the REHMA Community services.

Hameed:

> During one of the early Eid dinners in Hamilton in the late 1960s, Muin Muinuddin of Toronto was invited as a keynote speaker. At that time, I was a secretary of the Hamilton Muslim Association, and he introduced himself and acknowledged the effort that went into the

planning of the event by me. This meeting was the beginning of our working and personal relationship. It is to be noted that most of my CMCC involvement took place while I was living in Hamilton.

I became involved in different projects of the CMCC after my initial meeting with Muin Muinuddin. I found these projects both intriguing and challenging, and I enjoying working with both Qasem Mahmud, who was still in Hamilton, and Muin. As I became more involved, I was elected as the CMCC treasurer and became part of the decision-making team. The project which I enjoyed the most was organizing CMCC's annual conventions, as it allowed me an opportunity to connect with community leaders throughout Canada and experts on important issues facing the Muslim community.

During the heydays of CMCC, close to thirty project concepts and plans were developed by the team of executives and other volunteers. These included a Muslim census in Canada, a monthly magazine, *Islam Canada,* a series of introductory booklets on Islam, and youth summer camps. Financial aid was also extended to newly established and struggling Muslim community organizations. After the initial success, many of these projects were unfortunately abandoned due to lack of funds and committed volunteers.

Muin Muinuddin and Sudha and Abdullah Khandwani came up with the idea of promoting Canadian Muslims and their contributions through a visual presentation. A portable photographic exhibition by the Khandwanis became part of the Canadian Hijra Centennial Celebration and was shown in a [large number] of Canadian cities. They also produced a thirty-minute documentary film, *A Tale of Two Mosques,* about the 1938 Edmonton Al Rashid Mosque and its 1980s move to a historical park setting. The script was written by Professor Rasesh Thakkar, Muin Muinuddin, and the Khandwanis and received a grant from the Canada Council. It was shown abroad by the Ministry of Foreign Affairs and in Canada as part of the Canadian Hijra Centennial Celebration in 1979. This Hijra Celebration was a successful endeavour led by Azmat Khan, Mohamed Bhabha, Muin Muinuddin, and Hameed Shaikh. CMCC also took advantage of federal multiculturalism grants to organize seminars on the Muslim presence in Canada and Muslim contributions to the Canadian cultural mosaic.

Muin was first elected as the secretary of CMCC. After a few years he was the president. He remained a key decision-maker, since other presidents of the CMCC were from out of Toronto. The CMCC had no staff person, so Muin played the key role in consultation with the office-bearers. Keeping in mind that the CMCC was formed by the trio of Qasem Mahmud, Muin Muinuddin, and Fuad Şahin, the organizational role was played by Qasem and Muin, and they complemented each other. After the loss of Qasem [to Ottawa], it was Muin and to a lesser degree myself who were the torch-bearers of the CMCC.

Muin Muinuddin recognized the importance of establishing an interfaith relationship with Christian churches. A series of dialogue sessions were held with many church groups in Toronto and the major cities. Later, this hand of friendship was extended to the Jewish community as well. The association with the churches was instrumental when the CMCC formed the International Development and Refugee Foundation [IDRF] as a grassroots Muslim Canadian charity. Formation of the IDRF was based on the Islamic principles of self-reliance, social justice and human dignity. The IDRF was introduced to key government bureaucrats and politicians and other communities. It was invited to participate in the advocacy bodies such as the Inter-church Committee for Refugees.

A major role was played in the development of the IDRF by the Canadian Council of Churches in general and the United Church of Canada in particular. "Innocent Victims of the Iraqi War" was the Canadian aid project led by the IDRF. It focused on providing Canadian assistance to Iraqi displaced people . . . More Canadian Christian and Muslim projects were developed to continue interfaith assistance to poor people living in dire poverty throughout the world.

The African famine in Ethiopia focused attention on the plight of refugees in the mid-to-late 1980s worldwide. Canadian government policies assisted charity organizations to open their homes to refugees . . . The CMCC formed the IDRF to sponsor refugees to Canada

and secure matching government grants for international development projects . . . Later, the IDRF office moved to Toronto to better
serve the needs of refugees and to establish core support from a larger
Muslim community in Toronto. The IDRF became one of the most
reputable Canadian charities.

10. The Niagara Region: Aside from the Falls

TWO OF THE MUSLIM COMMUNITY'S MAIN PILLARS IN THE NIAGARA region were the respected elder, the Turkish urologist Dr Fuad Şahin (pronounced Shaheen) and the Bosnian chemical engineer and founder of Niagara Protective Coatings, the late Hassan Karachi. I interviewed Dr Şahin at his Niagara-on-the-Lake home in the summer of 2015.

Dr Şahin explained that after the Christian Reconquista of Moorish Andalusia in Spain, many Muslims fled to what became Algeria and Tunisia. There they called on the Ottoman sultan to help them fight back. In response, in 1460 Sultan Selim II sent Turkish Ottoman volunteers to fight the Spaniards, and these Turks ended up settling in Tlemcen, in present-day Algeria, and other cities.

> My father's name was Muhammed Salih and he was born in Tlemcen, Algeria in approximately 1892 . . . In Algeria, my father didn't like the French occupation. His parents had died and so at the age of seventeen—the year 1909 approximately—he went to Tunis and took a job in the trams and made enough money and left for Damascus [then still part of the Ottoman Empire]. He made a living there by teaching French.

Dr Şahin's father went on the hajj to Mecca and then made contact with people in Istanbul who were close to the sultan's court. Through them he was able to get into the Ottoman military officers' academy, and was there when the "Young Turk" rebellion broke out against the sultan's regime in Istanbul. It was led by Kemal Ataturk, and it was 1908. In 1911, when Italy attacked Libya (which was under the Ottomans), young volunteers were encouraged from all over the Ottoman Empire to go fight the Italians. Dr Şahin's father joined these Mujahideen. They fought for ten years.[90] He married there, and Dr Şahin was their third child, born on September 6, 1922. The fighting had to stop and the Ottoman forces retreated.

> I was forty days old. They put me on the back of a camel with my mother and our convoy started travelling through North Africa all the way eastward to Egypt. It took us eighteen months to reach Egypt!
>
> There were snakes and scorpions along the way. To protect me from scorpion bites, they fed me a cooked scorpion. I then had immunity to scorpion bites. I actually remember being bitten by a scorpion in the south of Turkey, as a young man, and the bite was inconsequential to me.
>
> When my father and mother reached Egypt, they entered a home and I supposedly started to scream whenever I came inside the house because I had only known the desert and tents. My mother always put me to sleep outside and only brought me inside after I fell asleep . . .
>
> Once back in Turkey, in 1924, my father resigned from the army. He had joined the army for *jihad*—not to be part of the [regular] Turkish army. He started working for the railway that was supposed to go all the way to Baghdad and it was called the Toros Express. He found a job and was sent to Aleppo in Syria when I was five years old . . .
>
> My father was then transferred to the eastern part of the railway—350 kilometres east of Aleppo. My parents left me with a family there . . . and I studied in Aleppo until 1937. I never had better teachers in my whole life like the ones in Syria . . . After six years of primary school, I went to a French school—Mission Laique Francaise. It was a secondary school . . . Living with a Syrian family, life was not ideal. My father then took me to Adana, Turkey, to study further. Then I was taken to Tarsus, where there was an American school, but the school quota was full so we went to Istanbul. We went to a special school named Galatasaray High School, established by the Ottomans to prepare people for government positions and learn French . . .
>
> I studied at Galatasaray until 1943. My father was still working for the railway as a mechanical technician. His income was not enough and he had a hard time. They made great sacrifices to get me through

high school. One year after graduating, I worked for the Turkish Business Bank, before starting medical school. I graduated in 1950.

When I was in high school, in the ninth grade, we were given a choice to learn German or English. My father told me, "Learn English well, because by the time you grow up the whole world will be speaking English." I was therefore studying English on top of the other high school courses . . .

In 1950, I went into military service for one year and served as a doctor. All the Turks, once they graduated, wanted to go to America . . . Every day I went to the hospital and attended clinics to get more experience—internal medicine, radiology, etc. I was able to speak French and I knew medicine very well, but I didn't want to leave Turkey after my military service. I felt my country needed me.

[However,] the US Marshall Plan was recruiting Turks and giving scholarships. I won a scholarship . . . but I felt that I should serve the people. My parents brought me up with great sacrifice so I declined the scholarship and the opportunity to go to the US. I was always called "crazy" and ended up in Suruc [near the Syrian border, in 1953] . . .

My parents and sister were not far from there. I took a small bag with a stethoscope and samples and went to Suruc, which had a population of 5,000. Today there is a population of over 100,000. I entered the small town and a man came from the village saying they needed a doctor—the midwife was with a woman who had miscarried and was bleeding! I took my bag and went to this primitive place. Houses were domes of mud brick, dirt floors . . . [there was] a young woman lying on the ground and losing blood. I told them to get a pot and water and throw in a spoon and boil it. I had iodine tincture and cleaned myself and . . . and performed a D&C using a spoon. The womb needed to be evacuated. Her bleeding stopped and I told the family to take her to the hospital fifty kilometres away. A week later, the woman came and kissed my hand. She had never gone to the hospital! . . .

I healed a lot of people and stayed there two years. Then my parents came and said, "You are established here. You need furniture. Let's go to Urfa and buy furniture."

Dr Şahin told his parents they should go to shop for better furniture in Gaziantep, and there with his parents at a dinner with a friend, Emin Bey, he met his future wife, Solmaz. They were married in 1954 in Gaziantep. In 1957, they moved to Istanbul and he applied to a hospital in order to specialize. "My friends told me to go to America, 'Don't stay in Turkey.' [After applying] I received an acceptance from the US and also one offer from Hotel Dieu Hospital in Kingston [Ontario]."

He said that his decision to try Canada was based on his high regard for Lester B Pearson's stand against the British, French, and Israelis during the crisis in 1956 when Egyptian President Gamal Abdel Nasser nationalized the Suez Canal. At the time, Pearson was the Secretary of State for External Affairs and later won the Nobel Prize for Peace for his work in establishing peace in 1957:

> I was filled with admiration for Pearson and I also liked that Canada had both French and English languages . . . I came to Canada in 1958, but I didn't bring my wife and our three daughters. But Kingston General Hospital had a connection with Liverpool Hospital and sent me there for surgical training in 1960, so I went to England and sent for my family . . .
>
> When I was in Hotel Dieu Hospital, there were nuns there and they were also responsible for the cafeteria. One nun approached me and said they noticed that I wasn't eating the food that was displayed. I explained that I was Muslim and didn't eat pork. The nuns then made sure that I had other food to eat that was suitable, and one nun then found me fried eggs and cold turkey. A Canadian doctor asked for the same food and the nun said, "No. It is special for Dr Şahin!" One day the nuns noticed that I wasn't coming for breakfast and lunch. I explained that I was fasting [during Ramadan] and that I ate at sunset only. They arranged a special meal for me for *sahoor* [the pre-dawn meal] and iftar [at sunset]. This was the country of Lester B Pearson! It was a special Canada!

Dr Şahin then took a year of pathology at Kingston General Hospital and then went on to study urology for a year. After he finished his training he decided to go to Matheson in Northern Ontario for general practice to complete his studies. Then he went to Hamilton General Hospital to finish his residency in urology.

> At the cafeteria [at Hamilton General] one day, I met a pharmacist, Syedul Zaffar, and a GP from Trinidad, Unus Omarali. I was told that Muslims were meeting at a centre on Dundas Street [West] in Toronto and teaching kids Islam. So [Solmaz and I] went to the centre on a Sunday. There I made the mistake of saying something about the Qur'an and became known as an expert in Islam.
>
> A Pakistani professor in Islamic Studies [at the University of Toronto], Dr [Mirza Q] Baig, was the president [of the Muslim Society of Toronto] . . . [The community split as a result of a conflict] and a group rented a Portuguese church on Bathurst Street [where they would meet]. Later they bought a place on Rhodes Avenue, called the Orange Hall, and established the Islamic Foundation. They raised some money and repaired the place. Soon after they separated, the Muslim Society of Toronto bought a retired Presbyterian church on Boustead Avenue in High Park and started the Jami Mosque. Seitali Kerim and Regep Assim, the Albanian imam, got together and established it.

Meanwhile, a doctor friend in Hamilton suggested that he go to Niagara Falls, because they needed a urologist there, so he went and settled in Niagara-on-the-Lake in 1966 with his wife, Solmaz. He still had connections with the Muslims in Toronto.

> The number of Muslims [in Toronto] kept increasing and when Eid arrived, I was made president of the Islamic Foundation, but I explained that I couldn't be president because I lived in Niagara Falls and wasn't a local. Muin Muinuddin, Hasib Khan, and others were involved in the Foundation. When Eid came, I said I would go to the Jami Mosque to see my friends, because I didn't believe in the division [of the community].

In about 1970, internal politics and cultural differences finally broke up the Muslim Society of Toronto's Jami Mosque leadership and congregation. The Society's leaders eventually decided to get out of the turmoil and in 1973 they sold the Mosque indirectly to the Muslim Students Association, or MSA, according to the Jami Mosque's website. Dr Şahin said he had suggested that Hisham Badran be hired to work as imam and caretaker of the mosque.[91]

Dr Şahin recalled how at a conference of the FIA (the Federation of Islamic Associations of the United States and Canada), in about 1972, he and other Canadian leaders decided to form the Council of Muslim Communities of Canada, CMCC, and Qasem Mahmud, a Palestinian member of the Ottawa Mosque, was elected its first president. It was funded on the basis of each member community's membership numbers and held meetings and worked on projects, but subsequent funding shortages caused it to wind down its activities.

> I recognized that the MSA [the Muslim Students Association of the United States and Canada] didn't recognize the CMCC and worked against us. The CMCC had meetings where women and men came together; the CMCC did interfaith work, but the MSA didn't like that . . .
>
> One day at a [CMCC] meeting [in Winnipeg], I explained that MSA was going forward but we were going backward at CMCC. The problem was that we didn't have individual memberships for our members and that they needed to pay yearly dues . . . I explained that the Muslims needed something tangible to work around . . . That is why in 1983 I established the IDRF [the now-thriving International Development and Relief Foundation].

The Muslim Students Association was founded in 1963 in the United States and, soon after, in Canada. It had stricter practice and Islamist politics. It was, as Şahin says, not in agreement with the more liberal CMCC but did a lot of good "Islamic" work and mosque-building. It was well funded.

The IDRF was founded in 1984 as a refugee-oriented agency, but it soon broadened its mandate and still delivers aid and assistance around the world, including to Syrian refugees of the civil war in 2011, and the

Rohingyas in Bangladesh. Meanwhile, Dr Şahin continued with the development of the community in Niagara Falls.

> I would still travel from Niagara Falls to Toronto for special events. Solmaz would cook food on Eid and for iftars. Every Friday, we would get together for juma prayers at the Hassan Karachi house [in Niagara Falls]. On Sundays Nimet Karachi would take their kids to the Jami Mosque in Toronto to learn Islam.
>
> We started having Islamic classes at the Karachi house, and on Saturday evenings we started having tafseer [learned interpretation] of the Qur'an. Eid prayers were held on the front lawn of our house, and Solmaz and the girls would have cooked for days prior to the Eid to have lovely sweets to serve.
>
> When Solmaz and I and the family came to Niagara Falls in 1966, Hassan Karachi and his wife Nimet were the only ones here . . . Gradually a few more people came and so we started to have juma prayers at his house. There were quite a few families, the Karachis' and ours and [the families of] Parvez Ansari, an orthopedic

Hassan Karachi, young Bosnian chemist and entrepreneur.
Photo courtesy of Nimet Karachi.

surgeon, Dr Syed Tayab from Bangladesh, some Mauritians like Abid Fakim, and South Africans like Dr Ebrahim Sayed and Ibrahim Valli.

Later, the number of Muslims grew further, particularly after [Ugandan dictator] Idi Amin kicked out [people of Indian origin, among whom were Muslims] . . . A few of us got together and we bought a lot on Lyons Creek Road in Niagara Falls. The ground-breaking ceremony took place in October 1985 and the building was completed in 1986.

According to a marker at the first mosque, the Islamic Society of Niagara Region was established in 1978, the Lyons Creek Road land was purchased two years later in 1980, and the mosque was completed in 1986. The first full-time imam was Rizk Akoush. There was space for a school but no hall for gatherings. Hassan Karachi had died meanwhile, and at a CMCC meeting in Toronto Dr Şahin spoke about Karachi's vision of a multipurpose hall. A member of the Ontario NDP government was present and offered help. Finally $250,000 was obtained for a community centre attached to the Niagara Falls mosque. It opened in October 1994. It included two minarets and a copper dome, in addition to a kitchen, a gym, a library, school classrooms, and a meeting hall.

A few years later . . . Hussein Hamdani came to Niagara Falls [from Uganda via England]. He had a very good business in dry cleaning and did very well in real estate, so he bought a factory in the centre of St Catharines and converted it into a mosque . . . [Masjid An-Noor].

Dr Şahin died on November 4, 2019 and after traditional funeral prayers at the Islamic Society of Niagara Peninsula mosque, he was buried in the nearby Islamic Cemetery of the Niagara Cemetery.

His wife Solmaz Şahin was always a great support to her heavily engaged activist husband. They had four children, Selma, Hulya, Leyla, and Mustafa. In an interview in Sadia Zaman's *At My Mother's Feet: Stories of Muslim Women*, Solmaz Şahin said:

Although I am proud of the important work Fuad and other Muslim leaders did during those pioneering years, I also recognize the many sacrifices made by the families. We women were often the unsung heroes who toiled in the background, cooking for community dinners, and managing our homes and families so that our husbands could do this volunteer work. Our children sacrificed by not being able to spend more time with their father. Everything has a price, so that is how we paid for this work.[92]

In January 2017, I interviewed Hassan Karachi's wife Nimet and one of their three children.

My husband, Hassan—Harry in Canada—Karachi, was born Hassan Karacic in Sarajevo, Yugoslavia, on September 1, 1924. He came from a middle-class family. His father had a coffee shop, and his mother came from an upper middle-class family. He was the eldest of four children, three boys and the youngest was a girl. His primary education was in Sarajevo, and his middle school as well . . . When he was fourteen years old, he ran away from school because his teacher gave him a zero for conduct. Hassan knew it was because he wore a fez—you know at that time the fez was an identifiable Muslim symbol . . . He was eventually brought back home. Hassan finished high school in Sarajevo. While there, he belonged to an underground young Muslim organization. Hassan's family was not overly religious, but he did attend madrassah to learn Qur'an.

Even before he completed high school, he was taken to the army and served in Tito's [wartime partisan] army, at the age of seventeen or eighteen. Because he was educated and could read and write all the different dialects, he served as the secretary . . . Hassan had a young sister, Camila. When she was in kindergarten, the Germans bombed her school. She was killed in that attack on Sarajevo.

After high school, he went to Zagreb, Croatia, and joined the chemical engineering faculty. The Communists were gathering young Muslim boys and girls. At the time all his young friends were getting arrested, including his friend Alija Izetbegovic—who became much later the president of the country of Bosnia in the 1990s. They were very intelligent people. Hassan knew his fate would be to be arrested and sent to fight for Tito. So he decided to run away with a Catholic friend, Bronco Obradovich, to the border to try to escape . . . on his second attempt, he was able to escape to [Trieste], Italy. I think this took place about 1947, approximately . . .

Hassan was in a refugee camp for quite some time. He started learning Italian and he got a job making hats and selling postcards. He next went to Rome and enrolled himself in the University of Rome. He attended one year of chemical engineering.

At that point, he heard that Canada was looking for young men to work on the farms. He did not speak a word of English, but he found out where to go and he went there and had a medical check. He was young and healthy and I think twenty-three years old, and was put on a boat to Canada with other young men. He ended up near Ottawa, at Carleton Place, on a farm in 1949. That was the year I was born!

He started working on a farm . . . [He would walk] to school every morning to learn English, and then would work on the farm in the afternoons. One day, Hassan was walking back in that cold Ottawa weather, freezing, [when] a car stopped and a man offered him a lift. The gentleman talked to him and asked him what he was doing in the area. Hassan told him he was a chemical engineer and had gone to school in Zagreb, Yugoslavia . . . he had come to Canada as a refu-gee and was working on a farm . . . This gentleman ended up being a famous scientist, Dr Aimsley, with the National Research Council. He said, "I am going to help you get out of your duties at the farm so you can go back to school." Hassan applied to the necessary govern-ment agencies and in six months he was released from his farming duties . . . He did different odd jobs in Ottawa. He worked at a soda fountain, learning English and sending money back to his mother and father in Yugoslavia.[93]

Hassan moved to Hamilton and worked at National Steel Car. He spoke all the Slavic languages and was speaking English by this time, so they gave him a good position and he was hiring all the immigrants and translating for them. Eventually, he brought his brother Redzep from Czechoslovakia . . .

Hassan started his studies at the University of Toronto and grad-uated in chemical engineering in 1952 . . . While he was attending university, he was also working at the Banting Institute as a chemical research fellow with Dr Best. [Frederick Banting and Charles Best are credited with having discovered insulin.] He also worked for Dr [Wilson Gordon] Bigelow, who was credited with the discovery of the pacemaker. Hassan was on the research team when the pacemaker was developed. There is a book called *Cold Hearts*, and Hassan is mentioned in the book.

He graduated and worked at the Ontario Research Foundation. One day a project started and he was supposed to work on a certain coating for a large American company. He developed a couple of formulations and they were submitted to McNaughton Brooks, a huge American company. This is when he realized: "I developed the products and someone else is making the money, so why don't I do something about it?" . . . A few young doctor friends from the Banting Institute gave him two or three thousand dollars each to help him purchase a bankrupt paint company in Toronto, back in 1957. He was developing coatings, making paint, finding customers, and delivering. He had a distribution company to find customers and orders. He started getting a lot of orders from the United States . . . so he started manufacturing in Niagara Falls, New York.

[Eventually he moved to Niagara Falls, Ontario and built a factory there. His company was called Everguard Coatings International and operated under the name Niagara Protective Coatings. The plant was next to their home.]

Nimet Karachi has her own story of struggle and success:

I was born in 1949 in Izmir, Turkey, and was raised in Istanbul after I was two years old. My father was a big businessman, and my mother was from a prominent family, descendants of Sokullu Mehmet Pasha, the grand vizier of Sultan Suleyman. I was educated in the American School of Istanbul.

Hassan had opened a paint factory in Turkey with my father, Ahmet Karaosmanoglu. I was translating for my father and that's when Hassan saw me and asked for my hand in marriage, and my father said, "Okay." I married Hassan on December 8, 1965 and came to Canada on December 15 at sixteen years of age. I have been living in the same house for fifty-one years!

I came as a young bride and I got into learning about all the Muslims in Toronto, and Hassan was part of an organization in the States. He was vice-president of the Federation of Islamic Associations of the United States and Canada, and of course he was very much involved in Toronto with the Bosnians and the Muslims.

I worked from the moment I came to Canada in the paint business. I am still part of it, and I worked for over forty years—the office, store, and helped produce paint. Everything, you name it. I ran the business with Hassan.

Our children? Nina was born on December 10, 1966, and Nadine was born March 5, 1968 and Ahmet (Dean) on January 26, 1969. I was nineteen with three young babies and a business and husband and my Islamic work. I remember how I would go to work and put each baby in a five-gallon paint can. That was their play pen. The ground floor of my house was a mosque for fifteen years—seven days a week, for twenty-four hours. We held Friday juma prayers, tafseer [Qur'anic commentary] one night a week and children's classes as often as Dr Şahin had the time, which at times felt like every day!

We established the Islamic Society of Niagara Peninsula in 1978, and we built the mosque on Lyon's Creek Road in Niagara Falls in 1985. From at least 1970 until 1985 our house was used as the mosque.

Hassan was part of the establishment of the Bosnian Muslim community in Toronto, called the Islamic Society of Gazi Husrev Beg. It was named after a Bosnian leader and there's a big mosque with his name in Sarajevo next to the covered bazaar in the middle of Sarajevo. I think it was from the Ottoman times, in the sixteenth century. I was there last summer [2016].

I asked Hassan's eldest daughter, Nina Karachi-Khaled, about her father.

He was a typical Type A, a self-made man. He came to Canada with a quarter in his pocket. He was driven. He had so much energy and impatience. He didn't suffer fools lightly. He had to do everything and be everything. This type of man, they burn out fast. His health suffered, his knees. If there was a thousand-gallon drum in the factory that had to be moved from point A to point B, instead of getting a machine and lifting the barrel with the machine, no, my father would rather go and push that thing himself. He was *not* a walk in the park, but he was *never* boring . . .

He was very active. He was intelligent, well-read, spoke many languages, travelled the world, enjoyed good food and good company. He was an amazing host and friend to many people. His door was always open. He was famous for his hospitality and his coffee. He could not have done any of that without his wife. Together they were an amazing team and worked day and night in the business and the Muslim community.

Hassan was shrouded in mystery. He would often throw out quotes—from Winston Churchill to Shakespeare to Bernard Shaw. Oftentimes the company would not understand his anecdotes, but Hassan would be quietly amusing himself. He could converse with anyone. He revelled in being around converts and survivors of any kind, people like Cat Stevens [later Yusuf Islam], Siraj Wahaj, political activists, prisoners of war, even a survivor of the Iranian hostage incident. Hassan was a ferocious learner and therefore could speak on any subject. Perhaps for that reason so many people loved to drop by for a cup of coffee and hear what thoughts came to mind for Hassan.

Nimet and Hassan [her parents] housed so many newcomers and helped them get started in Canada. How many people put a house trailer on their property just to house newcomers to Canada? This was one of the many seemingly crazy things that Hassan did. Naturally, there was a steady flow of newcomers to Canada being housed in the three-bedroom motor home next to Karachi headquarters. Amongst the many people that stayed rent free for an extended period of time was Mohamed Abdulrahman. In the 1980s, during the famine in Ethiopia, Hassan received a letter from a teenaged Ethiopian boy who was trying to get to Canada. What does Hassan do? He sponsors Mohammed Gato and brings him to live in his house for ten years! Hassan and Nimet educate Mohammed, take care of him and basically act as Mohammed's parents all during his teenage and young adult life.

Hassan was very generous and kind, especially to animals. He loved plants and flowers and had huge gardens on the property. He loved fruit trees and would plant them on every property he owned. For him, if you had land and fruit trees then you would always be secure. He worked hard and donated his money generously. He would always talk about being blessed with so much and having to give what he had accumulated. He knew that whatever he gave, Allah would reward him tenfold.

He loved being a Canadian Muslim. He was so proud to be a Muslim in Canada. You know he came from a communist country where you couldn't even tell people you were a Muslim. You had to hide everything. You couldn't talk to anyone. You were persecuted.

He would always talk about the beauty of this country, the freedom, the space, the opportunity, the goodness . . . He was a very positive person. He was a kind man. He would always see the good in people. He was often cheated in business because he trusted everyone. He had such a strong faith and he knew that everything would always be okay. He had faith in himself and he knew that he could work hard and earn more. He always insisted that his children learn and study. He encouraged us to learn about other religions and get to know what our neighbours and friends believed. He used to say that the best Muslim knows just as much about the other religions—this is also how you spread understanding and tolerance.

He was so funny. He was an amazing father and provider. He loved us and our friends. He would be so happy when the house was full. He always wanted people around him. He appreciated his friends and loved young children. He would laugh so easily. He told countless stories and jokes and could remember details from years ago. He had friends all over the world. He was a prolific letter-writer. He loved corresponding with people all over the world. He had many heroes in his life. He was a huge fan of Muhammed Ali, Malcolm X, Professor Tom Irving,[94] Professors Ismail and Lamia Faruqi, Alija Izetbegovic, and many others.

Prior to his death, he was paralyzed for six or seven years after back surgery and then he had a massive stroke during surgery. My mother nursed him, dressed him, bathed him, but she didn't have to feed him.

She took him to countless doctors' appointments and treatments—and she ran the business. It was a stressful and difficult time in my mom's life. After that, he never wanted to go into the factory again, even though it was right next door to the house. It was too painful for him.

For us children, it was a beautiful time. He was unable to run around and work from morning to night anymore. We were able to have our father to ourselves. He was not mobile and he was "stuck" with us. We were able to spend time with him and enjoy his company. He was not the same man anymore, but he was still our beloved father.

Hassan Karachi died on August 1, 1993.

11. *Toronto: Muslims En Masse*

TORONTO HAS CONTINUED TO DRAW PEOPLE SINCE THE TIMES OF the first Indigenous settlers and later the United Empire Loyalists. Over the years these settlers have included a small minority of Muslims, principally Albanians, but also a few Syrian Lebanese. Toronto is now home to more than half a million Muslims of many nationalities, including South Asian and Middle Eastern.

In 2001 Amir Hussain, now a professor of theological studies at Loyola Marymount University in Los Angeles, completed his doctoral thesis at the University of Toronto. Entitled "The Canadian Face of Islam: Muslim Communities in Toronto," it is a very useful study of how the Muslim minority in all its variety was adapting to life in Toronto two decades and more ago,[95] and I am grateful to be able to draw on it.

When I moved to Toronto in 1958, one of the first Muslims I met there was Fatime Kerim (Shaben, after her remarriage in 1963). She was born Fatime Feizo in Montreal in 1924, of Albanian parents,[96] and lived all her life in Toronto. I interviewed her in 1979.

> I didn't get much religious teaching through my parents because they came from the old country—Albania [in 1915]—where they didn't get it themselves. I really got into religion when I got married. I was twenty years old and married a Muslim man from Albania, and that is really where I got my knowledge of Islam.
>
> When we were growing up we had little teaching [but] we were told we were Muslims, even to the point that we were not allowed to do many things that our Canadian friends did. I feel old-fashioned even today. When I was in my late teens I became very attached to an

Albanian man but he was an Orthodox Christian and there was no way my parents would let him into our home. We were never allowed to go out or dress like our friends. It would be scorching hot outside but we weren't allowed to go out without stockings. We were never allowed to wear a bathing suit. I can't even skate today because we didn't go skating because there were boys at the rink!

We were *very* sheltered. We wore sleeves to the elbow, no sundresses, and dating was out of the question. We met men through our parents or friends, or someone would bring someone to meet you. One day I was talking to a male friend on the street when my mother came by, and I ran away [from him] . . . I worked in my father's restaurant and he drove me to work and home again. I only went to [school up to] grade eight because my parents felt girls didn't need an education. I regret this . . . After school we just stayed around the house, learned to cook, and helped mother.

I got married in December 1944. A close friend of mine was getting married in Toronto and I met my [first] husband Sami Kerim there. A week after we met we were engaged and three months later we were married. My parents approved of him because he was a Muslim Albanian. His religion meant more to him than his nationality. With Albanians their nationality usually supersedes their religion.

Fatime (later Shaben) and Sami Kerim's wedding, Toronto, 1944.
Photo courtesy of Eileen Spencer.

We lived in Toronto after we were married. When we first heard of any Muslim [who had arrived] in Canada, my husband would always bring them to the house and help them get started . . .

Our first child, Alia—Eileen[97]—was born in 1947, Maureen in 1949,[98] and Bob four years later.[99] When we were children the others used to make fun of our foreign names so this is why I gave my children Canadian names, but they have Albanian names as well. Had I known times would change it would have made a difference.

There were no classes on religion in Toronto so my husband [Sami Kerim] used to sit in the living room and read the Qur'an to the children and explain it to them . . .

The first [Muslim] person we met was Ali Tayyeb [a Pakistani professor of geography at the University of Toronto], and through him we met more Muslims and they all brought their children to the house. We opened our basement and Ali became the teacher . . . This would be about 1957–58. There were about fifteen children, mostly Pakistanis and Albanians . . .

Regep Assim, called "Effendi" and also "Mister Assim," was the imam of the Albanian Muslim Society of Toronto. He had been an Albanian revolutionary nationalist against the Ottoman Empire, and had to flee to Canada, arriving in Toronto with his two cousins in 1912.[100] They became self-employed because, in those pre-World War I days, your employer asked your religion, and a Muslim was automatically a "heathen" Turk. To make a living, they opened a confectionary store called High Park Sweets, which lasted until the 1970s. They also had a farm near Barrie. Sami Kerim, Fatime's first husband, was also a partner in Toronto's Club Kingsway with his brothers Seitali and Fazli Kerim.

According to Eileen Kerim, now Eileen Spencer and eldest daughter of Fatime and Sami, Regep Assim and Neim Sali registered the Albanian Muslim Society in 1954. In 1958 her father suggested that "Albanian" be dropped due to the growing presence of non-Albanians Muslims in Toronto. Mr Assim was immensely generous in his support of the fledgling Muslim Society of Toronto and of individuals.

Fatime Shaben recalled of Mr Assim:

Regep Assim, founder and imam of the Muslim Society of Toronto.
Photo courtesy of Eileen Spencer.

Mr Assim and my husband were first cousins. They both came from
Bilisht, Albania. I don't recall if there was an Albanian association or
not, but Zakria Malik, Sami, and Mr Assim were the organizers of the
Muslim Society of Toronto and registered it at City Hall.[101] We used
to have Eid dinners at the Club Kingsway. My husband donated the
club because he wanted friends to get together . . .

Fatime and Sami Kerim had five children: Eileen, Maureen, Robert,
Doreen, and Lori. Sami died in 1959 and in 1963 Fatime got married
again, to Albert Mohammad Shaben, a widower. He brought his youngest child, Mary Shaben, into the marriage. He was born in Lebanon and
grew up in Edmonton, Alberta. The couple went to Europe on their
honeymoon and then to Lebanon to visit the family home, but tragically
Albert Shaben suffered a heart attack and died there. On her return to
Toronto as a second-time widow, Fatime found that she was pregnant
with their son, Albert Mohammed Shaben. Fatime Shaben died on
February 28, 2000.

Mary Hafeeza Ahmet was born about 1906 in a small town in Quebec, some one hundred miles from Montreal, of Lebanese parents. She got married in 1924 and had several children, including a daughter, Violet. Violet duly married Walter Howell of Toronto and both became active members of the Muslim Society of Toronto of the 1960s. In her 1979 interview, Mary Hafeeza Ahmet said:

> My father peddled from a suitcase, things like ribbons, bows, jewelry, and clothes . . . People that didn't have the cash traded with hay or eggs or 'most anything. He then opened a store in the country, a good business, and mother and I ran the store while he went out with the horse and buggy. Then he heard about the Ford plant in Windsor paying $4 per day. We moved there in 1918 and bought a house on Glengarry Street . . . Father [who came from the Lebanese fortress town of Hassan] opened a store called Hassan Grocery. All us children worked in the store except Aunt Ethel who taught Sunday School outside. The third youngest sister of mine, Jeannie, went out and worked and paid her way through university . . . She got married and went to the United States . . .
>
> Mother never let us have a social life. She would kill us if we went out with an English fellow. There were no Muslims there but they started to come over from Detroit. My husband came over with Jim Walker, Ali Joseph, Frank and Harry Egypt, and Charlie Boose [their anglicized names]. A lot of people changed their names because they couldn't get jobs. Some people were surprised to hear us say we were Arabs—they thought we would be black. They were smuggled over . . .
>
> There was no mosque but we celebrated Eid. They didn't teach us much, but we held to our religion. Half the time we weren't accepted at school and were told to go back to our own country. We went to the Catholic school but my father told the teacher we weren't Catholic, we were Muslims. We held Eid at home, prayed and fasted . . .
>
> I was married at eighteen. We said "hello" and that was all. We were married in the United Church in Windsor . . . [102]
>
> There were no Muslims in Windsor when we came, but they started to [come] in the 1940s and 1950s. The only trouble we had was when

[my daughter] Helen went to Neilson's chocolate factory to look for a job, and when they asked who and what she was she didn't get the job. This was in the 1930s or 1940s. Helen later got a BA from Guelph [the University of Guelph].

Restaurateur Neim Sali came to Canada from Albania as an adult in 1927. He gained his religious education by observing his parents. They prayed five times a day and fasted forty-two days a year. He recalled:[103]

> In the old country we had big families. They didn't just have their own families but they had one great big house and if there were four or five brothers they all lived in there. Their wives were in there, their children were in there and their parents. In those days we didn't have what they call "old men's homes." They had to take care of each other and I thought that was great.
>
> I came because I knew I could make a better living out here and I loved every minute of it, and I still love it. When I came over here, I first worked as a dishwasher, but then after a short time I got behind that kitchen stove, cooking, and I became second chef. I learned how to do all the roasting, the pies, and how to do ham and eggs and everything . . .
>
> But it wasn't more than about a year and a half when I had picked up a bit of the English language and I opened up a store [a restaurant] on my own and I thought that was the greatest. It was down at Broadview and Gerrard, at the corner, and I called it "Toronto Lunch," and to me it was a great time. It was beautiful to be with the English-speaking Canadians. I loved them all, especially some of my own age, but by golly it was marvellous. I was so happy and so proud to be such a good fella that people came there and [when they] saw the store full with customers, they wouldn't walk away but they'd wait behind [outside] the doors there in the coldest of weathers until there's a seat there for them. As soon as they get in—oh, golly, it was great—they'd say "Long time no see, friend." They all called me by name, "Sal, how are you tonight?"
>
> Business was booming and being in the free world out here I did whatever I pleased with my own money. Every time I got so much

money I sent it to the old country because I got my mother there, I got my brothers married there, I got my sisters—the younger ones not married—and I tried to get everything for them as good as possible, everything [including] a big house. The one my father left us was a small one but I sold that one and I gave them a big one and everyone was there.

Neim Sali described the difficulties he had when he returned to Albania late in 1934 to get married. The girl's father was a friend of King Zog and away with him in the capital, Tirana. Therefore the decision was dragged out for six weeks. Later when Sali wanted to bring his wife, Kibe, to Canada, her family objected and he had to return alone. She didn't arrive until 1937, with their first-born child, a son named Sali. He was followed by a daughter, Dolores Mina Sali.

Neim Sali:

When we came here there was no way in which [we Muslims] could distinguish ourselves. We called ourselves Canadians but being believers in God Almighty we had no mosque to go to, but we went to a United Church for our own prayers and we loved it there too. This country has been beautiful to us. I remember when we started to go to church and the minister would come in the store and speak to us and they [the Christians] came to the house to drop in for coffee and my wife got into gatherings with them . . . They knew we were Muslims [but] they accepted us as people . . . As far as I'm concerned, I have no complaints about Canada, my beautiful heaven . . .

There were very few Albanian families . . . Nearly everybody came out here and gathered up so much money, like I did the first time, and ran off to their homes. Most of them stayed over there . . . The reason was, I guess, they didn't want to lose their own people and ways of living out there, and most Muslims are against the pig—eating pork—and I guess that's what chased them back there . . .

[In Albania] I bought a woolen mill and cows and horses and sheep and goats and even a buffalo and a farm with hayfields. But by 1943 those miserable, criminal Communists took everything and they left absolutely nothing for my mother to live on, and because they called my brother a capitalist, they [the family] suffered more . . .

By 1940 [in Toronto] we started to see what we can do with the Muslim religion, having a little mosque of our own. We called it a *jami* in those days. In 1947, me and Sami Kerim tried to gather up all the Albanians together, but somehow we didn't succeed . . . Finally, Mr Regep Assim and some Pakistani boys got together and we came to where we are today [in 1979].

The history of the Albanian Muslim Society of Toronto is ultimately a rather sad one. As explained earlier, the Albanians had opened their association to us newcomers from a variety of nationalities in the late 1950s and heavily supported the initial Muslim Society of Toronto's Islamic Centre on Dundas Street West starting in 1961. They carried on with us in the purchase and alteration of the Boustead Avenue church into the Jami Mosque in 1969. However, newer arrivals with different and more literalist ideas in effect drove them away. Regep Assim died cleaning in the new mosque in 1972, purportedly in part of a broken heart over this situation. In the 1970s, the society's Albanian-led management ended up selling the mosque on Boustead Avenue to the MSA, and the Albanians retired to their own mosque at 564 Annette Street, where Mr. Assim's portrait still hangs.

Of their new location, Neim Sali recalled:

We gather there quite often for Bayram and Mevlud for the dead ones and the ladies meet there on Friday night. It's keeping the place quite busy and at least the Albanians have some place to call their own. And every time they want to hold a little party they've got the upstairs, and the downstairs is for prayers. I think it's a nicely run *jami* . . .

[But] it's fading. The reason I say this is because the youngsters have such a great desire to be "Canadian," with the English language, and they just love to go on with the Canadian and to heck with the culture of Albania. Now I could be all wrong, but this is the only thing that's worrying me. In ten years, the old people will be gone.

Another early Albanian immigrant was Haki Yashar, born in 1904 in Bilisht. He came to Canada having trained for eighteen months in an Albanian machine gun unit.

> I came to this country in 1929 from Albania.[104] My parents were farmers, a small farm, just to make a living. I came to this country because I could make a better living than staying over there.
>
> I had an uncle here [in Toronto] who had a little shoe-repair shop at Keele and Dundas. His name was Suleiman. He came here in 1913 and he died in 1973. He left Albania to go away and make some more money to buy some farmland. He went to Romania to work in building, in construction. From there he went to Turkey, for I don't know how many years. He used to work for a rich guy who used to ride on a horse to look at the workers there—they used to call him "effendi, effendi." After that, the war started, the Balkan Wars in 1912, and he left Turkey and came over here. He never married . . .

Haki Yashar and wife Meleke with children, Agim (or Gary) on left in brother Suli's lap, and Neggie on right. Ca. 1950. Photo courtesy of Agim Yashar.

I started working for him [in 1929] and then there was the Depression in 1930, '31, '32 to '33, but I was making good wages, and at the time you could get a full-course meal for twenty-five cents. I used to make nine dollars a week and paid a dollar and a half for a room. After that it started to be busier . . .

I went back to the old country in 1938 and stayed there nine months, and so we got a connection with my wife Meleke and we got an agreement and I married her—if she doesn't come over here, I don't marry her—and we came back [to Canada] just before the War started in 1939.

I worked for my uncle till 1940, and he gave me the shop. I called it Haki's Shoe Shine and Repair. It was not bad. I made a living and I sent my three boys to school—two are printers, and one teaches French. My wife Meleke died in 1964, and after 1965 I got sick.

Haki Yashar's son Gary (Agim) Yashar added the following in November 2017:

Many of the immigrants who fled Albania through the late '50s and through the '60s gave Pop's business address as their mailing address. I guess they never knew how long they would be in one place, so Pop's store became their "post office." We had a daily group of guys coming in to pick up their mail. We can only assume that the Albanian government got wind of this, and kind of "blackballed" Pop. He applied every year for a visa to go to visit Albania and was always denied, until he was finally granted one at the age of eighty-two, long after retiring. I guess the government figured that an eighty-two-year-old guy couldn't do much damage.

Haki Yashar died in 1990.

Margaret Banka, née Ahmet, was another Albanian.

I was born in Toronto [on September 12, 1933], a Canadian Muslim, two years after my mother arrived in Canada. I was the oldest of three girls.[105] My father came to the United States in 1917, went back to Albania and then returned to Canada in 1922. He was a labourer at

Canada Packers and when I was five years old he went into the restaurant business. His name was Nevrus Ahmet . . .

Islam meant to us that we couldn't date, wear makeup, didn't talk to boys, and were never late to get home. We had little training [in Islam], only moral laws. We were without any basic knowledge except for Allah and the Prophet . . .

Most of our people were farmers from a certain region and were taught the ways of our [forefathers]. Until we were in our teens we were taught stories mainly. I was married at sixteen. There were about ten [Albanian] families and they all lived close by as they needed each other. They didn't speak English and my mother learned Macedonian and became friends with a Macedonian lady for someone to talk to. The group of families lived mostly in the west end [of Toronto, the Junction] and came from my father's village in the southeastern region of Albania . . .

When I was five, a few other men brought in their wives, and that is when our community started. Before that most of them had families back in the old country and just came out to work and send money back home . . .

My husband [Rizvan Banka] came from a different class in the old country. His grandfather was a Member of Parliament in 1922, and most of the Albanians at that time didn't know how to read and write. My people were farmers. My father learned to read and write from an Albanian newspaper that was published in Boston. Some with a little education would teach the others to read and write, and this is how they learned, from each other, so as to make their way in the new world. The men had to learn English because they had to go out to work, but the women kept the dietary laws, etc. The women were the best Muslims.

Margaret Ahmet and Rizvan Banka were married in the summer of 1949 by the Albanian leader Imam Vehbi Ismail of Detroit.[106]

Our children were luckier than we were. Imam Vehbi Ismail opened a school in Detroit and the [Islamic] literature started coming in. They tried to form organizations so children could learn. [And so the children] were more knowledgeable than we were at nine and ten years old. The school in Detroit was the focal point of Albanians. We had relatives there and [our] children would go there for three or four weeks and attend the school . . .

I think there was an advantage to being Muslim—our daughter never had to worry about what she would do when she went out with a boy, or whether she would get pregnant. Our daughter chose her own husband, as did I. She was allowed to go to group outings with brothers for religious or national events. I would like to see our sons marry Albanian Muslims . . . My sisters married Canadians and one husband turned to Islam. The children consider themselves Muslim.

At the time I went to school in Toronto, Albanian Muslims were rare. One teacher came to the class to look at me to see if I looked different. I mostly kept to myself but had one or two friends. I made friends with a Jewish girl because at that time Jews had a difficult time and we were both different . . .

Today, women won't eat in restaurants because they don't know what really goes on in the kitchens—they don't trust the people who cook. We used to have a restaurant and my mother cooked all kinds of foods such as ham and bacon and eggs, but she kept her dishes separate, never mixed them with those of the restaurant . . .

When I was a child, my father used to buy live chickens from a Jewish man. He would buy five or six of them and feed them and kill them as we needed them. As we got older we used to buy from stores. Most Albanian Muslims ate the right food—we ate lamb, chicken, beef but never ate pork. Albanians drink alcohol with moderation, they never overdo it. We didn't really do our prayers but did keep the customs and thanked God. We managed to raise our children [Luan, Miriam, and Gazmir] as Muslims. Luan was president of the [Muslim Society of Toronto] youth group, I was treasurer of the Muslim Society of Toronto and vice-president of the Albanian Muslim Society . . . The children don't speak Albanian well, not as much as we wanted them to . . . The only music we listen to is Albanian records, tapes, and we do Albanian dancing [the *dubke*] . . .

I am a Muslim in my heart, but I don't always fast.

Margaret Banka died on August 11, 1987. Rizvan Banka, her husband, was born on April 4, 1923. I interviewed him in July 1979. He was a big, straightforward man with a shock of hair that jutted out above his forehead:

> I came from the city of Tirana which is the capital of Albania. I came from a Muslim family of ten, with six children—four brothers, two sisters—and my paternal grandmother and grandfather. One brother was killed after I left the old country. My grandfather prayed five times daily, went to Mecca twice. He was a very religious and a very honest person. He took me from the public school to a religious school for several years. The school closed down and then I went back to public school and finished high school, and then the war came. Grandfather didn't insist that we go to the mosque, and as a child I wasn't that interested. He used to take us especially during Ramadan and during that time we all fasted. Grandfather would get up and go to early prayer and come home with something for us for breakfast and then we would go off to school. We were just Muslims, we didn't belong to any sect . . .
>
> I escaped from Communist pressure in 1944. During the war I was in the Underground versus the Italians and Germans. At the end of '44 we saw that we had lost because of the Allies, and I got a boat and went to Italy. I was politically involved in Balli Kombetar, the Democratic Front, and this is why I left Albania . . . There were no job opportunities in Italy and the Italian government wouldn't let foreigners work.
>
> [At the end of the war] the Canadian mission came to find people for the labour force and I applied and came to Canada in 1948, and started a new life, got married and had a family. Where can you find a country like Canada where I came with just my bare hands and made it? I bought a house and paid for it . . .
>
> I was hired as a woodcutter in the bush at Kapuskasing, in northern Ontario. I didn't find a contract because of the wound I had in my arm from the war. I had no relatives but I read a [Albanian] newspaper from Boston and got addresses [of Albanians in Toronto] from the secretary-general of my party. Some of the addresses included

[those of] Sami Kerim and Haki Yashar, and I went to meet them at a shoe store at 378 Keele Street. [Haki Yashar] took me home and then to Sami's house and got me a job in [the Kerims'] Club Kingsway. I stayed there for a while and then left to work in a restaurant as a waiter.

I met my wife's family and we got married [in 1949] a year after we met. Her father and I went into a restaurant business together, and I finally got a job with the Steel Company of Canada as a hot-nut operator, and now I am a heat-treatment operator and have been there for twenty-eight years.

There was no religious organization [in Toronto], but Regep Assim showed us books and we met with him a few times. He was simple and modest and we were very fond of him. He treated people nicely, scholar or not. We were organized for weddings, Bayram and Eid. The food was prepared by the ladies, and we had a band and music and folk dancing. It was more nationalist than religious, being Albanians more than Muslims. We didn't pray together but Mr Assim prayed . . . he was the imam. He buried the dead, gave funeral rites . . .

There was no Muslim paper but later on Imam Vehbi Ismail had a monthly paper, *Our Life*, [from Detroit] which was all Islamic.

Rizvan Banka also served on the executive of the Muslim Society of Toronto. According to his son Luan, Rizvan retired early from Stelco, in 1978, and died on November 27, 1986.

Mary Kole Kerim, a prominent member and a secretary of the Muslim Society of Toronto and later of the Albanian Muslim Society of Toronto, was born Mary Kole in Detroit. She married Toronto Albanian businessman Seitali (Babe) Kerim in 1946 and took his name. I interviewed her in 2011–12. She died in 2014.

I was born in Detroit in 1927. I don't know when my dad arrived. He left Albania around the 1900s, so he would not be conscripted by the Turkish army. First he went to some other city, but then he went to Detroit and there were six or seven men who rented a house and lived together . . .

My dad had a restaurant in the factory area of Detroit, so we never suffered during the Depression. My mother was a stay-at-home regular mother. I had one brother and one sister. My brother was sixteen months older and my sister was six years younger. My brother was born in Albania but my sister and I were born in the States . . .

We went to Albania in around 1935, and we were there for about two years and then Mum and Dad decided they were not going to live in Albania. So the five of us came back to Detroit because Dad wouldn't separate the family. We came to Detroit and we were there for a couple of years and then Dad rented out the house and he took his cousin into partnership in his restaurant. Then he got a Philco and a Norge contract to sell radios and refrigerators and appliances from the States in Albania. So we went back to Albania but we came back in March 1940, when Albania was invaded by the Italians. I remember that . . .

There was no mosque or anything in Detroit when we were growing up. But when Imam Vehbi Ismail came to Detroit [1949] . . . there was by then a mosque in Detroit. It was Albanian. They had bought an old church and converted it into a mosque, so when Imam Vehbi came, he was our first imam. We had Friday prayers, but we would gather as families on Sunday and we went to the mosque. After a few years they sold the church and built a new mosque on Harper Avenue, which is still there.

The men didn't go in for prayers [during the week] because they were working, and of course in Albania the women didn't go to the mosque except on special occasions . . . but the men said their prayers at the mosque on Sundays.

We were in the east end of Detroit, and there were no Albanians around us, so I literally grew up with Americans. We were surrounded by Americans, and we only saw Albanians on Sunday or Saturday. There were hundreds of Albanians in Detroit.

We didn't discuss Islam. I was raised with all these Christians and I had a lot of Catholic and Protestant friends and as I said we only met [Muslim] Albanians on a Sunday. I literally grew up with the Christians. There were a lot of Baptists in Detroit . . .

When I was a girl in Albania before the war, my mother and aunt would go to the dressmakers and they would have fashion magazines from Paris and my mum and my aunt would pick out fashions and then buy material and have dresses made. My grandma had a headscarf, but my mother and my aunt, none of them did, but [since then] extremism has taken over. In Albania, the Christians and the Muslims were friends. You know, for Easter and Christmas, the Muslims would go visiting their Christian friends and wish them happy Easter or whatever, and when we had Eid or Ramadan, they would come and visit us. It was a whole community . . .

I went to grade school and then to high school, and then I went to the University of Michigan, in the general course. I was there for two years and then I met Babe in 1945, and we got married. He [and his brothers Sami and Fazli Kerim] had the Club Kingsway in Toronto and we had mutual friends in London, Ontario, the Hasan family . . . Mr Hasan had a restaurant in London that was called Zed Lunch . . . When Babe had the club, he was promoting bands, and the band would be in Toronto one night and in Hamilton another and in Guelph another and in London another, so whenever the band was playing in London he would stay at the Hasans' home . . . Babe used to go to the Albanian Flag Day celebrations in Detroit on November 28, and that's where we met.

There were five [Kerim] brothers[107] that were in Toronto before the [Second World] War started, and they brought their mother over because she was widowed. There was one brother left in Albania and the rest of the boys were in Toronto. They bought a house on Indian Road, and the brothers and the mother lived in that lovely old home.

Babe was born in Albania in 1914 . . . he came to Canada in 1928 with his brother Sami. His older brothers were here already . . . He got involved with the Muslim Society of Toronto to help out Regep Assim, his first cousin. Before that, they had invited the Albanians to hold their Eid dinners at the [Kingsway] Club . . .

Babe's religious experience was a private thing with him. He was very religious within himself, but it wasn't there for publicity . . . He never drank and he didn't smoke, and of course I didn't either. My dad liked his beer, he would have a bottle of beer before dinner every night, but my mother wasn't much of a drinker. She loved her coffee . . .

Regep Assim lived in an apartment above the restaurant in Toronto and all the Albanian bachelors would go and visit him. I remember when Mr Assim passed away, there were a lot of bachelors who said to me: "Now we have no one to confide in." He was a very private person and it didn't matter what you said to him, it stayed with him. He acted as our imam for years and he got a licence to perform marriages . . .

Mr Assim died on November 8, 1972, after a long struggle to keep the community from becoming too radical at the Boustead Avenue Jami Mosque . . . He wanted all of the Muslims, no matter what country they came from or what heritage they came from, to be together, and of course they fell apart. There were these radicals and they literally broke his heart.

Babe Kerim died in 1980, and Mary Kole Kerim in 2014.

In the late 1950s and early '60s, Toronto's Muslim community began to receive members who were neither Lebanese nor Albanian but South Asians—from newly independent India, Pakistan, Bangladesh, and Sri Lanka—and even from further east and south. One of the earliest arrivals was Khaliq Mohamed Khan:[108]

My name is Khaliq Mohamed Khan, and I was born in 1932 into a well-known Pathan family of Khurja in UP [United Provinces], India. My family was in a mixture of landownership and government service. I was the only son and I have two sisters in Pakistan. My father was Rafiq Mohamed Khan, and my mother was Khatoon Begum. My father was a senior police officer, so every three years we were transferred from one city to another. He retired in 1947. I had my primary and secondary education in different cities of UP. I did my undergraduate BSc degree in geology at Aligarh Muslim University in 1952.

In the early years after Partition [in 1947], life was difficult for Muslims in India. Violence and riots were widespread, and Muslims were afraid and insecure. It was hard to see the way ahead because the future to them was uncertain. You did not know what the next week or the next month and sometimes the next day would bring. I left India for Pakistan in late 1952.

In Pakistan, I managed to land an executive position in a British mining company called Pakistan Chrome Mines. They had no Pakistani in an executive position and were under pressure by the government to hire one, and it happened to be me. Within a year they posted me to the position of group mines manager. It was a chromite mining company and was located in Hindubagh in Zhobe Agency of Baluchistan, a tribal area. I stayed in Hindubagh until my departure to Canada in the summer of 1957.

The main purpose for coming to Canada was to study. I had an acceptance from the University of Toronto for a master's program in geology. I was advised by a Canadian who was visiting Pakistan on an area photographic mapping assignment that, if possible, to take an immigration visa. That would give me a choice to stay in Canada. Also, for summer jobs no permission would be required. In those days there was a quota of fifty immigrants a year from Pakistan. I applied for immigration and got it . . .

On arrival, I ran into money-transfer difficulties and decided to look for a job without knowing where to find mining company offices. After going through several buildings on Bay Street and reading the companies listed, I found one and got a job in underground mine survey in a uranium mine—Can Met Explorations in the Elliot Lake area. I returned to Toronto a year later with a decision that mining or geology was not the right career for me, but I did not know what the right one would be. Since my admission in geology was already approved I decided to proceed with it in the academic year 1958–59. By the end of January I had decided on town and regional planning, in geography . . . and dropped out of the geology program . . . I took admission in the town and regional planning department and graduated in 1962.

Life in the early days was rough. I came across many good people and also some very nasty people. The concept of political correctness was nonexistent. It came more than a decade later. For Muslims, halal meat was not available. Identifying pork-free food was also a challenge. I used to look forward to Fridays when fish and chips were available everywhere—Catholics in those days observed meat-free Fridays. For me, coming from Pakistan, food tasted very bland. Very little or no spices were used, and Indian and Pakistani spices were not available until the late '60s.

For people like me, who held good positions and had good social status in Pakistan, to drop to zero was hard . . . In those days, most Indians and Pakistanis were students, professionals or academics, but outside the university their status was not generally recognized. The later Charter of Rights and the recognition of Canada as a multicultural society were a breath of fresh air for me.

In January 1959 I met my wife, Brigitte, and we got married in 1960 in the London Mosque. Murray and Alia [Hogben] and Badr and Fatima Hasan drove there and attended the wedding. Saghir Ahmed[109] was also there. I had met Alia on campus in 1959 and Murray soon after, and we became family friends.

On my return to Toronto from the Elliot Lake area in 1958, I met Ali Tayyeb and his wife Husna. They came [to Canada] in 1952.[110] He was a professor in the geography department. He became my mentor and was a close friend and advisor. Another immigrant family was that of Malik Rabbani, who came in 1954. All other Pakistanis were here on student visas. Among them ten were on one-year Colombo Plan visas and four PhD students . . . With these friends, things became much easier . . .

Our Sunday meetings were informal, but we did have a speaker. I was responsible for the speakers, and Badr [Hasan] did the organizing and calling people to attend and putting a guilt trip on those who did not attend. According to my memory, I asked Murray [Hogben] to be the secretary and he kept that position for several years. At the head table only Murray and the speaker sat. Regep Assim was the honorary president who took a back seat and kept paying the bills.

In about five years, attendance grew to one hundred for an Eid *namaz*. As is customary among Muslims, there are as many opinions as there are Muslims. A faction broke off and established the Islamic Foundation of Toronto[111] mosque near India Town off Gerrard Street. At the Islamic Centre, money was being raised to purchase a church on Boustead Avenue. Dr Qadir Baig, the president and an Islamic studies professor at the University of Toronto, got involved and through his contacts obtained the bulk of the funds from Saudi Arabia. The money was channelled through MSA [Muslim Students Association], later ISNA [Islamic Society of North America], and this gave them some control of the mosque. Soon after opening, in the late '60s, things became unruly in the mosque and ISNA took full control and still runs it today. I more or less dropped out because I found [these proceedings] quite disturbing.

In 1962, my career of thirty years in city planning began. Most of it was with the planning department of the City of Toronto. There I worked as a planner, then as a principal planner, and for nineteen years as an area manager, of which sixteen years were as a manager of North District and three years as manager of West District. Also, I worked for one year as a manager of the zoning and legislation division. I took early retirement in 1991.

In addition to serving with the Dundas Street Islamic Centre, I served on the boards of the Riverdale Immigrant Women's Centre, the Bloor Street Legal Clinic, the Brampton Muslim Community Centre, the Rotary Club of Toronto, Eglinton, and as chair for over fifteen years of the Rotary Foundation Scholarship Committee of District 7070, covering clubs from Toronto to Belleville.

I also received the Paul Harris Fellow award from the Rotary Club of Toronto, Eglinton, the Citation for Meritorious Service from the Rotary Foundation of Rotary International, and the fifty-five-year anniversary of graduation medal for elevation to the Chancellor Circle from the University of Toronto.

Our daughter Zarina was born in 1962. We now have two grandchildren, Safiyah and Rashad. They and their mother Zarina all graduated from York University, and Safiyah is also a graduate of Windsor Law School.

Khaliq's wife Brigitte's story follows.

I was born Brigitte Adamaitis in 1938 in Riga, Latvia. My family were Baltic Germans, a community which had settled in Latvia during the Middle Ages and had kept their German language and customs. It was at the beginning of the Second World War, when Russia invaded

Latvia, that the Germans had to leave. My family survived the war and in December 1952 came to Canada, where some relatives had already settled and had managed to convince my parents that life here was better than in postwar Germany. We arrived in Weston, Ontario, at that time a small Anglo-Saxon Protestant town, which was eventually amalgamated with the City of Toronto.

For me, a fourteen-year-old teenager, coming to Canada and settling down here was a big adventure. Everything was different, the abundance of food, the language, and even the clothes people wore. I was placed in Grade 9, which was equivalent to my grade in Germany. Although I had learned English there and had basic reading and writing skills, I could speak very little and understood almost nothing. Audio equipment was not available to us then. However, since I was the only new immigrant in the whole school, both the teachers and students were very welcoming and helpful. I was assigned a helper for the first week. She guided me to the different classrooms, introduced me to my fellow students, and let me copy her notes. When my German clothes were replaced with the school uniform, I felt that I fitted in and could settle down. My English skills improved fast, but my accent has remained to this day.

I finished high school in 1957 and got an Ontario government job. I had intended to go to university later, but in January 1959 I met my future husband, Khaliq. We both remember this day every year. We sat beside each other at a social function and started talking to each other. This is how the handsome Muslim man from Pakistan and the shy young German girl became friends. It was more than that from the very beginning, but we both pretended to be only good friends, with the formality that this relationship seemed to require. Eventually, when all the hurdles with our families had been overcome, we married.

We were married in 1960 but at that time there was no Muslim in the Toronto area who was licensed to perform weddings. Khaliq did not want separate civil and religious ceremonies. The only person licensed to perform marriages lived in Detroit and would not travel beyond London, Ontario. London already had a small but active Muslim community. So we were married there by Imam Vehbi Ismail. Our daughter Zarina was born in 1962.

A condition of my marriage was conversion to Islam. I had already left my church while still in my teens and was reading about Buddhism. The prescriptions for a good life and the empathy toward all living beings appealed to me, but I missed the concept of God. I never ceased believing and praying to God. When I picked up my English translation of the Qur'an, it was the first time I had ever read anything about Islam. I was surprised to find the biblical prophets and references to biblical stories there. It was not exotic and strange as I had expected, and my belief in God could remain.

To be truthful, the purpose of my conversion was to get married so that I could forever be with Khaliq, so I did not find it difficult. Abstinence from alcohol and pork was also not hard, as my family rarely drank and I already avoided pork products on the orders of my dermatologist. Halal meat was not available; we bought kosher meat when it was convenient but were not strict about it. As well, the hostility toward Islam, which sprang up in later years, was not there. I was told, but not by Khaliq, that I had to have a Muslim name. I agreed,

Khaliq and Brigitte Khan of Toronto, married in the new London mosque in 1960. Photo courtesy of Brigitte Khan.

thinking that it would be easier to be accepted by Khaliq's family, which was important to him. I chose the name Aisha but dropped it before going for hajj, the Muslim pilgrimage, in 1997. I felt that the name given to me by my parents was my true identity, and that's how I wanted to visit God's house.

My initial involvement with the Muslim community was in the Muslim Society of Toronto's first Islamic Centre. It was just a storefront on Dundas Street West, bought by the small mainly Balkan community of Toronto, with the help of some of the Pakistani graduate students at the time. The person who made it happen and contributed the most was Regep Assim, an old, much-respected but humble man, called *effendi* by his Albanian community. There were no Friday community prayers. We gathered on Sunday mornings, discussed religious issues around a table, and offered the noon prayer. On special occasions and festivals, such as Eid, the whole community gathered for prayer in the morning and for dinner and socialization in the evening.

In the beginning there were at most forty or fifty people on these occasions, although the number soon increased when the existence of the centre became known and more Muslims came to Canada. I still have fond memories of those early days, when this little community felt like one family. Sunnis, Shi'as, and Ahmadis prayed and celebrated together. Later in 1968, when the community had grown further, a former Presbyterian church on Boustead Avenue in Toronto was bought and converted into the Jami Mosque. With the arrival of more Muslims, mainly from South Asia in the late 1960s and '70s, new centres and mosques were established for a more culturally and religiously diverse Muslim community.

My own understanding and practice of Islam also grew. As I learned more, my belief became stronger, but it was not until I visited India and Pakistan many years later that I actually saw how Islam is lived. I saw my in-laws living by the tenets of the Qur'an, never missing a prayer, remembering God in all their activities but never questioning me about my beliefs and practices or lack thereof. In the northern areas of Pakistan I saw rough truck drivers stopping on narrow roads and spreading out their prayer mats to kneel down and pray. I felt the hospitality of poor village people who gave me, a foreigner, presents of fruit, blessing it, so that I might enjoy it. At hajj, the pilgrimage, I learned the meaning of the Muslim ummah, acceptance of each other as part of a world community.

Now in 2018, the Muslim community has grown, mainly through immigration. Muslims have become active and respected participants in Canadian society. The Muslim community is the most culturally, socially, and religiously diverse group in the Greater Toronto Area. This allows Muslims to practice their faith according to their own interpretation. In Sunni Islam, the main branch of the religion, there is no central authority which must be followed. Unfortunately, the various Muslim groups have not always been united and are only now learning to stand together for their common good.

It pleases me that my family has been a part of this evolving community. Our daughter grew up and married Fuad, a Muslim whose family came from Guyana, and our adult grandchildren Rashad and Safiyah are continuing the practice of Islam on a personal and societal level.

Syed Badrul Hasan was a graduate student at the University of Toronto starting in 1958 and an active of the fledgling Muslim Society of Toronto. His story follows.

I came [from Pakistan] to Toronto in June 1958, and my family joined me in September. My interest in the Muslims of Toronto [was aroused] after the sad demise of brother Sami Kerim, formerly of Albania. On the evening of his funeral unfortunately very, very few people from the very big gathering lined up for the *namaz-e-janaza* [funeral prayer], which was led by the late brother [Imam Vehbi] Ismail, from Detroit, formerly of Albania.

Brothers Khaliq, Mastoor, and Waheeduzzaman met at my house [on Brunswick Avenue] and pondered over the miserable [circumstance] that Muslims were not properly organized to perform their religious obligations . . . We collected ten dollars each (totaling forty dollars) to start work and approached Regep Assim, who was the focal point of Albanian Muslims, to lead us. We then organized shab-miraj (night of Isra) with the late professor Dr Fazlur Rahman to speak and we raised $10,000.

What I remember is that before organizing the Muslim Society of Toronto, or reorganizing the former Albanian Muslim Society of Toronto, brother Kazi R Ahmed from East Pakistan (now Bangladesh) was active in organizing Eid prayers, religious functions and Pakistani holidays. Brother Dr Waheeduzzaman was very active in the propagation of Islam to our Canadian friends who were very eager to learn about the religion. So also was brother Dr Mastoor, who used to lead prayers at Eid congregations. Some other Muslim students from Pakistan and the Mid-East also contributed in various ways.[112]

Two members of the 1960s Muslim Society of Toronto were Trinidadians, Dr Unus Omarali and his wife Phirosa Omarali. Her story, recorded in 2015, and her account of her late husband's life, are as follows:

I was born in the island of Trinidad in the West Indies, one of seven children in a busy and loving household. My mother, Khateijah, was a businesswoman who was very successful and ventured into many enterprises. Khateijah was the original micro-entrepreneur who had little but was able to establish her own storefront with clothing she designed with a team of local women who sewed for her. She was an innovator with the gift of insight into people's needs and fulfilling that niche market. Real estate was her forte. She was active in the community until she passed away at ninety-five years of age.

My grandfathers on both sides of the family were imams and played a significant role in propagating and preserving Islam in Trinidad.

When I finished high school in Trinidad, I went to McGill University in Montreal in 1955. I was introduced to my future husband, Unus, when I went home to Trinidad from McGill in the summer. We met just twice, and the third time we met, we were getting married! After our marriage, we moved to England where I pursued a career as an audiologist at the Royal National Throat, Nose, and Ear Hospital in London.

We immigrated to Canada in 1965 because it was a progressive country and had many opportunities for us . . .

My father, Haidar Ali, was one of the first East Indian analysts for

Dr Unus Omarali and his wife, educator Phirosa Omarali.
Photos courtesy of Phirosa Omarali.

Shell Oil. When he retired, he became involved in building and the real-estate business. From humble beginnings, my parents' work ethic and success enabled them to build the Point Fortin Masjid [mosque] in Trinidad for the community.

I always valued education. One of my dreams was to become a teacher. I also wanted to understand the Canadian system that my children were experiencing, so I applied to the faculty of education and earned my teaching qualification. I taught at Harrison Road Public School for many years. Then I applied for and received a bursary to teach deaf education. I learned sign language and teaching techniques at James Whitney School for the Deaf in Belleville, Ontario.

As a specialist in deaf education, I worked with the Toronto District School Board at the Metropolitan School for the Deaf, on Davisville Avenue. I retired in 1999. Now I had more time to travel, volunteer, and garden. I do enjoy tending to my garden and watch the flowers bloom and vegetables grow. I enjoy cooking and experimenting with recipes, reminiscing about the spicy and sumptuous foods of Trinidad. My curry chicken, roti, dal puri with goat meat and pone are always appreciated at our gatherings.

During all those years, I supported my husband in his endeavours while raising our three children. Haidar is a business analyst, known as Nasr; Iqbal is a cardiologist in San Francisco; and Zenobia is now an educator and guidance counsellor.

Looking back, I well remember that the first year we were here, we hardly met any Muslims, and I remember our first Ramadan—in the 1960s—and keeping the fast on the day of Eid al-Fitr because we were unable to see the Eid moon . . . We eventually met other Muslims and in time we were able to come together and meet at the newly established [Muslim Society of Toronto] 3047 Dundas Street West masjid, where we not only prayed but enjoyed meeting Muslims from different ethnic backgrounds.

We became aware that the Federation of Islamic Associations held annual conventions where Muslims from North America attended in the summer. We travelled with our children to Dearborn, Michigan, to Toledo, Ohio, and to other cities in the United States. There were lectures, prayers, dinners, and social events for the youth. These conventions were not as large as today's Reviving the Islamic Spirit [annual conferences in Toronto], but we had the same intention . . .

Never in my dreams did I think that there would be Islamic schools and so many masjids serving the Muslim community in Toronto, alhamdolillah.

Phirosa Omarali also told me about her late husband, Dr Unus Omarali, a pillar of the early Muslim community in Toronto. He came from a devout Trinidadian Muslim family with ancestors from Uttar Pradesh, India, in the 1870s. His father, Omar Enaithali, was a successful businessman, and his mother, Afrose, was a housewife. Unus Omarali was born in San Fernando, Trinidad, the eldest of nine children. He did very well in school and won a bursary to attend Naparima College, and subsequently taught mathematics and geography.

In 1948 he came to Canada and attended the University of Saskatchewan and obtained a diploma in business. He later went to Dublin and then graduated from the Royal College of Surgeons in medicine in 1955, completed his internship at the Beth-El Hospital in Brooklyn, New York, and received more training in London, England. Unus then returned to Trinidad where he helped the Muslim community with his medical expertise a day per week.

After he and Phirosa were married they came to Toronto in 1965 where he practised family medicine from 1972 until retirement in 1997. He was active with the new Muslim Society of Toronto on Dundas Street West and was among the core elders who established the society's Jami Mosque on Boustead Avenue, working with Seitali (Babe) Kerim, Ayube Ally,[113] and Rassool Auckbaraully.

Phirosa said that her husband Unus's Danforth Avenue office became a hub for the Muslim community in Toronto where new immigrants came for advice and for their immigration physical examinations. He also helped Muslim men and women have marriage introductions in his waiting room and performed countless marriages in his medical office and elsewhere in southern Ontario as a rare registered Muslim marriage officer. He also immunized pilgrims going on the hajj at cost and was for many a "life coach," based on Islamic principles. Unus encouraged the birth of various Islamic organizations and was active with the Doctors' Lions Club that focused on supporting medical needs in developing nations. He was also active in the medical community in Toronto and elsewhere. He died at age 75 in 2005.

One of the most influential pioneer Muslims was Muin Muinuddin, who inspired this project of writing a book on Muslims in Canada back in the late 1970s. In 2017, I interviewed his wife, Talat Muinuddin, who was involved with him in his activities and went on to become president of the Canadian Council of Muslim Women and later of Reh'ma Community Services.

> My name is Talat and I was born in October 1936 in Parbhani, a town in the former [princely] Hyderabad State, central India. It is now part of Maharashtra. We later moved to Aurangabad, which was bigger than Parbhani and was also a historic city in Hyderabad State. I attended elementary school there.
>
> My father's name was Mohammad Baquir Ali, and he was an engineer by profession. My mother, Sakina Khatoon, had closely studied Islam and Islamic history under the guidance of her uncles, who were

great scholars of Islam. They were founders of the world-renowned Deoband Islamic Seminary. My mother was also keenly interested in current affairs and had a habit of reading several newspapers every day along with listening to a variety of radio programs. She was a visionary and forward-looking person.

The year 1947 was traumatic and harrowing. The British Partition of India was bloody and cruel, displacing over fourteen million people and creating an overwhelming refugee crisis in both [new] countries. It was a nightmare for all of us. I remember right after Partition that Muslims were migrating to Pakistan or moving to larger cities within the newly independent India where Muslims were in larger number. Many Muslims moved to Hyderabad, which was a Muslim state and to Aurangabad, as these cities provided a sense of security. This was a very devastating experience for the people who left everything behind and migrated to unknown places and an uncertain future.

During that time of crisis, my family became involved in relief activities in Aurangabad. My brothers owned a pharmacy and were able to provide free medicine to people who had taken shelter in refugee camps. My mother cooked big pots of rice along with meat and vegetables and sent them to the camp. I also remember some families came and stayed with us.

The fall of Hyderabad to Indian troops [in September 1948] pushed my parents to move to Pakistan. It was not an easy decision as it was not safe to travel by train to Bombay to board a ship to Pakistan. There was so much unrest, suspicion, and hatred between Hindus and Muslims. The Hindus and Sikhs were slaughtering Muslims trying to flee to Pakistan. They were taking young girls and women as hostages. There was sexual violence and theft and death. Trains arriving in Pakistan and Hyderabad were full of dead bodies of Muslims . . .

On the train ride to Bombay to begin our journey to Pakistan, our compartment was raided by the police along with some government officials. They came to arrest my brother whom they had mistaken for our other brother, Kamil Nadir. Kamil was studying at Usmania University Medical College at that time and was also receiving Razacar or freedom-fighter training. Those officers wanted to take my brother back to Aurangabad for further interrogation. It was very scary for us and we were extremely frightened. The Indian officials told my mother that we could continue our journey but they would take my brother back to Aurangabad. My mother refused. She decided that the family would also turn back and go with my brother to defend him. My brother was taken into custody. We were terrified for my brother and what could happen next, but my father's Hindu friends, Uncle Panditji and Uncle Asaram, came to our rescue. They helped us and were able to set my brother free. There were always good people around who stepped up to help. We were thankful to our Hindu uncles for their timely support.

We began our journey again about a month later and arrived in Pakistan safely on September 27, 1948. I already had two brothers in Karachi and we were finally reunited. We all stayed together in a small apartment until we could build our own home in the new suburb of Nazimabad. It was the beginning of our life in a newly created Pakistan. I was twelve years old.

I attended Waseem Girls High School in Karachi along with my two younger sisters. I then joined Sindh Muslim Intermediate Science College and after completion applied to the medical school, but was unsuccessful. I then joined the University of Karachi and studied zoology and microbiology. I topped in my BSc honours, and enrolled in the master's program in parasitology. I graduated with the highest marks at the university. First class, first position!

After a year of working as a fellow in the zoology department, I received a Colombo Plan Scholarship to do research in London, England, on malaria at the London School of Hygiene and Tropical Medicine. My goal was to do a PhD and join the World Health Organization (WHO). However, when I reached London, I was told my supervisor had to leave for Nigeria. I decided instead to complete the diploma course in parasitology and medical entomology and then apply to the University of Alberta in Canada in 1962 for my teacher's training, which I went on to complete. I always loved teaching.

It is worth mentioning that my mother was a source of inspiration for all of us brothers and sisters. It was her mission to give her daughters the same opportunity to get an education as boys would normally receive. She always believed in equal opportunities for girls and boys and wanted for her daughters to have the same kind of independence as her sons. As a result of her efforts and determination, all her children were encouraged to be whatever they wanted to be . . .

After arriving in Edmonton in 1962 and completing my teacher's training, I started teaching in Edmonton in 1963. I met Muin Muinuddin in Edmonton. He had accepted a teaching position with the Edmonton school board and was taking some courses at the University of Alberta. As Pakistani students, we started a Pakistan Students Association (PSA). Muin was the founding president, and I was the secretary of the PSA. We organized social programs for students and the community . . .

We started to take a keen interest in the socioreligious activities of the Al Rashid Mosque in Edmonton. It was built in 1938 by the early Lebanese Community . . . Because of our active participation in community affairs, Muin and I had established a good relationship with the mosque congregants, particularly Mrs Alma Shaben, Mrs Hilwie Hamdon, Larry Shaben, and Alia Bogra.

Muin was born on the first of July 1928 in Aligarh, India. Aligarh is home to the first Muslim university in India, and it was founded by Sir Sayed Ahmad Khan, a great Muslim leader and a visionary. Muin was an extraordinary and brilliant student. He topped the All-India Matric examination. After that, he continued to receive the highest marks from his BA all the way to his MEd [master of education]. Muin went on to receive a Fulbright scholarship to study in the USA. In 1959, he came to Canada to take on the job of vice-principal at a school in Estevan, Saskatchewan.

Muin and I were working together on social issues and projects, and we grew to like each other very much . . . We got married in 1966 in London, England, since my mother and many of my siblings were there at the time. After our honeymoon in Europe, we decided to settle in Toronto. The city had a larger Muslim community and the weather was also better compared to Edmonton.

We came to Toronto in late August 1966. It was too late to find a teaching position, as the teachers were already hired for that year, but the following year I was lucky to get a teaching position at Gordon

Graydon High School in Mississauga. We later moved to Thornhill and I switched to the Durham Board of Education where I taught for thirty-four years. I retired in 1998. We had two sons, Ahmad and Tariq.

In Toronto, Muin and I met Murray Hogben, Alia, Dr M A Rauf, Mrs Rauf, Khaliq Khan, Dr Abdul Qadir Baig, his wife Nighat, and many more friends. Alia's family became very good friends, and we were considered part of the family. Meanwhile, Muin took an active part in activities at the local [Muslim Society of Toronto] Islamic Centre. At that time, we used to meet at the Islamic Centre on Dundas Street West. It was a time of beginnings . . .

Soon enough, Muin and a group of people including Dr [Fuad] Şahin, Hasib Khan, Hameed Bhayat, Mahmood Khial, Moladina, Abdul Basit, and Abdul Wahid started to meet at a church on Bathurst Street. They provided volunteer services and contributed financially to purchase a place which used to be an Orange Hall, at 184 Rhodes Avenue, and establish the Islamic Foundation of Toronto.

Muin was also instrumental, along with Ahmad Tatunji and Ahmad Sakr, in forming the Muslim Students Association of Canada (MSA). Muin and I were active in MSA for some time. However, as it was an organization for students, Muin thought that there should be an organization for the families who opted to make Canada their

Muin Muinuddin and his wife Talat Muinuddin in the later 1960s.
Photo courtesy of Dr Ahmed Muinuddin.

home . . . This led to the formation of CMCC (1972), the Council of Muslim Communities of Canada . . .

Within a short time, a large number of Muslim associations were affiliated with CMCC chapters across Canada. With support from the Organization of Islamic Cooperation, CMCC sponsored a number of programs and held an annual convention in different Canadian cities. *Islam Canada*, a monthly magazine, was published under the editorship of Muin. It covered news from the community organizations and focused on the major issues facing the Muslim community. Dr Daood Hamdani, who worked for Statistics Canada, was requested to undertake the collection of data on Muslim Canadians and to advise and assist Census Canada. Dr Hamdani had published a number of research papers on Muslim Canadians including the first demographic analysis of the Canadian Muslim presence . . . [114]

Muin also had a strong relationship with the Canadian Council of Churches. CMCC initiated an interfaith dialogue between churches and mosques at the local, regional and national level. This forum helped a great deal in clearing misunderstandings and confusions based on ignorance. This engagement ultimately resulted in the National Christian-Muslim Liaison Committee.

Eventually, CMCC decided Muslim women should have an autonomous national organization affiliated with CMCC and, so, gave seed money to Dr Lila Fahlman, then vice-president of CMCC, to travel across Canada and connect with Muslim women and organize them so they could have a national voice. This effort led to the creation of the Canadian Council of Muslim Women . . .

In the early 1990s, Muin, Hameed Shaikh, and I, in cooperation with the University of Toronto, did a feasibility study looking at the potential future needs of Muslim seniors. The work continued under the guidance of Hameed Shaikh, Ebrahim Sayed, Ally Esmail, Munir Jan, and myself. In 1999, we established an organization dedicated to this work called Reh'ma Community Services. Reh'ma is an organization for seniors, run by seniors . . .

Muin's one unfinished project was the PhD he had started that he had hoped would culminate in writing a history of Canadian Muslims. Knowing Muin and his deep commitment to honouring and respecting people's stories and experiences, such a history would have been a necessary and critical contribution.

Muin Muinuddin passed away from a massive heart attack on November 19, 1998 while attending an interfaith meeting.

One of the earlier South Asian members of the Toronto Muslim community was Amjad R M Syed, who arrived from India in November 1965, to join the family of his brother-in-law, Dr Rahman Syed. The following was recorded in March 2019.

> I was born in Mysore City in 1936. It was a place where Tipu Sultan had a palace and it was a very historic place, seventy or eighty miles from Bangalore. My father, Syed Abdur Rahim, was born in India near Bombay and his forefathers were from Baghdad, a long time ago. My father was a teacher and gave a very good education to all the family members, three brothers and five sisters. They all became university graduates.
>
> It was a very good thing that my father was a teacher himself because he gave his first-born daughter, my sister, Afzalunnisa Rahman, in marriage to Dr Rahman [Syed]—he is also my first cousin. They came to Ohio State University in 1958, and she did her PhD in education and he did a PhD in chemistry. They were both Fulbright Scholars. After that they came back to Bangalore.
>
> But they did not like the environment there in Bangalore because with their very good education they both expected a lot better positions, so they decided to come back to North America. He came to Canada in 1964, and my sister in early 1965, to Toronto.
>
> In India, I had done my BSc degree in agricultural science and I was involved there for six years in cytogenetics in the department of agriculture in Bangalore. In November 1965 I came to Canada . . .
>
> Before coming to this country we used to hear from my sister and Dr Rahman, and there were pictures of people wearing heavy long woollen clothes, winter jackets, when in the background there was snow. I didn't know what cold was, and I [wondered] how, when there was lots of sun around, they were wearing heavy clothing . . . But after

coming over here I found a completely different picture! I did not know that all the people here were not PhDs and doctors, and I realized that there were janitors and poor people also, poorer than I used to think. I realized not everyone had a car! . . .

Of course, after coming to Canada I had to change my field in order to survive here. Because Dr Rahman was already here—he worked as a clinical chemist in the Toronto East General Hospital—he gave me a lead, and so I also joined the hospital and worked as a laboratory technologist. After about one year I moved to Sunnybrook Hospital and that was also the time that Dr Rahman moved with his family to Erie, Pennsylvania . . . My parents called and said come back and get married to Malika and then go back [to Canada]. That was the system in those days. The parents would see that their children got married, not like these days. So I got married in 1967. Now we have two sons and one daughter and grandchildren, all well settled, alhamdolillah.

In the early days there was a lot of luxury. All that we did was hold mushairas [recitations of Urdu poems] and Urdu debates, community picnics and dinners. Also, we were involved at the same time in holding meetings and brainstorming about acquiring a place for a masjid, and we used to get together in our small houses for prayers.

Then there was the Islamic Centre . . . Those were *really great days* . . . When I was standing in line for the zuhr [afternoon] prayer I used to get thrilled like anything because I could see Albanians, white people, brown people from India and Pakistan and different races. It was very thrilling for me because back home in India I had never said prayers with a white person. Here we were shoulder to shoulder, white, brown, short and tall, men and women. Back home there was no place for women in the masjids [mosques]. Here they had their own section [in rows behind the men]. It was amazing. Really, tears came into my eyes. It was an unforgettable thing . . .

Unfortunately, the community split. It was the worst thing I could think of. Anyway, it was all the will of Allah. Instead of one jamat [congregation], He wanted two jamats. So Regep Assim, yourself [Murray Hogben], the Albanians, and Dr M Q Baig formed a group [and remained in the Muslim Society of Toronto]. Others,

Dr Rahman and Haseeb Khan, an Indian and a Pakistani, formed another [the Islamic Foundation of Toronto]. In those days there was no such thing as "Indian" and "Pakistani," because we were all Urdu speaking. Later on, we [the Islamic Foundation] rented St Mary's Catholic Church basement at Bloor and Bathurst for our zuhr prayers [on Sundays]. That was the time when a lot of Indian and Pakistani young people were here for their higher education. They were so eager to come to this particular masjid because Malika and Dr Rahman's wife and Haseeb Khan's wife Saleha cooked a lot of nice spicy food and all the young people would run to grab the food.

A series of five articles linked to the Islamic Foundation website, written by Muneeb Nasir, originally from Guyana and son of long-standing president of the board of directors, Mohamed Nasir,[115] tells the story of the community. In brief, the group that had left the Muslim Society of Toronto and was meeting weekly in various locations decided in May 1968 to form the Muslim Foundation of Toronto. Amjad Syed provided a copy of a list, dated August 17, 1969, giving the following as the board of trustees: Nabil S Ali, Moin Ansari, Nasim Butt, Izzet Cevik, Y A Kalik Coovadia, Assim Hayat, Hasib H Khan (treasurer), Muin Muinuddin, Dr Ahmed Fuad Şahin (chair; see Niagara Region chapter), Amjad R M Syed, and Dr Rahman A Syed.

A handwritten annotation in one corner says: "Fatih Mosque, 182 Rhodes Ave, Toronto—Coxwell & Gerrard," referring to the two-storey Orange Hall in East York that the group purchased in 1968 and converted to their mosque.[116] According to Muneeb Nasir, in 1981 the Foundation directors decided to build a bigger mosque in Scarborough for their expanding membership and put in an offer to purchase 2.35 acres of land on Nugget Avenue. After a long battle with a neighbouring restaurateur, a large mosque, complete with dome and minaret, was completed in 1992.

Meanwhile, in 1969, the original core group of Albanians and others bought the Presbyterian church on Boustead Avenue, naming it the Jami Mosque. Tragically, within a few years, ongoing personality and cultural differences divided the community again, to the extent that the Muslim

Society of Toronto's Albanians in particular, who had funded the original Dundas Street West Islamic Centre, sold the Jami Mosque to the Muslim Students Association (MSA). The Albanians then bought their own smaller building on Annette Street. The Jami Mosque was able to get money from King Feisal of Saudi Arabia in about 1970.[117] The mosque property is now owned by MSA's parent organization, the Islamic Society of North America (ISNA).

Amjad Syed:

> At Sunnybrook Hospital there was no place for zuhr prayers during lunchtime. Just myself and a very good friend, Nazeer Ahmed, and Dr Naqvi, a cardiologist, used to do our zuhr prayers in the hospital chapel. This continued for about twenty-five years . . . [Finally] I contacted the chapel minister and he said if you give me some money you can spread your carpet and make it your prayer place. But we had no money. Ultimately, with Allah's grace, the chapel people themselves helped us and they gave us a small hall with a capacity for about thirty people and they carpeted it and said, alright there's your masjid . . . There is now a synagogue, a church, and a masjid there today. May Allah reward them for that . . .
>
> During my service in the hospital, at lunchtime I used to visit one or two Muslim patients. It was really rare in those days to see a Muslim patient. I used to run and sit on their beds during lunchtime and the patients liked this so much because there was no one to talk to. Naturally their children were working and had no time to come and visit their father or mother . . . This service became my passion.
>
> Immediately after my retirement in 1995, I recollected my experience of visiting patients at Sunnybrook Hospital and put this practice into action by starting a program at two Mississauga hospitals. Today, this program is a well-established [function] of the Islamic Society of North America (ISNA). We keep a limit of ten volunteers. Also, my dear wife Malika and I have been giving orientation training in Greater Toronto. The experience led me to write a book of 160 pages under the title *Islamic Perspectives on Prayers and Coping with Sickness*. Dr Ashraf, who was the secretary-general of ISNA, printed 20,000 copies of this book to give to hospital patients . . . Also, eleven

different brochures are prepared for the patients as well as for the hospital staff . . . We give small talks to the doctors and nurses regarding the needs of Muslim patients, also on how to handle Muslim bodies. We even introduced halal food for the patients at Credit Valley and Mississauga Trillium Hospitals.

Another service that I did was to establish the funeral system, including setting up of a ghusal [body-washing room] at the ISNA facility in 1998 . . . This experience led me to write a 226-page book under the title *Textbook of Muslim Funerals in the West* . . .

When the ISNA building was in planning stage, I was one of the three people who decided where this masjid [mosque] was going to be and where it is standing today [on QEW highway in Mississauga]. Once the construction started, we made plans for gathering the community. In that connection, I rented a nearby community hall and arranged for juma [Friday] prayer. The juma congregation continued there for the next five years there—1995 to 2000—nonstop until the masjid building was ready to take this congregation.

In those early days, roughly 1965 to 1968, we were involved more in fun activities and dinners but not too much in the advancement of Islam. But still we did lay some foundations . . . Malika and I arranged for evening weekly Islamic classes at our home. Brother Hisham Badran, an enthusiastic young volunteer, helped us. The classes ran for six years. Today, those kids are parents and well-established.

Muslim immigrants today have taken for granted that all the facilities for prayers, Ramadan activities and banquet halls are all "existing." Besides, they have jobs and are making good money. Nothing to worry about. They even have Islamic schools. They do not know how these things came into existence. There is awareness, no doubt. Not everyone is sleeping, though. Besides, there are anti-Muslim elements and activities going on by known and latent organizations. We have to be vigilant and keep on working hard physically, financially, and with the power of dua, insha'allah. In fact there was a lot of opposition by the local [non-Muslim] community to masjid construction. I was one of the lead local [Muslim] community members to represent the masjid to the Ontario Municipal Board.

Amjad and Malika received a number of awards, Amjad the ISNA Canada Community Service Award in 2002, and Malika the Queen Elizabeth Medal in 2013; Malika and Amjad together were awarded a hajj trip in 2001 by Rabitat al-Alam al-Islami (Muslim World League), a lifelong award in the Husband and Wife Team category by the Canadian Islamic Congress in 2004.

12. Kingston: University Town

MY WIFE ALIA AND I HAVE NOW LIVED CLOSE TO KINGSTON, Ontario, for more than forty years. This historic Loyalist military, commercial, and educational site was briefly the capital of Canada in the 1840s. Although it has long had an active Jewish community, it was only in the 1960s that the first Muslims arrived in Kingston: a Pakistani and an Egyptian.

Imtiaz Azhar, from South Asia, seems to have been the first Muslim immigrant to this city. The following was recorded in September 2017.

> My father's name was Chaudhry Mohammed Hussain and my mother's name was Zainab Bibi, and I was born on January 1, 1932, in Pakistan [then British India], in a village or *chak* . . .
>
> I went to primary school and then to a school with grades nine and ten which was further away and in English. Then I went to college in Lahore. It was a very famous college, Government College Lahore, it was very selective. I graduated after four years with a BSc in sciences, in 1955.
>
> When Partition came in 1947, I was in grade nine, and I was on the Pakistan side of the line where there was a majority of Muslims. There was fighting and sometimes killing. The Hindus and Sikhs were mostly friendly, but they lived in different communities. People stuck to their religions.
>
> After graduation . . . a very kind teacher, bless his soul, guided me and decided I should go for further education in England. I went to Manchester College and spent three years to do a bachelor of science in textiles. From there I didn't want to go back to Pakistan because I liked Europe and wanted a little bit more, so the next two years I spent

214 • MINARETS ON THE HORIZON

in Germany, working in the textile industry.

I was back in Karachi in 1960, and that is when by accident I learned that Canada had opened its doors to Asians. Before that, you had to be European.

I landed in Montreal and was looking for a job when I got a letter from CIL [Canadian Industries Limited, October 21, 1960] that said they were desperately looking for an engineer at their Millhaven plant [outside Kingston] because Dupont was beating them very hard in fibre [research], and they couldn't find one . . . After I came to Kingston in 1960, I worked with CIL for five years. I got married on January 20, 1963 to Ismat Nawaz, in Pakistan. We met and then we got married in Bhalwal, in Sargodha Province. We had three daughters—one died only recently [in 2017]—and one son. Then after five years with CIL, we wanted to go back [to Pakistan], so I spent the next years in the Terylene plant near Lahore and I had a good job there until 1979. Then in 1979 we came back. I started looking for another job here, and when I couldn't find one for some time, I worked at something a little different, as a driving instructor, as a classroom teacher and behind the wheel, and I carried that on until very recently . . .

I have encountered zero racism. I have been here for years and years, and I found that Canada is the least, if at all, racist country. I have never come across it . . . this place is the most friendly place.[118]

When I came, I was the first Muslim immigrant in Kingston. [There were three Muslim students] and when she [his wife] came, there were five [of us Muslims]. When we left in 1965 [to return to Pakistan], Dr Moustafa Fahmy had arrived, and later some Pakistanis . . . There was no Islamic Society of Kingston nor any Islamic Centre.

Moustafa Fahmy, PhD, now of London, Ontario, was the founder of the Muslim community in Kingston. Originally from Egypt, he arrived in Canada from the United States in 1965 with his wife Fatma and became a professor of electrical engineering at Queen's University and a president of the Islamic Society of Kingston. In October 2017, he told me his family's story.

I was born in Alexandria, Egypt, in 1929 and raised in Alexandria in particular, and I did all my undergraduate studies there. I got my bachelor's degree in electrical engineering from Alexandria University. At that time it was called Farouk University, because Egypt was a monarchy and King Farouk was the king. I graduated in 1950 at the top of my class. So I was appointed as a teaching assistant in the Department of Electrical Engineering at the same university. I continued 'til I got my master's degree, an MSc, in electrical engineering, about 1960, and then within a year I got a government scholarship to pursue my PhD abroad.

My father was working with a British mining company in Alexandria, Egypt . . . My mother was a housewife and I had two other brothers and three sisters, and all of them are dead now, so I am the only one left . . . Our family were practising Muslims, and my siblings were university graduates.

Being a recipient of a government scholarship, it was up to me to find a university for admission, and the only restriction was the area or field of study was assigned by the Egyptian government. I had a friend who happened to be teaching as a professor at the State University of New Mexico in Las Cruces, and so he helped me to go there and start my PhD studies in the summer of 1962. When I went there, I did not find the particular area that I was supposed to study at Las Cruces, so while I started the summer session in Las Cruces I searched for another university where I could find professors in my area of research, called instrumentation. So I settled on the University of Michigan at Ann Arbor, and then I focused on an area that is close to instrumentation, which is control systems. I started my studies at the University of Michigan in the fall of 1962. [That winter] was the first time I saw snow in my life and I remember that it was such a cold winter!

We [he and his wife Fatma] had got married before leaving Egypt in 1961. She came from a business-oriented family. They have wholesale grocery stores and so on, and in fact now they have expanded into something like Loblaws Superstores. She finished her high school diploma in home economics in 1961, just before we got engaged. I stayed at the University of Michigan until '65 when I had completed my PhD thesis.

216 ON THE HORIZON

I will tell you how I came to Canada. I had a classmate at the University of Michigan. It happened that he was associated with Queen's University in Kingston, and he kept persuading me to go to spend a few years at Queen's University. At first I was not welcoming the idea, but after so much persuasion I agreed to it. I went to Queen's for an interview with the Department of Electrical Engineering, and it didn't take much time [for me] to receive an offer. You see, the Department of Electrical Engineering was so small. It consisted of about seven faculty members and only two of them were holding PhDs and the rest were holding masters' degrees . . . My appointment as an assistant professor was the first appointment of a Muslim in the Department of Electrical Engineering and in fact in the whole Faculty of Applied Science . . . Socially, the members of the department and their families were accommodating and welcoming and in fact we so much appreciate how much they helped us in starting our lives in Kingston. I retired in 1994 . . .

When we arrived in Kingston in December 1965, we were looking for a piece of used furniture to buy, and we found an ad in the paper and the person who put in the ad happened to be Imtiaz Azhar [see above]. So for the first time we met a Muslim in Kingston. His was the first and only [Muslim] family we met in Kingston.

At Queen's itself, there were a few international Muslim graduate students from different countries, and I was surprised to find that they prayed the juma prayer [on Fridays] at the home of one of them. So coming from the University of Michigan where we had a room on campus for the Friday prayers, I persuaded them that we should request the university administration to provide us with a room to pray juma. So, alhamdolillah, our request was approved and we got the Memorial Room, which had a memorial to the Unknown Soldier, and so we started using this as a place to hold the juma prayer. It was only maybe six or seven people. Then we started thinking of where we could pray the zuhr and asr prayers, and so again I approached the university administration, and they were willing to reserve for us some vacant classrooms at that time, so we used to get together for zuhr and asr prayers in the assigned classrooms, which changed from day to day.

Professor Moustafa Fahmy leads prayers in Queen's University's Memorial Room in the later 1960s. Photo courtesy of Moustafa Fahmy.

There were very few families. I remember that Qamar Al-Tawheed—may Allah's mercy be upon him—was working in the Correctional Service, so we started to get together, and then some more people came. We had a medical doctor, a Dr Ahmed, who came to the city, but he moved to Toledo in the US and I think he's still there. A few more people came and we established a relationship with them and we tried sometimes to get together and study Qur'an . . . The number of international students increased and some of them were undergraduates, so we started to establish what was known as the Muslim Students Association. In fact I remember that one year we hosted the annual conference of the Muslim Students Associations of Canada.

Some years after that, the Islamic Society of Kingston was founded [September 9, 1982],[119] and the Muslim Students Association of Queen's was considered [to be] under its wing . . . [Later on the MSA at Queen's students] withdrew from the Islamic Society of Kingston and formed what was called QUMSA, the Queen's University Muslim Students Association, in the mid-1980s. In fact the first chair of QUMSA was my daughter, Eanass Fahmy. Then the idea of having an Islamic centre started to gain acceptance and there was fundraising,[120] and it was opened in February 1996, and the first congregational prayer was for the Eid prayer in 1996 or 1997.

From the beginning we made it a point that we would not accept any overseas funding for this project. The funding came locally and from within North America. I was the president [of the Islamic Society of Kingston] for one term. It was after 1998, but for sure at the time of 9/11 [September 11, 2001] I was president.

We left for London [Ontario] in 2011. We have five daughters. Two of the children, the eldest, Eaman, and the youngest Mihad, are in London, Eanass is in New Jersey, and Hoda is in Mississauga. Hebba is living in Ancaster, which is a suburb of Hamilton . . .

The best experience of living in Canada was that we gave our children the opportunity to live within a diverse community. While they were studying in Kingston, they had friends from Malaysia, the Philippines, [and] from Indonesia in addition to their Canadian friends, so their view of the world has expanded. It was a great benefit to them, and it is reflected in their lives later on as activists. What we regret most, really, is that our children are not as fluent in the Arabic language as we would like . . .

I would like to see the Muslims here in Canada get really involved in the affairs of the Canadian community at large. They have to have a physical presence within the social services, helping the poor and so on, and helping the indigenous people. The Muslims should help in this field and also in the political area . . . Non-Muslims in Canadian society [will not] know Muslims . . . through lectures or articles. They have to see them really as examples of Islam. This is really what Muslims should recognize and should work hard for. This is really the thing that I would like to see, that Canadian Muslims will behave in the community at large as Muslims adhering to the values of Islam.

Two of Moustafa Fahmy's earliest colleagues as professors of electrical engineering at Queen's were Hafiz Rahman, who arrived from East Pakistan, now Bangladesh, in 1968, and Mohammed Bayoumi, who arrived from Egypt in 1969. Both became hardworking presidents of the Islamic Society of Kingston in later years and are still active with it.

13. Ottawa: Capital Ideas

OTTAWA, BECAUSE OF ITS GREATER SAFETY FROM THE REACH OF American armies than Montreal, Kingston, or Toronto, was the city that eventually became Canada's capital. It has had a Syrian Muslim presence since at least the start of the twentieth century. By the late 1950s and early '60s, several Pakistanis had arrived—including a university student and an experienced journalist—as well as an Indian South African teacher. All three made their mark on the Muslim history of Canada.

My first interviewee and one of the leading pioneer Muslims in Ottawa was Eva Wahab, with whom I spoke in 1979. Born in Ottawa in September 1914, she was a well-known personality. She died on April 23, 2005.

In the early years, the Muslim community was a minority here in Ottawa. We were about fifteen or twenty and were all related. This included my mother and father, aunts and uncles. My father was Hassan Mohammed Al-Wahab [d. November 3, 1962] and my mother's maiden name was Sherify Saddaka [d. December 19, 1945]. They were originally from Lebanon, which was known as Greater Syria at that time. My mother's brother was Mohammed Saddaka, and my father's brother was Mohammed Al-Wahab, and they all came from the village of Fermisky. Our family was the only Muslim family in that village. All the rest were Christians.

We were six children—four girls and two boys. I was the first born in Canada. My parents were married in Lebanon, and when my sister was three months old, my father came to the New World to make his fortune. It took a month to come from Lebanon to Canada by boat, and when they arrived everything was strange to them and they didn't

Eva Wahab, an Ottawa pioneer and federal civil servant.
Photo courtesy of Muslim Link.

know the language, so it was difficult to find jobs.

My father became a peddler and bought items in a store and went into the country and sold them to the farmers. He carried such things as yard goods, thread, needles, and hosiery in packsacks on his back. Sometimes they would walk for miles before they would reach a farmhouse and when they got there they found they needed nothing. Sometimes they asked if they could stay, and some would say yes and some would say no. Sometimes in return they would give the farmers something they would ask for. He never complained of the hardships they had. At times when they were refused accommodation, they would spend the night in the snow.

It was some time before my father opened a dry goods store. He had saved his money while peddling . . . I remember he had a dry goods store at St Laurent and St Henri in Hull [now Gatineau, Quebec]. It was called "'Assan's" . . . He had a lot of stock and we often sent parcels home to my sister and grandmother [in Lebanon]. He got along well with everyone, and the priests and nuns would come for donations and Father would give. The Capuchins came for money or goods and Father would contribute, as we were part of the community. They knew he was a Muslim and they would talk about religion, but the only thing they knew about the Muslim religion was that Father could have four wives! Father would explain to them, but it was not that easy!

Religion never came up in school. At that time we were called "Mohammedans," not "Muslims" . . . No one said anything offensive because we were all together—French, English, Jewish—and we were all the same. There was no difference . . . Father taught us our prayers at home and he taught us all he knew, for which I am grateful, because both he and my mother put religion in our blood. Father taught a few other children who were Muslim as well . . . In the 1940s we had to bring Imam Kharoub from Detroit to Ottawa for weddings and funerals.

Through the years we celebrated the holy days, and our parents would figure out the dates themselves. My father would look up at the moon and tell us it would soon be Ramadan. He could tell by the crescent of the moon what date it would be approximately, and what season it was. He would bring out the thread to see if we could distinguish it in the dark. This was done for fasting purposes.[121] There were no Muslim calendars in those days . . . We never had pork in the house. My father would go out and buy a live sheep, goose, or turkey from a farmer; Mother would hold the animal and Father would slaughter it in an Islamic way. They kept the traditions the way that they were brought up. Food and cooking were strictly Islamic. Mother bought wheat and ground her own flour for bread, and we children had to rub it between our hands. Everything she learned in the old country she brought here with her . . .

When Eid came around, the food was strictly Islamic and Arab— no pork or liquor. Some of the single men and some of the men whose families had not come over [to join them from Lebanon] yet were invited to eat on those days . . .

[My father] was very strict when it came to bringing up children. We girls were not allowed to go out [with boys] even though we were attending Canadian schools. We were not allowed to wear lipstick, makeup, go to dances or walk home with a boy. Father ruled the home—anything we wanted to do we had to ask his permission. I am grateful and thankful that we were brought up in this kind of environment. We saw the other girls going out with boys and being teens and wearing lipstick, but it was not that way for us. Mother made our clothes, . . . and we also wore clothes from his [Father's] store. We were modestly dressed to go to school—nothing above the knee and nothing sleeveless—but we were never extreme—with our heads covered and covered to the ankles . . .

We all learned three languages—Arabic, English, and French. I later took private lessons in Spanish as I was always interested in languages . . . Later, I worked as a [federal] civil servant and became supervisor of the Department of Munitions and Supply—it was called that during the [Second World] War, but it was later changed to Reconstruction.

After some time we opened a confectionery business, and I resigned from the government and went into business. It was later turned into a restaurant called Eva's Coffee Shoppe. We operated it for about seventeen years and for two [more] years after Father died. I found it interesting to be with people. It was a wonderful education, the kind of education that does not come from books . . .

This is our country and there isn't a day that goes by that I don't get down on my hands and knees and thank Allah for having been born Canadian. Canada is not just French and English. It's all of us together. Everyone came from somewhere, and this is what makes our country strong and beautiful and we have a lot to be proud of.

There was a long gap between the late-nineteenth and early twentieth-century arrivals of Syrian Lebanese immigrants like Eva's family and the arrivals of South Asian and other immigrants beginning the 1960s, when the racist immigration laws were relaxed. Among the latter was Mohammad Naeem Malik, a founder and repeat president of the 1962 Ottawa Muslim Association. He was interviewed in August 2017.

I was born on the eighth of September 1937 in the city of Amritsar, India. My father was a businessman. He had a printing press and a stationery store, wholesale, and when we came to Lahore, Pakistan, he carried on the same business, but he had to start from scratch because we left everything back in India. My mother was just a housewife. We were five boys and one girl and I was the youngest in the family.

Partition [in 1947] was terrible. I was separated from the rest of the family. You see, I was staying with my father. My mother and my other siblings came to the railway station in order to get to Pakistan and in the meantime things got worse, with communal riots. My mother sent me to tell my father that they were going to Lahore and that we were going to have to go our own way, myself and my father, and I never made it to my house. There was fighting going on and killing and whatnot and I was just a young boy then [aged ten]. Anyway, then my father—when things got really worse—he sent me with a couple of other people who were going to Lahore just to save my life. On the train when we were coming there were seven Sikhs holding bombs under the train. Some people noticed they were hiding under the train and so they stopped the train and killed all seven of them. Sikhs had long hair, and they tied their legs and arms with their long hair and threw them in the river—and I saw all that! So we came to Lahore with no money and no nothing. It was terrible!

In due time, Naeem had completed his grade 10 matriculation and followed by two years of college in Pakistan. In 1958, one of his brothers, who had won a scholarship to take a master's degree at the University of Texas, became a Pakistani diplomat and invited him to Ottawa. Naeem came and worked for a few years.

When I arrived in Ottawa I was very lonely—I was eighteen or nineteen—because there were very few Pakistani teenagers in Ottawa at that time. I think there was another family that had a son in high school. The father was a Pakistani army colonel who had come as a landed immigrant. So had I. [His son's] name was Saleem, and we became good friends, but they lived in Ottawa, quite a distance from where my brother was, in Aylmer on the Quebec side, across the river. But slowly, slowly, I got used to living in Ottawa.

I finished my bachelor's degree, a BSc, at Carleton University in 1967 . . . I started working with the Ontario Department of Health, in the provincial government. They trained me on the job and I became a research biologist. [Later] I switched to the federal government—again the Ministry of Health—as a research biologist, always in Ottawa.

In 1966, I went back home to Lahore to get married. Her name was Shahida Malik. Malik is a tribal name. There are lots of Maliks in Pakistan . . . they were from Afghanistan and they settled in India.

I was in Ottawa for sixty years. I didn't move. I worked for forty-two years, and then I retired in 2005. The reason I retired is that my wife had cancer. My four kids and I—three boys and a girl—didn't want to put her in a hospital, because if they put you as a cancer patient in a hospital, you become a number . . . so we kept her home here . . . She died in 2005.

When I was a student here, there were four or five Muslim families, very few, because at that time the only people who came to Canada from India and Pakistan were under the Colombo Plan—that was a plan that used to send civil servants for training. Besides that, I think there were only one or two people who came as landed immigrants, not too many people. They didn't like the climate here—it was too cold and people were afraid to come—but slowly, slowly, they came.

But there were a lot of racial problems. You wouldn't get a job easily, and they wanted somebody with Canadian experience and this and that. Also, people were hardly used to seeing people with a brown skin in Canada—and now, my God! When I came, if you saw some-body with a brown skin walking, you would run to talk to them, it didn't matter if they were Hindu or Muslim. You were just so glad to see someone who looked like you . . .

There were only a handful of Muslims in Ottawa . . . so few that the Eid prayer had to be held at the Pakistan High Commission, which was on Wilbrod Street downtown. That was it. Then slowly people started coming to Ottawa and the number of Muslims increased . . . people started coming from the Middle East and from Iran and all that, and now we have sixty thousand Muslims in Ottawa. We were so bad [in terms of numbers] that we approached Western United Church—they had a church at Bronson and Wellington Street—for space to pray. Then later on, the city wanted to set up a water pumping station where the church was, so the city gave them some land in the west end, on Northwestern Avenue. That's where our mosque is now. They [the church] asked us if we wanted to use their basement for our prayers, so we started using it.

In 1962, we founded the Ottawa Muslim Association, but we didn't have land, no mosque, no nothing, so when there were two small private cottages [available], we bought them for $50,000, both houses. But we had no money to develop further, because you need money to make a building. In the meantime, the prime minister of Pakistan, Zulfikhar Ali Bhutto [president, 1971–73, prime minister, 1973–77] came here for a visit and we invited him to see where we wanted to build our mosque. I was part of the board then and so he asked us what he could do, so we said give us some money because we want to build a mosque. The poor guy wanted to say a hundred thousand rupees, but he said a $100,000, so when he went back he wanted to change his story. He said I'll give you a hundred thousand rupees, I didn't mean a $100,000. But we said no, in the house of God you said dollars, so give us dollars because we want to build a mosque, so he gave us $100,000. That was Zulfikhar Ali Bhutto, who was hanged later [in 1979]. Then we approached a lot of Middle Eastern countries. Saudi Arabia was another financier of this mosque in Ottawa.

The Ottawa Muslim Association mosque was finally built in 1972. Naeem continued:

So far we have had three imams and all three came from Egypt, all of them graduates from Al-Azhar University [Cairo's famous Islamic school]. The first imam, [Dr] Tawfiq Shaheen [1980–97],[122] was very well known throughout the Muslim world. I think he wanted $50,000 dollars as a salary, and that was a lot of money in those days, but in the meantime the Saudi Arabian oil shaikh, [Ahmad] Zaki Yamani, came to Ottawa and he said, "Don't worry, I will pay the imam's salary out of my pocket."

So he paid 'til he was kicked out of the oil ministry. When the poor guy lost his job, fired by King Fahd in 1986, he came to us and said, "I'm sorry I can't pay any more," so we started paying the imam ourselves . . . Then some people said, "Shaikh, we have to cut down your salary," and the poor imam called me . . . and I told the him, "Don't worry. We will pay you ourselves, or I will pay you out of my pocket." I was president [of the Association] at the time. Every time nobody wanted to be president, they would bring me in.

Now, my God, we have sixty thousand people [in Ottawa], mostly Somalis. Now there are thirteen mosques and ours is the oldest mosque. They call it the mother of all the mosques in Ottawa . . . We got the land in 1968, and the mosque was built in 1972. The women's section is on the second floor. They can see us but we can't see them[123] . . . I made sure when I was running [for president] that I would bring in some ladies on the board. In our mosque at least a minimum of one thousand people come for juma [Friday prayers].

Last summer [2016] we bought the church that had given us space to pray . . . The neighbourhood is very nice to us. [Once] we had racial slurs written on the mosque windows and walls and we cleaned it up. All the neighbours came—it was a very cold day in October. And on the day after the Quebec City massacre [January 29, 2017], they came and they formed a human chain around the mosque. They brought hot coffee and sandwiches. [Later] we had an open house at the mosque for the whole neighbourhood and they came and we served them food . . .

We have had internal problems quite often.[124] They are not between Sunni and Shi'a but between ethnic groups. You see, different countries have adopted something local. It is not a product of Islam but it is part of their culture, and they bring it here and we try to accommodate everybody, especially in Ramadan. The women's section wanted to come down and eat with the men, and we had to put up a partition and this and that. And sometimes it gets a bit out of hand but we have calmed down everybody . . .

Now the thirteen mosques [in Ottawa] tend to represent different ethnic groups . . . I sometimes go to the other mosques and I feel very much the stranger. But when I go to ours [the Ottawa Muslim Association mosque] on Northwestern Avenue, I feel very much at home . . . People wanted to expand it for thirteen years but they didn't get the money because of the in-fighting and things like that . . . When I became president again he said, [Imam Shaheen said,] "Naeem let's do the expansion." But I said, "Shaikh, we have only half a million dollars and we can't build it. It will take a million dollars. But he said, take me to the houses of the Muslims, [which I did] and we never came out of any house without some money . . . Not only did we expand the mosque but also we acquired a parking lot, because parking had been a big problem . . .

Most of the money [however] came from Pakistan, Saudi Arabia, and even Libya and Malaysia. Most of the ambassadors used to come and pray in our mosque . . . The bulk of the community at that time was Lebanese. They didn't have a decent education but worked in restaurants and grocery stores, and the majority of the educated people came from India, Pakistan, and Egypt.

The Lebanese are still with us . . . Every second year when we hold an election, the majority [of voters] are the Lebanese people because their children got educated and all that. The Lebanese group work very hard for the mosque. I remember whenever we had the annual dinner you would first buy groceries from your pocket and then take it to your house and your wife or your daughter or somebody would cook it. Then you would bring it to the hall where you were holding the dinner and you served the food and then you paid five dollars to get a ticket, even if you brought the food! After the dinner you ended up washing the dishes, so it wasn't all white shirts and suits because you had to work. Alhamdolillah, we came a long way. Now when I tell some of the young kids these stories, they laugh and say, you people did all that work? And I say, yes. I will be eighty in November [2017].

Another person who was here a long time was Dr Farid Ahmed. He was from Egypt . . . Another old-timer was the late Qasem Mahmud, who passed away in July 2017. I knew him from day one when he first came to Ottawa. He translated some books from Arabic to English, children's books, and gave them free of charge to most of the mosques in Canada. Also, Qasem [helped] buy some land to set up a children's camp for all the young Muslim children in the summertime free of charge, and I think that camp is still running.[125]

A third long-term and widely known member of the Muslim community in Ottawa was Mohammed Azhar Ali Khan, who had an international reach due to his lengthy journalistic and government commission work. He was interviewed in August 2017.

I was born in Bhopal, central India, in 1932. My father was the chief conservator of forests and then the secretary for commerce, industry and labour . . . and then revenue 'til he retired. His family members held different positions in Bhopal, a state ruled by a Muslim. The majority were Hindus. We lived in peace and friendship without friction and attended the same schools. I went to an English school and then a local one. My father chose a Hindu tutor for me, showing that he harbored no prejudice based on religion. Then came independence and Partition in 1947, and the troubles began.

Though Bhopal was peaceful, it was located in central India and was a junction of railways. We saw dead bodies in the trains that went through Bhopal. A lot of Hindu refugees who had fled from Sind Province in Pakistan settled in Bhopal. They were full of sorrow and anger. At the same time, Muslims from the neighbouring Hindu states of Gwalior and Indore came to Bhopal seeking refuge. Though Bhopal remained peaceful, you sensed fear and uncertainty. Some of my elder sisters were married in Pakistan, and my family felt that probably we would be safer in Pakistan. Bhopal was peaceful, but we did not know for how long. I still have relatives in Bhopal who live in peace in an island of tolerance.

I went to Karachi in June 1950, where I completed my studies in political science and economics and got a scholarship from the University of the Philippines in 1953. I studied in Quezon City near Manila for one year, specializing in journalism. I came back to Pakistan in 1955 and worked and then got a fellowship from the University of Michigan in 1956. I studied in the US for three years. I came back in December 1959 and joined *Morning News*, the only paper published at that time simultaneously from Karachi and Dhaka, East Pakistan [now Bangladesh]. I became assistant editor and then news editor and also wrote for the *Christian Science Monitor*, the *Baltimore Sun*, and the *Indianapolis Star.* In 1965, I moved to Canada.

I wrote about my plans to several Canadian papers, and they said to see them when I arrived. I had started writing occasionally for the *Ottawa Citizen*, and editor Christopher Young told me that he'd give me a chance if they had a vacancy when I came. They had no vacancy when I saw Mr Young, but he still hired me and I started working within two days. After two weeks they said I'd be better off as a copy editor. They soon made me the telegraph editor, which meant copy editing and going through incoming reports to enable the news editor to decide which stories deserved the front page. After about a year they took me on the editorial board as a foreign affairs analyst, writing editorials on foreign affairs and a weekly column on world affairs, and editing the op-ed page.

Soon after my arrival, I met a Muslim in the post office who told me of a Qur'anic reading and invited me. I met a few people and learned of the very small Muslim community. We did not have a mosque and prayed on Sunday afternoons in a church because people couldn't take time off work on Fridays. We had our annual dinner also in the church, which was very supportive. We have had excellent relations since that time. The Ottawa Muslim Association had just been formed . . . and I joined it . . .

My wife, Nishat Khanum, is from Quetta, Baluchistan. My father knew her father because when my father was conservator of forests, her father used to come to Bhopal to buy wood. Her father was chief secretary to the Khan of Kalat—the ruler of Kalat. They had both gone to the Muslim University in Aligarh in India. Some of my relatives, including an uncle, also lived in Quetta. So the families knew each other and I saw her occasionally. Everybody spoke very highly of her. I proposed to her and we got married in 1965—and then came to Canada . . .

She expected that Canada would have very few people and vast open spaces and wilderness. She was pleasantly surprised when our plane descended from the clouds over Montreal and she saw glittering lights illuminating a huge city.

Nishat had taken child psychology courses in her school in Karachi, which was affiliated with Oklahoma State University. In Ottawa she got a job as a psychometrist and started taking evening courses. She did her BA in psychology, then her MA and PhD. She worked for the Carleton School Board, which became a part of the Ottawa School Board.

I served as president, vice-president, and secretary of the Ottawa Muslim Association. Naeem Malik was the first president and then Dr Farid Ahmed, of Egyptian origin, who served for many years as president. That was a big advantage for the Lebanese, most of whom could not speak or understand English much.

Ottawa has a large Lebanese community, but most were not professionals and left the leadership mostly to Farid Ahmed and Hussain Gawad, who were from Egypt, and some Pakistanis, such as Ghulam Khaliq Chaudhry. At that time, many Shi'a were members of the Ottawa Muslim Association, because there was no Shi'a mosque or association. They joined in building OMA's mosque and we prayed together. We got along very well. Gradually the number of Muslims grew, so new organizations and mosques came into being to serve particular localities or ethnic groups. The Shi'a developed their own organizations and mosques. It was not a matter of friction, but simply one of convenience. In winter, in particular, it is hard to drive in the snow to a distant place, so people preferred going to a mosque in their own neighbourhoods . . .

The community's basic problem has been that [although most of its] organizations build and maintain mosques and arrange religious programs, they do not act to meet the needs of a growing community and its most vulnerable members, such as widows, single parents, women who are victims of violence, youth being lured to crime, drugs, alcoholism, and extremism, and . . . the sick, the mentally ill, the elderly, and so on. All the mainstream Muslim organizations have more or less sidelined women—they have no leadership positions and have very little say in these organizations. The only exception to my knowledge is the Muslim Association of Canada, whose head in Ottawa is a woman.

I worked for the *Citizen* for twenty-five years. One day editor Gord Fisher told me he had received a call from Keith Spicer, the chairman of the Canadian Radio-television and Telecommunications Commission [CRTC]. He had been appointed the chair of the royal commission, the Citizens' Forum on Canada's Future, which Prime Minister Brian Mulroney had set up to consult Canadians from coast to coast on their vision for Canada in the next century. With Fisher's permission, Spicer told me, "You have worked for the *Ottawa Citizen* for twenty-five years. What charm do you have in working there now? You are doing the same thing over and over again." He wanted me to become the director of multiculturalism in the Citizens' Forum and take charge of all discussions with all the ethnic communities of the country. That lasted for a year, about 1990–91. I was extremely successful. All the ethnic organizations responded positively to our messages, and there was a very high level of participation.

After Spicer had submitted his report to the prime minister and the Citizens' Forum ended its job, executive director David Broadbent introduced me to the deputy minister of the Department of Multiculturalism and Citizenship and said my experience with the *Citizen* and the Citizens' Forum would be invaluable to the department. The deputy minister gave me a contract and later encouraged me to enter into a competition, which I did and so got a permanent job. Then it became a part of the Department of Canadian Heritage, so I worked there.

Later, the federal cabinet appointed me a member of the Immigration and Refugee Board, a refugee judge. The Prime Minister's Office made the appointment but told me the appointment would have to be approved by the Parliament and I would have to appear before a parliamentary committee to answer their questions. I was grilled and approved. I was appointed for two years but was given two extensions and served with them for ten years, the maximum they give. [This was from 1996 to 2006] I retired after that but continued some community work and occasional writing.

I think the Muslim community has been a success mostly because of individual members making great contributions . . . In Canada, more than in most countries, all citizens enjoy opportunities. I say to young people: There is discrimination, racism, and difficulties in Canada . . . but don't lose heart. You will not find countries with a better record. I can't think of any Muslim country which treats Muslims and all its citizens with so much respect . . . For all its problems, this is an ideal country. I myself have been awarded the Order of Canada, the Order of Ontario, and the Queen's Diamond and Golden Jubilee awards.

Khadija Haffajee was another civic-minded member of the Ottawa Muslim community. She was interviewed in 2017.

I was born in Pietermaritzburg, Natal, South Africa, in August 1937. My grandparents came from India at the turn of the century, 1900 or thereabouts, and my father was the eldest child born in South Africa [in 1905] . . .

We were a large family . . . We were six siblings that I remember, because only six [of us] survived out of thirteen. I got a regular schooling in South Africa. I went to primary school and I was taught by nuns. Yes, the classes were segregated . . . Then I went to high school. It was an all-girls high school where I did my matric. By then my father was deceased and my mother was not in a good financial state. I was fortunate to receive bursaries to attend teachers' college. They were all segregated—it was black, coloured, Indian, and white—I was in the midst of all that. I did a three-year diploma and started my teaching career in Pietermaritzburg. I was the first nonwhite young person to teach at the local high school . . . It was the reality of Apartheid. We had different salary scales even though we taught the same curriculum to the same students . . . That was one of the reasons I decided that I would leave South Africa. I went to England first, where I taught at a grammar school . . .

In the summer of 1965, I was attending the Edinburgh Music Festival where I met a young, newly married Canadian couple, Peggy and Bill Tyson. I mentioned to them about my plans to go to Canada in the spring of 1966. A day later I found a note from them under my door, saying that they did not have an address in Canada, but gave me Peggy's parents' address and asked me to get in touch with them when I arrived. I had applied to come to Canada . . . and I landed in Quebec City on April 18, 1966 . . . I came by boat across the Atlantic. I landed not knowing a single soul. I was a twenty-eight-year-old single Muslim woman immigrating to Canada on my own . . .

Lo and behold, when the ship docked in Quebec City, there was a letter of welcome from Peggy sent via the shipping line, giving me their Toronto address and phone number. What a welcome to Canada! I did call them, as due to unforeseen circumstances I was taking a late train to Toronto. They kindly met me at Union Station and took me home for the night. The next morning I left Toronto [for Hamilton]. My qualifications had been accepted, so all I had to do was see if I could get a job. [Finally] I ended up in Burlington, Ontario . . .

Burlington was a very small place then, a village. I was teaching middle school, grades seven and eight, and I was a home-room teacher and . . . taught language arts and maths . . . After three years I moved to Ottawa . . . The Muslim community there was very small. There were no mosques . . . [but] initially I was the treasurer of the Ottawa Muslim Association while the mosque was being built in 1974–75 . . . Eva [Wahab] was a good friend. [See previous interview.] She had started the women's auxiliary in Ottawa . . . I took over from her and became the next president after Eva of the Ottawa Muslim Women's Auxiliary. That's when CMCC asked me to become involved with the women's programming for CMCC. I travelled across the country and encouraged women to become involved at the mosque level because there were very few people and they needed them to be active at the mosques. I had done a survey on my own. I sent a survey across the country to all the mosques that I knew, even to BC, so that I could speak with some authority to say I know that there are no women involved in any of these organizations and there should be.

Khadija was in the CMCC for four years, after which she was followed by Lila Fahlman and the founding of the Canadian Council of Muslim Women (CCMW). In the years that followed, Khadija was member of several organizations, including the ISNA (Islamic Society of North America), mentioned before, and became more involved as a community person. She was the first ISNA women's representative for Canada and in 1997 was the first woman elected to the Majlis Ashura [advisory council] of continental ISNA. She was on the Majlis for ten years. Since the late 1990s until her death she was on the board of the National Council of Canadian Muslims.[126] She worked with Human Concern International [HCI] on Afghan relief during the Soviet war, working in refugee camps in Peshawar and Quetta, Pakistan, later did many public lectures to raise awareness of the situation. She returned to Afghanistan in the spring of 2003 as a member of an interfaith delegation funded by the Canadian International Development Agency to work on programs for women and orphans in Kabul. She was also part of an Interfaith Peace-Builders delegation to Palestine/Israel in 2004.[127] Later in her life she became a member of the Council on Aging of Ottawa and the Christian/Muslim Dialogue of Ottawa, and on the advisory committee for the Multi-Faith Housing Initiative. She received the City of Ottawa's Interfaith Award in 1999 and the Distinguished Civic Humanitarian Award in 2009.

> For the past forty years I have been holding a weekly *halaqa*[128] at my place for new Muslim sisters. It is really an educational support group based on interaction and discussion by all participants. It was for women converts who were not so well accepted, and the aim was to make them more comfortable with themselves as Muslim women and not just part of a cultural group. I am the facilitator. Over the years, some move on and others join. In September 2017, we had a *Halaqa* Reunion of more than a hundred women in Ottawa . . .
>
> We got the first wave of Somali refugees in the 1980s . . . They came in large numbers, and some of them were not refugees but came as independents—they have really survived very well as a community and took off on their own, and became very, very active. In fact there is a lesson to be learned here, because they were very independent. They knew how to get things done, and they've made a name for themselves. They became involved in politics—we have a minister [Hon Ahmed Hussen, Minister of Immigration, Refugees and Citizenship] . . . They were gung-ho and they helped each other as well, so I think that is a very good example that the rest of us didn't really pay attention to. We had already built the mosques so they could use that and they had that advantage and they went ahead . . .
>
> We have not moved on from concentrating on schools and education to become engaged citizens of our new home. We still have an immigrant mentality. We still do not see ourselves as full citizens with civic responsibilities. That is a very big part that is missing . . . We are still floundering. There is no direction. There is no strong focus to lead us. We have too many smaller organizations all repeating the same thing without emphasizing citizenship. As long as we don't do that, it is always going to be to our detriment because we are always going to be considered as immigrants . . .

It's civic responsibility that we need to emphasize. I used to do that on my own. I've always been involved because I come from a Western country and I was raised in that way . . . But now I feel that we have a critical mass, and it's encouraging to see that there is a younger generation going into politics and banking and other fields and not just having a narrow emphasis, insha'allah.

Khadija Haffajee died on September 17, 2020.

14. Montreal: Neither French Nor Catholic

IN THE LATE NINETEENTH AND EARLY TWENTIETH CENTURIES, when young Syrian-Lebanese Muslim men, and occasionally women, were heading for North America, the Province of Quebec seemed to have had no special pull for them. Some may have learned French in Lebanon, which might have made things easier in Quebec. It certainly has made it easier for the North Africans who came decades later, when knowledge of one of Canada's two official languages was a distinct aid to entry to Canada. Quebec's Muslim North African population swelled, as did its French-speaking North African Jewish population.

Professor Baha Abu-Laban's study, *An Olive Branch on the Family Tree*, made use of half a dozen types of research materials. These included a 1974 survey of Arabs living in Quebec and Ontario, where 90 percent of the population of this group was living.[129] That estimate is still roughly true. In 2001, some 39 percent of Canadian Arab immigrants lived in Quebec and 43 percent in Ontario. In 2016, 40.8 percent lived in Quebec and 40.2 percent in Ontario.[130] Abu-Laban found that about 70 percent of the respondents to his survey were Christians, the remaining 30 percent being Muslims, including Druze.[131]

It has been suggested that "the first Arab immigrant to Canada was Abraham Bounadere (Ibrahim Abu Nadir) from Zahley in Lebanon. He arrived in Montreal in 1882. By 1890, there were about fifty [Arab] immigrants in Quebec."[132]

A chapter by Sheila McDonough, "Muslims of Montreal" in *Muslim Communities in North America*,[133] indicates that at that time the population of about 50,000 Muslims in Montreal was "more or less evenly divided" between South Asians and Arabs. She writes:

Although a few Muslims from Syria and Lebanon came to Montreal before World War II, the community began to develop more rapidly in the early 1950s when a number of immigrants from South Asia and the Arab world, mainly professionals, began to arrive. The oldest mosque in the city, the Islamic Centre of Quebec (ICQ), dates back to 1958 . . . In the 1950s and 1960s the Pakistanis and other South Asians were the more numerous group and were active on the board of the ICQ and in other community affairs. More recently, because South Asians are normally English speaking, they have tended to go elsewhere in Canada, as Quebec has become more predominantly Francophone. During the 1970s and 1980s immigration from Lebanon and North Africa has increased significantly. These French-speaking Muslims usually find it easier to adapt to Quebec society than do those who speak only English . . . The second mosque built in the city is that owned by the Muslim Community of Quebec (MCQ), which dates from 1979.[134]

McDonough's brief sketch of the Montreal scene is borne out by my interviews with two South Asian professionals, who both moved to Ontario in later life.

Hamdani's 2015 *Canadian Muslims: A Statistical Review*, noted that Muslims in Quebec stood out from non-Muslim immigrant communities in their adoption of French. This was especially true of young girls.[135] Muslims in Quebec numbered only ten in 1901, but as in the case of Muslims across Canada, their numbers jumped—to 8,380 by 1971, to 12,115 by 1981,[136] to 44,930 in 1991, to 108,620 by 2001, and to 243,430 by the time of the time of the 2011 voluntary household survey.[137]

Among the handful of active pioneer Muslims in Montreal in the early 1950s were two Pakistanis. The first, Mumtaz Haque Rehman, became a distinguished civil engineer and a prime mover in the founding of the Muslim community in that city. In 2004, he wrote a very useful article, "The Story of Indo-Pakistani Muslim Community in Montreal, Quebec," for the Montreal Religious Sites Project.[138] I interviewed him in 2017.

I was born in colonial India in 1928, in a small town, Aminpur, in

the district of Lyallpur, now called Faisalabad [in Punjab, Pakistan]. My father and grandfathers worked generally in the forest and the irrigation departments of Punjab Province. My great-grandfather was a Sohal Rajput from Rajasthan, India, and had converted to Islam and moved from Rajasthan west to Gurdaspur District in Punjab. He was a forest ranger. His sons were all bureaucrats—nobody was in business. As far as I can remember, my father and mother were very practising Muslims. My maternal grandfather built a mosque in Dina Nagar in the Gurdaspur District, adjacent to his home, where he had settled.

I had a very good childhood. I was the youngest in a family of nine. I had five sisters and three brothers. My father was Fazal Rehman and my mother was Khadija, first cousin of my father . . .

While my father had died in January 1947, I had one brother in Multan district in West Punjab, later Pakistan. Since I was in the last year of a bachelor of arts program at Government College in Lyallpur, part of the University of Panjab in Lahore,[139] I finished my exams and joined my family in Multan, before Partition that summer. During the subsequent mutual atrocities of Partition, one of my uncles and his wife died because he trusted his Hindu friends would protect him, in vain, but another couple of uncles decided to leave in time to escape the mutual violence along the new border.

I completed my bachelor of science in civil engineering from the Punjab College of Engineering and Technology, Lahore, in 1950, and worked for the Public Works Department, Buildings and Roads Branch, for four years before coming to Canada.

My purpose in coming to Canada [in September 1954] was to get my graduate degree in engineering, but when I came here I had to support myself [in Toronto]. So I had to look for a job and was lucky that I was recognized as an Ontario professional engineer and I started working for the Department of Highways, which is now called the Ministry of Transportation and Communications. I started working there after the Thanksgiving weekend, October 1954. I was there for one year and worked on the design of Highway 401 and some under-passes. Later, an opportunity to work for the federal Department of Public Works came in September 1955 and I worked there for one

Mumtaz Rehman and wife Shamim with young marrieds Shehla and Izhar Mirza, Montreal, 1967. Photo courtesy of Izhar Mirza.

year, also in Toronto. Then the St Lawrence Seaway project started and they needed engineers so I applied and was accepted. That's why I moved to Montreal in 1956.

My wife, Shamim, and two sons, Nadeem and Naeem, had joined me in August 1955 in Toronto. The kids were three and one and a half years old.

In Toronto, Ali Tayyeb was the first Muslim family I met, and then there was a gentleman named Zakaria Malik. He was a businessman, and then I met your brother-in-law Saleem [Rauf], who was at the University of Toronto pursuing graduate work. We [Muslims] used to get together once in a while on some Fridays . . .

At that time Montreal was the largest city in Canada. I remember it still had streetcars going, and the Sun Life building in Dominion Square was the biggest building in the [British] Commonwealth. Montreal was a big city at that time and flourishing, and nobody asked if you knew French or not. We felt the people, the French Canadians, were very friendly, and at that time there were a lot of Britishers after the war and I had a lot of colleagues who were from Britain. Although I knew them as a colonial power in Pakistan, when you met them here, they were all very friendly and all that. The same was true in Toronto when I went to the highways department. They were good friends.

The Muslim community in Montreal consisted of two or three families only. Before I came to Montreal there was Mr Habibullah Khan. He was a chartered accountant from Britain and he was working at McGill University looking after the internal audit of all the funds the federal government gave to McGill. He was a man in his fifties and he had four sons and two daughters. After retirement, around 1970, he moved to Los Angeles. He passed away probably thirty years ago or so. He was in Montreal since 1955 and I arrived in Montreal in September 1956.

There were some other Muslim families. Mr Masoud was from Lebanon and owned a real-estate company. He was one of the founding members of Islamic Centre of Montreal. There were a number of students at McGill and University of Montreal. There were a number of medical doctors, getting training at McGill to get their FRCS [Fellow of the Royal College of Surgeons]. Two names come to mind, Jalal Shamsi and Akhter Rashid. Both were being trained as psychiatrists at McGill. Both are good friends. In 1961, Akhter Rashid and his wife, Fatima, left for New Brunswick, where he was offered a position and later went to the US. Jalal Shamsi accepted a position at Verdun Protestant Hospital and became a renowned specialist in adolescent psychiatry . . .

The Institute of Islamic Studies at McGill [founded in 1952] gave us their premises to hold our functions, Eid al-Fitr, Eid al-Adha, for our prayers. In the late 1950s, Professor Fazlur Rahman came there, and Dr Ismail Faruqi and Dr M Rasjidi from Indonesia, [they] were all teaching at the Institute. That was a good boost to our aspirations in Montreal, and both Fazlur Rahman and Dr Faruqi were presidents of our [initial] Islamic Centre of Montreal. Dr Faruqi, when he was president, [made an arrangement] with the United Church of Canada in the Town of Mount Royal, and they gave us their basement for holding our functions and meetings. That would have been about 1958–59. Dr Wilfred Cantwell Smith was still the director of the Institute of Islamic Studies.[140] Altogether we had not more than twenty people.

I joined McGill as a graduate student in civil engineering in 1958, graduating with a master of engineering degree in the spring of 1961.

I think we used to meet at Habibullah Khan's place. He was very hospitable and invited us and all the students from McGill and the University of Montreal . . . That's where the discussions about having a Muslim association started. In 1958 the Islamic Centre of Montreal came into being. We got it registered in that city. I was the secretary and Habibullah Khan was the president. To make it a real centre, we rented a small apartment very close to the McGill campus on Sherbrooke Street. Mostly, we would have a function every month and we would invite a guest speaker like Fazlur Rahman or Ismail Faruqi to come and talk about Islam.

When Dr Faruqi was the president of Islamic Centre of Montreal in 1961, a lot people started to know about our centre, but all the births and marriages had to be registered only in churches. There was no civil status for anybody [in a predominantly French Catholic province]; you had to get married in a church. So that's how we started thinking about it, and the need for recognition of Islam as a minority religion became paramount. So we consulted Mr James Robb, one of the lawyers of the Stikeman and Elliot group, where the premier of Quebec, Jean Lesage, used to be a partner. Mr Robb said that he knew Lesage very well and he suggested we could get some private member of the National Assembly to propose a private member's bill to give the Islamic Centre of Montreal a Muslim minority status so we could get our births and marriages done in the mosque. He [also] advised us that the name Islamic Centre of Montreal should be changed to the Islamic Centre of Quebec. By a vote in a special general meeting of the membership, the name was changed to the Islamic Centre of Quebec.

An application was made on behalf of our members in 1964 to the Quebec Legislature, and Bill 194 was approved in August 1965 by the Quebec Legislature,[141] granting ICQ civil status. There is a picture of us when we went to Quebec [City] to attend and be present at the provincial legislature [to answer] any questions. Passing of Bill 194 was a momentous landmark in the history of Muslims in Montreal. Roohi Kurdi was a Syrian Muslim who was appointed imam of ICQ.

Mumtaz Rehman, third from left, and Habibullah Khan, third from right, with group petitioning the Quebec National Assembly, 1965.
Photo courtesy of Mumtaz Rehman.

He maintained the register of births and marriages. Later, Moeen Ghauri remained imam of ICQ for many years.

For prayers, there was no distinction made between Sunnis and Shi'as, and the Ahmadis [also came] in the beginning. Then one of their elders, Mian Ataullah, came from Rawalpindi [in the mid-1960s]. He was an older person, and when he came we used to have . . . our prayers and iftars and the taraweeh prayers and all that at Habibullah Khan's place or at my place. He [Mian Ataullah] said he would only come to our iftar party if he could lead the prayer. That was the first time the distinction between us and the Ahmadis happened. We accommodated him for the sake of unity and we said he could lead the prayers. The Shi'as were also coming and no one made any objection of any sort. This was before we had the [ICQ] building and iftar was only held in people's homes. We didn't have any place.

Friday prayers were seldom held; that's why when Bill 194 was approved in 1965 we started thinking about buying a place. In 1967 we got an old building [for $25,000].[142] It was a sort of barrack for the army in the Second World War. It was in Ville St Laurent and it still exists there, the Islamic Centre of Quebec [at 2520 Laval Road]—the enlarged mosque is still there. After some renovations by our own people we opened the mosque in 1967. It was a total of fifteen hundred square feet. There was room for Friday prayers, but it was mostly used on Saturdays and Sundays when more people came. If there was one row of people for prayer it was considered to be a good day . . . [He thought fifty to one hundred Muslims arrived in the 1960–65 period].[143]

When we opened the mosque at 2520 Laval Road in Montreal, there was a Muslim family from South Africa. He was in business and had quite a bit of money so he donated the carpet for the floor. The mosque was only one storey high at that time. Now it has two or three storeys, but at that time when it opened in 1967 it had only one room, the prayer hall, and a washroom and some space at the back and we put a ping pong table there. There was a kitchen, but there was not much cooking done. On Sundays I think some of the Muslim families brought food and the students came and we had zuhr [midday] prayer and refreshments and a bit of food. Also, some Arab Muslims, who were in business, started to come to our mosque, and some Muslims also started to buy housing around and near the mosque. The mosque was now open for five daily prayers and salatul juma [Friday congregational prayers].

Because the Muslim population in Montreal had by then reached about five thousand, work began in 1971 on a plan to expand the Centre. The construction committee, chaired by Rehman, who was president in 1972 and 1973, completed the extension for $61,000, and it opened in January 1973. His long-time associate Syed Ali Husain succeeded him as president in 1974, followed by Izhar Mirza. However, as the Muslim population continued to increase in the 1970s, it was necessary to expand the Islamic Centre again in the 1980s, on adjacent vacant land, again with Rehman chairing the construction committee. This expansion included a place for *wudu* or ablutions, washrooms, rooms for bathing and storing the bodies of the deceased, a kitchen, office, and library.[144]

After the end of the restrictive system of immigration in 1967 more and more people from India and Pakistan started arriving in the early 1970s, now as families, which brought about an explosion in population. However, now differing Muslim groups began to contest for influence and power, as happened in other cities, leading to painful divisions and new groups. Rehman explained:

> The Tablighi Jamaat[145] [touring missionaries usually from South Asia] were always welcome and we told them they could come and say their prayers. We didn't want them staying in the mosque but they [insisted on staying there]. When one group came—after I was no longer president but still living in Montreal—the president, Yuksel Oran [1978] proposed to them that the mosque would rent some rooms in an apartment nearby for them to stay. What happened is that they started coming regularly and would stay and sleep at night in the mosque, and so when the children came to study Qur'an or anything on Sunday morning, they were still sleeping, and that smells, you know. He told them that we don't mind all the worshipping and everything but sleeping we won't allow. So that didn't go well with those people of the Tablighi Jamaat and with a lot of people in the community who sympathized with them. At first they would never become members of the Islamic Centre, but when the president said they couldn't stay, they organized themselves and eighty people became members! Then they passed a no-confidence motion against the executive of Yuksel Oran and the executive was ousted!
>
> The above event divided our Muslim community—the people having enlightened and balanced views on one side and the conservatives who sided with the Tablighi Jamaat on the other side. The conservatives took over control of the Centre [ICQ] and declared that the existing by-laws were "un-Islamic." The by-laws had served us for ten to twelve years, but they brought in new by-laws. I was not part of the new group which took over control. At that time, Dr Mohammed Amin, a psychiatrist, working for Verdun Protestant Hospital, organized another group and he called it the Muslim Community of Quebec [MCQ]. He asked me to join, and I was sympathetic and I agreed with him in principle, but being the founding member of the ICQ, I didn't want to join that [new] group. I participated in their activities but I was never a member of that MCQ group. He did very good work while the Islamic Centre was decadent at that time and he started classes for the students and he had an elementary Muslim

school. They bought a building in another part of the town, in Notre Dame de Grace, and their activities started there. He also organized a school that was recognized by the provincial government, and now it's a high school, very well recognized!

Another issue, Rehman said, was the arrival of the Muslim Students' Association:

> The MSA was a rising group and they were trying to control most centres, including the Muslim Society of Toronto's Jami Masjid. In Montreal it so happened that five or six members who were among the original founders of the Centre didn't like the MSA's policies, which were dictated by Saudi Arabia. It was Wahabism . . . Although I had two members of my executive committee who wanted MSA to have control of the mosque, somehow we didn't let them . . .
>
> Regarding the CMCC [Council of Muslim Communities of Canada], I was president [when] in the summer of 1973 a meeting was held in Montreal at the Islamic Centre of Quebec, in our mosque, to finalize the constitution and by-laws of the CMCC. [Muin] Muinuddin and people from other centres attended the meeting. I think that's how CMCC started. The membership was open to all Muslim associations across Canada and annual dues were a small amount—twenty-five dollars. It was active for a few years until the funding dried up. I think it doesn't exist except on paper. Another thing was that people like Muinuddin and Dr Şahin took control of it and every year there were elections held but the same people came back. They wouldn't allow anyone to come in and that's another reason the CMCC didn't succeed.

Regarding the need for a Muslim Cemetery in Montreal, Rehman recalled:

> ICQ had a committee consisting of Zafar Abbas, Dr M Ishaque and Iftikhar Sheikh, who were looking for land in towns within fifty miles of Montreal. Their efforts did not succeed, because the city council refused to allow us to have a cemetery there. It was definitely prejudice. In 1973, an all-faith cemetery on Sources Boulevard, Rideau

Memorial Gardens, offered us fifty plots to make a Muslim Section. These plots were grabbed up quickly. Later the efforts of the Cemetery Committee were more successful. An existing cemetery in Laval was for sale. ICQ made an offer after a resolution was passed to go ahead with buying that property. I think it was around 1991 or 1992 . . .

In early 1992, the Religious Committee headed by the existing imam, Moeen Ghauri, recommended hiring a new imam, Syed Fida Bokhari, who was educated in Medina University [Saudi Arabia]. It had been decided that the imam's should be a salaried position. Fida Bokhari did not have a good command of English but was very fluent in Arabic. I was not in favour of hiring an imam who could not deliver a khutba in English . . . [but still, Fida Bukhari was hired].

The cemetery was supposed to be for all Muslims. But in one of the khutbas, Bokhari stated that Shi'as are not even Muslims, so they should have their own cemetery, separate from Sunnis. This resulted in dividing the cemetery . . . I was president of ICQ then, and I resigned . . .

It must be remembered en passant that in January 2017, before this interview, six members of the mosque in Quebec City, the provincial capital, were shot to death and others wounded by a white extremist. Then, later in the year, after months of controversy the community was finally able to buy a plot of land for a Muslim cemetery. Within days, the car of the president of the mosque was destroyed by fire outside his home, and in the summer two suspects were arrested.

In April 2017, a proposal to start a Muslim cemetery for 6,400 graves in Saint-Apollinaire, thirty-five kilometres southwest of Quebec City, was already raising controversy there.[146] In July, the plan was rejected over the issue of zoning. Mayor Bernard Ouellet blamed the negative vote on hearsay; Mohamed Kesri of the Quebec centre said it amounted to discrimination.[147] Two years later, a proposal to set aside five hundred plots in nearby St Augustin de Desmaures, which was apparently set up without mosque involvement, ran into problems.[148]

Rehman:

The Shi'as had their imambarah [Shi'a prayer hall] . . . Some other masallas [prayer rooms] and mosques sprang up in different areas where newcomers made their homes. Some Arabs from Lebanon bought a big Jewish centre in Dollard des Ormeaux and it became the largest mosque in Montreal. By the turn of the century, there were some twenty mosques in Montreal. There is a new mosque on the south shore [of the St. Lawrence] in the Brossard area [and] that's the biggest one in the Montreal area, the Islamic Community Centre of South Shore[149] . . .

Another pioneer Pakistani immigrant to Montreal was Izhar Mirza. I interviewed him in 2017. He was involved with the founding of both the Islamic Centre of Quebec and the Muslim Community of Quebec.

I was born in Hyderabad, India, in 1936. My family originally came from Delhi, but we settled in Hyderabad because my father was employed there. He was working as a superintendent of land excise for Hyderabad, a semi-independent state [ruled by the Nizam] . . .

My childhood was spent there, but in 1948 [after Partition] I moved to Pakistan . . . Actually, in 1947 I had a really sad experience. My parents [Hameed Mirza and Zakri Begum] were killed while travelling by train from Delhi to Hyderabad after being at my elder brother's wedding in Delhi. The newly-married couple flew to Kashmir for their honeymoon and the rest of the groom's party—my parents and my brother Shameem [aged twelve][150] and I [ten]—left by train for Hyderabad. We reserved a compartment bearing our names. The train was stopped by Sikh rioters. Discovering that we were Muslims they shot my father and mother. At gunpoint they made us [Izhar and his brother] disembark from the train and follow them. Crossing a hot sun-baked field they took out their kirpans or swords and attacked both of us. The rioters left us bleeding on the ground from where we were rescued and taken to a hospital by the police.

This was in September 1947. It was a very traumatic experience. The government of Hyderabad sent a military plane with my eldest brother to bring us back to our home. After hospitalization, surgery, and convalescence, we recovered. Our uncle subsequently took both of us by boat from Bombay to Karachi, Pakistan, where my sister was living, just for a visit. But when Hyderabad was attacked and annexed by India in 1948, we never returned there.

I lived with my sister and went to school in Karachi, and subsequently the rest of my siblings from Hyderabad also moved to Pakistan. I spent my time in schooling with my brothers and sister and finished my high school. Then I went to Forman Christian College, an American institution in Lahore, and obtained a bachelor of arts degree with economics and political science as my majors.

Finishing that, I completed a master of arts degree in economics from the University of Punjab, Lahore. I was very keen to continue my studies abroad and applied for admission and financial support abroad. McGill was one of the schools I applied to. It accepted me and I was awarded a postgraduate Bronfman Fellowship. So I came to Montreal and joined McGill for a master's degree. I arrived a week before classes started in September 1959.

At that time the Muslim community was rather small, yet it was truly cosmopolitan. Most of the people were either students or professionals. Everyone knew practically everyone else. We used to celebrate Eid in the homes of people with families. Afterwards, when the numbers grew, we started to use the basement of the United Church of the Town of Mount Royal. The community consisted of sixty or seventy members. Though small in size, it had many eminent scholars among its members. Among them were Dr Fazlur Rahman and Dr Ismail Faruqi, and Dr Rasjidi, from Indonesia, and Naguib Al-Attas from Malaysia. It was a very, very nice group. We used to have regular Friday prayers at McGill University's Institute of Islamic Studies. I recollect that the best khutbas of my whole life were delivered by the scholars I mentioned before. It was amazing. I have never had that experience ever since.

I finished my MA in three years and they admitted me to the PhD program, but it remained incomplete.

I got a job in St Marys' University in Halifax, Nova Scotia in 1967, and I got married the same year, going to Pakistan before starting my job. My wife Shehla was related to me—she is my cousin's daughter. Her maiden name was Zaheer. On her mother's side she is related to me. At St Mary's university I taught economics as an assistant professor. Then I was helping out the local Muslim group, the Islamic Association of the Maritime Provinces. The number of Muslims living in that area was so small that from Halifax it served the needs of all the three Maritime provinces, Prince Edward Island, New Brunswick and Nova Scotia. In that setup I was working as the editor of the newsletter and also helping in other activities of the organization. That was my first voluntary work in serving the Muslim community. I was in Halifax for six years, from 1967 to 1973.

In '73 I moved back to Montreal where I got a job at Dawson College in the economics department, and I stayed there for thirty-six years. By 1973 the Muslim community had grown . . . but still it was meeting in the United Church; but [in 1967] the foundation stone of the Islamic Centre of Quebec [had been] laid . . . and I was very closely associated with it. Mr Mumtaz Rehman was its president and I was helping him out as secretary and as editor of its newsletter. Subsequently I was elected as the president after Mr Rehman and in that capacity I remained for at least two years, about 1975–76.

The population had grown in the past five or six years to two or three thousand. Most of them were from South Asia, but there were also from North Africa—Algeria, Tunisia, Morocco—sub-Saharan Africa, West Africa, and Lebanon and Syria . . . but later somehow the Centre was penetrated by conservative elements, the Tablighi Jamaat and their like . . . The president of the Islamic Centre of Quebec at the time was a Turkish gentleman, Yuksel Oran. This group of Tablighi Jamaat overthrew the executive by a vote of no-confidence because all the Tablighi Jamaat became members overnight. Some people who didn't like this met at my residence, and we decided to set up the Muslim Community of Quebec [MCQ]. The mainspring behind that was Dr Mohammed Amin, who was a psychiatrist in Montreal, and he became the president of that organization and I was elected as chairman of the board of directors.

The Muslim Community of Quebec decided to set up a school, probably about 1976 or 1977 . . . It was not mainly a South Asian group, while the Islamic Centre of Quebec at that time was predominantly South Asian. There were a lot of non-South Asian members in the MCQ, North Africans and Egyptians and many others, so it was more cosmopolitan in its orientation, and its location made it easier for those people to attend the programs. It was an organization that invited many lecturers and speakers . . . it had a talented staff and volunteers. Dr Amin personally contributed a lot of time and energy as well personal funds, and he was able to find a place [for the MCQ], a big building which was a former warehouse. It was converted into a mosque and a school. The medium of instruction in the school was French. The school and its administrators were South Asians while the teaching staff were mostly French-speaking Arabs from North Africa.

The two groups got along very well. Gradually with each year they added a higher grade to the school and eventually it became a full-fledged high school . . . with all the facilities, a gym and everything and it became a very well-respected and good institution. Recently, it was evaluated as among the best schools in Quebec . . .

Given their numbers in Canada, I feel Muslims don't have any clout in Canada because they have no central organization representing Muslim rights. The CMCC was effective in dealing with that, but after its decline it was never replaced by any organization or group which could claim to [speak] for all Muslims living in Canada. And what I find now is that most of the mosques are organized mostly on linguistic and ethnic lines and most people now identify themselves with very local causes, no more than that. There was [in the past] a very strong feeling of one community or ummah, but not any longer . . .

I think that we have to be very careful in asserting our identity in some ways right now, because of the climate that prevails in North America . . .

15. Truro and New Glasgow: Small Town Merchants

ACCORDING TO THE ISLAMIC ASSOCIATION OF NOVA SCOTIA website, the first Muslim organization in the Maritimes was founded in December 1966 when Dr U S Merdsoy became president of a small group of immigrant professionals, including himself and five medical doctors calling themselves the Islamic Association of the Maritime Provinces (IAMP). They included Dr Vahdettin Ketene, secretary,[151] and the directors Dr K S Haque, Dr Khalid Hameed, Dr Fazlur Rahman, and Dr Faiz A Choudhari. The Association had its official location in Merdsoy's home in Dartmouth, where they met for weekly prayers on the more practical day of Sunday. At the time, there were only a few dozen Muslims living in the area. As numbers grew, they started in 1969 to meet on Sunday afternoons in Halifax's St Andrew's United Church gymnasium, with about thirty in attendance.

The small association began to plan for a mosque. Two members bought a double lot in Dartmouth in February 1968, transferring ownership to the Islamic Association of Nova Scotia in March 1969. Having begun planning a bit too ambitiously, they later obtained a building permit for a scaled-down Dartmouth Mosque in July 1971 and the community held its first Eid prayers inside in late fall that year. As the decade continued, Dr Jamal Badawi, a professor at St Mary's University, became their first imam. They added to their prayer room in 1986 and also leased a school building in 1996 for what became the Maritime Muslim Academy in 1998–99.[152]

However, while the largely South Asian community of Dartmouth-Halifax were building an urban Muslim community, there already existed a Syrian Lebanese Muslim community of immigrants and their

Canadian-born descendants in rural Nova Scotia. Like the Syrian Lebanese out west, they too had survived initially by peddling; their stories of hardships followed by successes are similar. In 1944 they had established a small cemetery in Truro, Nova Scotia.

Dr Gordon Jasey was one of those pioneer Syrian Lebanese Muslims, having arrived in Nova Scotia at the age of one. He later moved to Windsor, Ontario, and his story appears in the Windsor section of this book. Another man who became one of the leading figures among Nova Scotia Muslims was Murray Joseph. He was born in Truro in August 1931; his parents gave him a "Canadian" name, though "Joseph" is the equivalent of the Arabic "Yusuf." He became a leading merchant in Truro and was heavily involved in Muslim affairs in the Maritimes. In 1986 he retired with his family to join the Lebanese Canadian Muslim community in London, Ontario. He died there in April 2010. I interviewed him in 1979, while he was still living in Truro.

> My mother's name was Melikie Hamid and my father's name was Said Rafia. My father immigrated to Canada from Bekaa [Valley], Syria, around 1904, and lived in a town called Mahone Bay [southwest of Halifax]. He stayed there for about six months and peddled. He later went to Liverpool [further south on the coast] and opened a retail clothing store . . .
>
> Chief Justice Laurie Hall, who was Bob Stanfield's father-in-law,[153] was in Liverpool when [my father] went there and said to him: "Listen, Said Rafia is too hard [to say]. A R Joseph is your name from now on" . . . and we all became Josephs . . .

For the record, the gravestone in the "Moslem Cemetery," Truro, states that he was Said Rofihe—apparently another spelling of Rafia—and was born in 1885 in Becca [Bekaa], Lebanon, and died in 1967. It also states that his wife, Melikie Hamid, was born in Damascus, Syria in 1888 and died in 1968. A newspaper clipping of September 2, 2015, probably from Truro, explains that he "became Abraham Robert (A R) Joseph and with the help of his wife established several businesses in Truro and raised six sons."

"Moslem Cemetery," founded in Truro, Nova Scotia, in 1944.

Murray Joseph:

> There are many stories relating to the peddlers. In those days all peddlers were "Turks." They were from the Ottoman Empire and on the side of the Kaiser [in the First World War]. They had a reputation in Canada and it was said that they would eat children!
>
> One time, during winter, my father and his cousin were peddling and they knocked at a house and no one would let them in. They were freezing and my father decided he would have to do something. He knocked again and when they answered, he asked: "What is that building over there?" The man answered: "That's our church." My father took out a match and said: "I'm going to set it on fire," and the man said: "No, no, come in and have a cup of coffee. Stay, I want

to talk to you." They stayed, the people fed and looked after them and the next day they bought [some items] from them. Of course my father had no intention of setting fire to the church—they just wanted to get in from the cold . . .

Ibrahim Rafia, a cousin, was peddling and he went up to someone's door and asked if he could stay the night. The man said, "No, you should go across the road." He went across the road but that man answered "No, you can't spend the night here; you should go back across the road." By the time he got there, there was a man with a shotgun saying: "Don't you take another step."

This was not uncommon! We have had people who were killed while peddling. They have gone out peddling and were never seen again. In the old days I remember my father telling me stories about finding their bodies. They did have a hard time, they were robbed and beaten.

They also had a problem with the language. For example, they would be asked: "Did you have your dinner?" and they thought they said "Do you want your dinner?" They'd say "Yes," and they would wait and wait and there would be no food and they couldn't understand why. There were many nights they went hungry. They slept in fields and they starved rather than eat the wrong [non-halal] foods . . .

My father and mother [Melikie Hamid] were married in this country. They were both Muslims but didn't know one another. Someone told my father there was a Muslim girl in Springhill. By this time he had a store in Liverpool and he went to see her—you must remember there is no courtship [among traditional Muslims].

She had come here from Syria and she and a girlfriend had opened up a little business. The other woman was Salma Ibrahim. Salma had a family problem in the Middle East and she was divorced and immigrated here with her only daughter. She was older than my mother.

My mother was "promised" and was coming to the United States to marry her fiancé. When she arrived, she found her fiancé had taken a common-law wife, and things didn't work out between them so she was not allowed to enter the country, the United States, but she was allowed to enter Canada. She came to Carleton Place, Ontario, and from there went to Truro, Nova Scotia. There were a lot of Muslim men in Truro who [had come] from other areas to work at Stanfield's [the famous Truro clothing manufacturer] and in the mines . . . Many questions were asked, and some fellow said to them: "Listen why don't you come to Springhill? There's no one there and no one to bother you. You live your own lives and mind your own business."

Both these women were very depressed so they took off to a non-Muslim community in Springhill and opened up a little business, a small confectionery store.

Shortly after, my father wrote to her telling her he liked her, that they were both Muslims, and they should get acquainted. She didn't answer so he returned to Springhill and they became acquainted and were married shortly after that, about 1920, and she went to live with him in Liverpool.

I had five brothers.[154] We had a very strange life growing up. No matter what happened, we were different. We refused to learn the Arabic language. We wanted to be the same as everyone else. We objected to our heritage. When everyone else was going to [church] Sunday school, why couldn't we? [Our parents] weren't educated enough to be able to explain things to us, and we couldn't accept this, and we didn't. When we were with our own people, we found their love and spoke the language, so our childhood became very strange, very strange . . . We were a minority and we resisted . . .

Others from Syrian Lebanese families became Christians or married Christians, but not he:

I could have gone the same way. There were no teachers around. There were translations [of the Qur'an] but no one bothered to read them. I was going to marry a Catholic girl—it was very close—but something bothered me, so I made a trip to the Middle East . . . where I met my wife [Hayat Mansour] in the old country . . . She had been here in Canada, in Mulgrave, Nova Scotia, and her father passed away so she returned to the Middle East. Her mother had passed away earlier . . . Now, my father knew her family so one visited the other and I was a young man. I was twenty-nine years old and she was a young girl in her prime. I looked. I was interested. The families agreed and

we were married. There was no courting. I knew certain things and I
went along with it and we were married [in 1960].

In 1986, about six years after I interviewed him, Murray Joseph moved
with his wife and children from Truro to the much larger Muslim community of London, Ontario. According to his son, Faisal B Joseph, a law
partner with Lerners LLP, in London, his father became the president
of the Islamic Association of the Maritime Provinces in the early 1980s
and helped build the first mosque in Bible Hill, Nova Scotia, outside
Truro, in the 1970s. It still stands there today, along with the Moslem
Cemetery, which was the first cemetery east of Montreal and was begun
in 1944. Further, Faisal Joseph said that his father was very involved in
the Islamic community nationally and internationally and encouraged
him to become the president of the Association of London Muslims
and president of the Islamic Centre there as well. With his father's help
Faisal Joseph created one of the largest Islamic cemeteries in Canada in
London, which has a Muslim population of thirty-five thousand.

Murray Joseph and his wife Hayat had four children: daughter Melikie
Joseph, now a social worker with the Office of the Children's Lawyer,
Ontario; son Faisal; son Gehad Joseph, a former Jaguar dealership general manager; and daughter Nadia, a former Royal Bank official, all
residing in London.

According to the family of my second Nova Scotian interviewee (2019),
Wayne Murray Harris, he and his father were very good friends of
Murray Joseph. Wayne Harris was born on July 2, 1941, in New
Glasgow, Nova Scotia, the youngest of five children. His Arabic name
was Radwain [Radwan], but Wayne was easier. The addition of Murray
to his and other subsequent-generations male names seems attributable
to his father's second name, Merhi.

Unfortunately, past dates and events have presented challenges to
family memories and hence to this story. According to a 1997 Lebanese
attestation, Wayne Harris's father was Hussein Merhi and was born in
1884[155] in the small village of Mdoukha, in the Bekaa Valley. His father
was listed as just Merhi, and his mother as Nayefe Merhi, but no more

detail was given about either. The document then states that the future George Harris was "Moslem Sunni, married . . . immigrant to Canada in 1901."

According to family tradition, George Harris's brother Mohamed, later Fred, arrived first, followed in 1901 by George Harris, aged seventeen, and brother Mohmood, later John; they were all given Scottish names.

In our 2019 interview, Wayne Harris recalled, "I understand my father came [to Nova Scotia] in 1907 or 1908, and he eventually came to Pictou County, and I think he went on the road peddling. They [presumably he and his brothers] walked and they went to different houses in the country and they sold shirts and suitcases and all that stuff."

In about 1918, having made a success of himself as a peddler, George Harris opened a store in Westville. An undated family photo of a paper shopping bag announces: GEORGE HARRIS, Dry Goods, Ladies' & Gent's Furnishings, Boots & Shoes. WESTVILLE, NS, Phone 6-5106. George lived above his store.

George returned to the Middle East in 1932. Sometime during that trip he made the Islamic pilgrimage to Mecca, and so was thereafter known among his community as Hajj Hussein Merhi.

Wayne Harris:

> The first thing George did for his hometown was to pipe water from a hill in the mountains all the way down to the main street of Mdoukha . . . As a result, there was always a well there and there was always running water. They had never had water in the village before.[156]
>
> While he was there, the mayor came and introduced him to my [future] mother, Khanom Zrein [born in 1910 in the Bekaa Valley city of Zahle]. My father was twenty-five years older than my mother and they got married there in 1935 . . .
>
> In 1935 [or 1936], my father came back from Lebanon on the boat to Montreal with my mother. They came to Westville, where my father had a general clothing store. My father changed his name to a Scottish name, George Harris, because he was in the retail business

and it was so much easier to say "Harris" than "Merhi."[157] It was a Canadian name in a Canadian town. Then my mother and father had five children, and I was the youngest [born in 1941] . . .

Also, in 1944, my father's cousin [Murray Harris] passed away and there was no place to bury him so my father bought this land [near Truro] and started a cemetery called the Syrian Cemetery . . . So they had the mosque [later, in 1971] and they had the cemetery and until today the cemetery is registered under George Harris's name . . . [158]

Meanwhile, George Harris and his wife Khanom ran the clothing business and raised their family until he passed away in 1954 at the age of seventy, if the 1884 birth date is correct. Wayne Harris said that after his father's death, his mother refurbished the store.

She remodelled it, and she carried on the clothing business . . . I stayed with my mother and I ran a little furniture store next to my mother's clothing store . . .

Then when I was around twenty-one, I got married to a girl from New Glasgow in 1965. She was a nurse, Fran White. My mother remained upstairs, and downstairs she had the clothing store, and I was alongside of her for five or six years . . . My mother lived to be one hundred and two.

Wayne Harris moved to New Glasgow in 1970, where he owned two stores, including a large one selling furniture. He also went into real estate. He and his wife Fran had four kids, two boys and two girls. Each boy carries the middle name Murray.[159] Fran died in 2010, at the age of sixty-eight.

Wayne's mother, Khanom Harris, was a remarkable woman. According to her obituary of February 28, 2011,

After her husband's death in 1954, she continued to operate her store until 1990. A resident of Main Street, Westville, until her passing, she had nothing but warm feelings for the town and its people. She lived an amazing life full of love, charity, and good health. Mrs Harris, as she was known to all, a matriarch, was also [a] very active and engaged member of the Muslim community and supportive of all Islamic mosques. She had a strong faith and believed it was God's will that her time had come. 'To Allah do we belong and to Him we return' . . .

Following her Islamic faith, her funeral took place Tuesday, March 1 [2011], at the Islamic Mosque, Bible Hill, followed by her burial in the Muslim Cemetery [side by side in Truro].[160]

Wayne Harris:

The reason why people go to London is that there is a mosque there, and for a lot of people from Lebanon their village is all in London, so they want to go where the community is. In Pictou County we don't have the community. We don't have the people, we don't have the mosque . . . There was no mosque in New Glasgow [in 1970] . . . There was a mosque in Truro and it was built by the Kadrays and the Josephs and the other Lebanese people around there, who donated and built a mosque [in 1971] . . .

Now, in 2019, in Trenton [north of New Glasgow] we have a new mosque open. We bought a Catholic church and we now have thirty families. They are from Syria, Lebanon, Pakistan, Egypt, and different parts. Instead of travelling to Halifax or Truro we have our mosque here . . . Now the Canadian government has brought in seven or eight [Syrian refugee] families into Pictou County. People come from nearby, forty miles away, from Antigonish, from down east, from New Glasgow, to this mosque . . .

I think my father would have been more than happy to see people come in from elsewhere into Pictou County. You must remember that all these people who come in are doctors, professionals, and the reason why is that the government wants them to immigrate, hoping their kids would become good citizens and entrepreneurs. Without immigration, Canada will not grow. Without foreigners, we really wouldn't have much of a Canada. Who else builds things? . . .

[By way of remembering the early pioneers] You can mention the Mansours—Tofick Mansour and family—who resided in Pictou and ran a clothing store. They moved into Pictou and they raised a family of six or seven. Then you can mention that down towards the east

end of Cape Breton there was the Hassan family who were a lovely
family and had five or six children, and the Mansour family who lived
down in Havre Boucher and Mulgrave, and the Kondors who lived
in Monastery . . . [A A Mansour from Mulgrave] had three sons and
a couple of daughters who peddled on the road, Moodie, Chadi and
Ritchie. Then there was the Hammoud family who ran a clothing
store . . .

They're all history now. All A R Joseph's children, all are dead now.

It seems appropriate here, ending a chapter about Arab Muslims with
the names Abraham Robert Joseph, Murray Joseph, Said Jasey, Joseph
Edwards, George Harris, and Wayne Harris, to quote a poem "Dying
with the Wrong Name" by Sam Hamod:

> These men died with the wrong names,
> Na'im Jazeeny from the beautiful valley of
> Jezzine, died as Nephew Sam,
> Sine Hussein died without relatives, and
> because they cut away his last name
> at Ellis Island, there was no way to trace
> him back even to Lebanon . . . [161]

Hamod, an award-winning poet, hails from Gary, Indiana. His collection
Dying with the Wrong Name (1980) was nominated for the Pulitzer Prize.

16. St John's: Almost Alone on the Rock

DAOOD HAMDANI ARRIVED IN NEWFOUNDLAND IN 1965, AFTER receiving a doctorate in economics in Nashville, Tennessee. He was at Memorial University for eighteen months before moving to Kingston, Toronto, and finally Ottawa.

I was born in colonial India in the city of Ferozepur in 1939. In 1947, the British divided the sub-continent into two countries, India and Pakistan, along religious lines. This led to one of the greatest humanitarian tragedies with an estimated one million people massacred and ten million more uprooted from their homes. My family was one of them. Ferozepur was in East Punjab, which is in India, and Pakistan had West Punjab.

My father was a professor in Ferozepur at a college of the University of Punjab. He taught Persian and Arabic. When Partition came, Ferozepur was a part of the new India, and that meant that the Muslims in Ferozepur had to leave. Minutes before our house was attacked by mobs of Sikhs and Hindus a military officer, who had been a student of my father, whisked us away in a military truck to a refugee camp on the outskirts of Ferozepur. We were very lucky. The camp had no facilities whatsoever. It was just on open ground fenced by barbed wire. There was no food and there was only one tap for drinking water for the hundreds of people who were in the camp and we had to line up for it.

We stayed in the camp for two days and then a train came that was going to Pakistan and so we boarded that train and it arrived in Pakistani territory. It was very scary. When the army officer took us from our home to the camp I was seven or eight years old and I could see dead bodies lying in the streets and the marauding mobs of murderers shouting battle cries and people screaming in pain . . .

We ended up in a very small town called Jhang. It did have a college and school and I did my high school education in Islamia High School, and then I did my undergraduate studies at Government College, Jhang. I graduated with honours in economics from the University of Punjab, in 1960. In 1962, I received a scholarship offer from Vanderbilt University in Nashville, Tennessee, to do graduate work in economics. I spent three years there and I got my doctorate in economics in 1965, and that's when I came to Canada . . .

I came to Memorial University in St Johns, because I had a job offer there . . . [There were only two other Muslims there.]

After eighteen months I left Memorial and went to Kingston, to Queen's University, in 1966, and I worked as a research fellow at their Institute for Public Policy. There were some Muslims there in the university . . . Some Fridays we would get together and say our congregational prayers with Dr Moustafa Fahmy, and a number of times with Hussain Al-Shahristani, then an Iraqi graduate student at the University of Toronto [later an Iraqi government minister]. He came to Kingston a number of times and we got together with him . . .

In 1967 I went to Toronto as a teaching fellow at the University of Toronto . . . We used to go for Friday prayers on Sundays at St Mary's Church Parish Hall with Muin Muinuddin and Dr Fuad Şahin, probably an initial location used by the Islamic Foundation group.

I stayed in Toronto for six years until 1973, when I came to Ottawa. I have been in Ottawa since then. I was the first Muslim to work for the Department of Finance and held various important portfolios, including [that of] environment and natural resources; eventually I [was involved with] science and technology at Statistics Canada . . . I worked on conceptualizing and measuring the contribution of intellectual property such as the commercial value of a copyright, a patent, a trademark, [etc.] I became the special advisor on science and economy. Because of my pioneering work, I was also named by the US National Science Foundation to its blue-ribbon advisory panel on the measurement of innovation.

Asked how he became an expert on Muslim statistics and trends in Canada, he said he was not involved with the Muslim community as such but needed to answer questions that were posed to him.

> When in Canada the demonization of Muslims began with Saudi Arabia's King Faisal imposing the oil embargo in 1973, and later on in 1979 with the Islamic revolution in Iran, the Toronto School of Theology and the Catholics for Social Change held a week-long seminar. They wanted someone from the Muslim community to come there and take a one-day seminar. They asked me and . . . I reluctantly agreed. They grilled me very well. I didn't know much because there was no material on Muslims in Canada at the time. [However,] the talk that I gave was published in 1992 in a book commissioned for the US State Department. Its title was *Muslims and Christian Life in Canada.*
>
> After the seminar, I became curious. I used to work on science and technology during the daytime and in the evening I used to search for my Canadian Muslim "ancestors": Who they were, why they came, where they came from. Now at that time Statistics Canada had just released detailed profiles of families in the [1871] census.—I think they release them ninety years or a hundred years after the census. I went to the National Archives here in Ottawa and with the help of the librarian there we located the general geographical area where they were. Then I sat down with the microfiches and went [over them] one-by-one . . . [until] I came upon a family of "Mahometans." Now I wanted to make sure I was reading it right because the microfiches were not very clear. So I got two or three of the library staff and we took a magnifying glass and I asked them each separately to read that word. They all came up with "Mahometans," so I said "that's it." I counted them [the number in the family] and they were thirteen people, and so that's how my interest began.
>
> I retired in 2004, but Statistics Canada called me back and I worked for six years . . . to further advance the work in science and technology statistics . . . I was able to write about Muslims, do interviews, write in newspapers. I knew a columnist on the *Ottawa Citizen,* Bob Harvey, and he often used to call me to get information. I said to him, "I can talk about Muslims but not about Islam, because I don't

consider myself a knowledgeable person." In 2004, the year I retired, he did a full-page article on Muslims, "A Community in Change," or something like that, and there was a huge picture of me.

I think we should have paid more attention to community building and to introducing ourselves to the broader Canadian society. Even as we mark the 168th anniversary of our settlement in Canada, we are the most misunderstood faith community. We are seen as new immigrants unable or unwilling to integrate.

Some changes are beginning to occur with the emergence of forward-looking organizations. Many Muslims, who are predominantly economic migrants, were too busy earning a living to focus on what role they wanted to play in the new homeland. Discourses on integration were then being directed by religious organizations, which were preoccupied with preserving religious and cultural traditions. These new organization are moving Muslims from the sidelines to the mainstream of Canadian society.

There is also a generational shift under way. In 1991, 22 percent of Muslims were born in Canada. In 2001, they increased to 24 percent,

Economist and statistician Daood Hamdani. Photo courtesy of *Ottawa Citizen*.

but in 2011 they jumped to 28 percent. The Canadian-born Muslims are not as fixated on ethnicity and cultural traditions as their immigrant parents.

Also, young women are redefining their role in society. In choosing their pathway to education they have their eyes clearly set on the labour market. A higher percentage is entering community colleges to get technical training. In universities, they are opting for science, technology, engineering, and mathematics, in contrast to their immigrant mothers and grandmothers who majored in humanities because their patriarchal societies deemed those subjects fit for women . . . I should mention that in much of my work I am grateful to the Canadian Council of Women, particularly to Alia Hogben, for their financial support.

Daood Hamdani died on November 24, 2019, at the age of eighty. He was predeceased by his wife Oliveria (née Quiaoit) and survived by his son Al (Tobi) and two grandchildren.

Conclusions

IT IS TIME NOW TO REFLECT ON THE EXPERIENCES OF MUSLIMS IN Canada over time, from the early pioneers from Greater Syria (Lebanon) who traversed the west on horse buggy, motor car, and dog sleigh to the urban settlers from around the world and their descendents. Pioneer lives matter, because history matters, not only that of Canadian Muslims but also that of Canada. Considering differences in ethnicities, languages, cultures, and histories to what degree do Muslims present a unity? Is it possible and is it even desirable or does it simply add to a divisiveness in the Canadian multicultural reality and a dangerous confusion in the minds of Muslim youth? How much is Islam now part of modern Canada's religious makeup?

Muslim Pioneers

The earliest Muslim pioneers, mostly young and unmarried Lebanese men from what was known as Greater Syria, arrived in North America at the Canadian ports of Halifax and Montreal and in the United States at New York City. They, like their Christian counterparts, left their homes to avoid a dangerous and miserable life as young Ottoman conscripts and to escape their economic hardships.

Conscription began in the Ottoman Empire in the 1440s and had been ongoing thereafter. Wars in Europe and the Middle East in the late nineteenth and twentieth centuries notoriously used up young men's lives. Louis de Bernieres's novel, *Birds Without Wings*, about a mixed Turkish and Greek village in the times of the Balkan Wars and the Great War, poignantly conveys this reality for the area:

> A woman wailed somewhere out in the streets, and those who were awake shuddered. There had been a time when everyone had believed that the wailing woman was a ghost, but eventually it had transpired that it was just someone who had lost all her sons in the wars that the imperilled empire had been fighting year upon year. So many conscripted sons had been lost that at night the town consented to let the maddened woman wail for all of them. These days there were not enough men to bring in the harvest or build the houses, there were not enough men to make bridegrooms, no one to make the music for the weddings, and no one to father the babies for sacrifice in future wars.[162]

The immigrants' stories that I heard in western Canada frequently referred to the Ottoman draft. Eddy Saddy described his father as "probably one of the original draft dodgers . . . My father left the village from one end as the recruiters were coming into the village from the other end." Mickey Awid was told by his father, Ahmed or Ed Awid, that Ed left Lebanon because young Arabs were being conscripted into the Turkish army at the age of eighteen. As a result, many parents falsified their sons' records so that they appeared younger than the required age and then let them emigrate.

Economic and political instability were as important in driving away young men to set off for the New World to make money. According to Abu-Laban, "The economic conditions of the Syrian masses were miserable. The economy of the Lebanon, that is, the mountainous region of modern Lebanon, in particular, was hard hit by the decline of the silk industry, low agricultural productivity, and increasing population pressure."[163] Initially, however, most Muslim arrivals, as Hanny Hassan said, "didn't really see Canada as an ultimate destination." For this reason, they were reluctant to bring women to an unknown place. However, by the 1930s and 1940s many had decided to settle down and start building a community. I was told numerous stories of men who made money and returned to their homeland, usually Lebanon but also Albania, and got married and sailed back to Canada to raise families.

Mohammed Mustapha Fyith arrived in 1927, following in his father's successful footsteps in Canada and the United States. In 1919, his father had returned home to stay, having made $25,000, a considerable sum at the time. While his father had been in America, Mohammed Fyith had grown up poor in Lebanon. Going to Canada with his father's encouragement, he worked hard on a farm during his first year to earn his naturalization during the Depression. Hearing that there was big money in furs, he had the bad fortune to capture a skunk and (understandably) gave up that plan. Thereafter, he worked at peddling goods in the bitter northern cold, eventually opening a store and starting a mink ranch.

The Punjabi Muslims in British Columbia's timber industry also came for economic reasons, but with apparently no intention of returning to their homelands.

These poor early immigrants tended to be uneducated rather than well schooled and variously religiously inclined. Initially they were not interested in adding minarets to the skyline of the Canadian semiwilderness, leaving that thought for later, if they decided on settling. Money was the object of their individual struggles, not mosques; neither were cemeteries an objective, as they didn't expect to die here.

In contrast, starting the 1960s, the generally more educated Muslim immigrants, mainly English-speaking South Asians, came seeking better economic futures than were available in their homelands. Still later, today thousands of immigrants, including Muslims, continue to leave the Middle East, Africa, and South Asia to get to Europe and North America, for better opportunities. Others arrive having escaped the ravages of war. Thousands fled the troubles in Somalia, and more thousands fled the Iraqi invasion and the civil war in Syria. Some 25,000 Syrian refugees, privately and government sponsored, were welcomed in Canada during the period 2015-16.

Reception by Immigration Authorities

The immigration officials that the early Muslim immigrants encountered varied in sympathy and willingness to deal with strangers at the gates. One of the early Syrian Lebanese in Canada, Alex Hamilton, left his home in 1905 when he was twelve and arrived in Marseille in a party of fifteen with his uncle. The Canadian officials, he said, didn't like people from the Middle East and turned back all but three of them, saying their eyesight wasn't good enough for them to go to Canada. Syrian-Lebanese Mohammed Mustapha [later Mike] Fyith too recalled being screened by an official in France, perhaps also in Marseille. He was supposed to be able to read but couldn't make out a sign saying "Open the door." In his case, the official was kind: "I didn't even know how to read it [but] he was a good man."

In 1966, Fijian Indian Usman Ali was met by an official at Vancouver airport who told him that a government office he needed to visit would be closed next day for a holiday in honour of his arrival—a joke, because it was Labour Day! That kind of levity was certainly much to be preferred in the case of the hundreds of Indian migrants on the *Komagata Maru* who arrived in Vancouver in 1914, only to be denied entrance on the grounds that they had not sailed straight from their port of departure.

Jewish immigrants, perhaps because they arrived in larger numbers, suffered extensive anti-Semitism. In an infamous incident in 1933, known as the Christie Pits Riot, an anti-Semitic mob of pro-Nazis in Toronto rioted to protest the use of Toronto recreation facilities by Jews. The year 1939 saw perhaps the most shameful acts of discrimination in the annals of Canadian immigration: the turning away of MS *St Louis*, carrying 908 Jewish refugees from Europe. Of the passengers who were then relanded in Europe, 254 died in Nazi death camps.

Through the 1930s and 1940s these same sentiments limited Jewish immigration to about 5,000 per year. It was not until late in the 1940s that about 40,000 Holocaust survivors were admitted to Canada.[164]

Then there was the question of their names, which seemed unpronounceable to locals. Many early immigrants of non-Anglo Saxon backgrounds, including Muslims, had their names changed by immigration officials who couldn't or didn't want to make the effort to understand or record them. Said Mohammed Hejazi's last name was changed by an immigration official to Jasey. Alex Hamilton was asked to call himself Hamilton, because, "Then everybody can spell your name."

Sometimes the motivation was well-meaning, in the belief that immigrants would "fit in" better without exotic names. Said Rafia in Liverpool, Nova Scotia, was advised by Chief Justice Laurie Hall to change his name to A R Joseph. His close friend Hussein Merhi became George Harris. Of course, some Muslim immigrants took on names by choice, rather than having them officially imposed. Mary Hafeeza Ahmet of Toronto recalled from her childhood in Windsor that Muslims started acquiring somewhat anglicized names like Jim Walker, Ali Joseph, Frank and Harry Egypt, and Charlie Boose in an effort to obtain jobs. Others embraced nicknames.

Post-1950s immigrants, who included South Asian Muslims, did not feel this pressure. Times had changed; they were more educated and came from assertive independent nations; and Canadian racism could not be seen internationally to be so overt. Some, of course, took on nicknames, such as Moe, Mike, and Al, though their legal names remained the same.

Admission into Canada

In the earlier period, admission to Canada as a landed immigrant was the first step; naturalization—or acquiring citizenship—was the next. But many lived on in Canada without ever being naturalized, as this was not mandatory.[165]

Naturalization for the early immigrants usually required a year of useful nation-building work on farms, in the mines, or in the forests. Said Jasey worked for a year on a farm before becoming a naturalized Canadian. Joseph Edwards (Abdul Kareem Al-Kadri) and his brother (Mohammed Abdul Jalil Al-Kadri) had immigrated before the First World War and both worked in the Cape Breton coal mines for a year.

After the upheavals of the Second World War, Canada under Prime Minister W L Mackenzie King cautiously opened its gates between 1947 and 1953 to "displaced persons," the somewhat disdained "DPs," to help in the country's postwar growth. This immigration was allowed as long as it did not "make a fundamental alteration of the character of the nation"—meaning non-Europeans[166] were discouraged. Canadian officials toured refugee camps in places like Italy looking for young, able-bodied men to sign manual labour contracts that, once completed, resulted in the granting of landed immigrant status.[167] Bosnian Hassan Karachi escaped from fighting in Tito's Yugoslavia to Italy where he enrolled at a university; learning that Canada was looking for young men to work on farms, he signed up and was sent to a farm near Carleton Place in 1949 for a year. Albanian Rizvan Banka, who had also escaped to Italy, similarly encountered a Canadian mission that recruited him to work as a woodcutter.

Initial Reception

In the late nineteenth and early twentieth century there was some suspicion of Muslims, who were viewed as "Turks," because of their Ottoman Empire origins; some were even nicknamed "Turk." Baha Abu-Laban, in his book *An Olive Branch on the Family Tree*, cites some particularly negative comments from noted Canadians about the Arabs, then called Syrians.

The detractors included government officials. The superintendent of immigration in Ottawa, William Duncan Scott, who was in charge of immigration from 1903 to 1919, maintained that the Ottoman immigrants of his time—who included Christians—tended to be financially successful but lacked "a desire to assimilate," often suffered from eye diseases, and were largely urbanites, running stores to sell "goods of Eastern manufacture." They were generally seen as deceitful and habitual liars, tended to have "miserable physique[s] with infectious diseases," and were "unsanitary" and a "health menace."[168] Those who toiled in the countryside peddling small goods were often denied a place to sleep and spent the night outside even in the depth of winter in the north. Some peddlers were robbed and beaten, and some were never seen again.

The federal government was equally or more unwelcoming to people they considered "Asians." They were required to show they had $200 in hand on arrival and were not allowed, as were Europeans, to sponsor the same classes of relatives.[169]

Even Muslims born in Canada could be made to feel alien or inferior: by being called names, by a refusal to say or accept their names, by being stared at. Those from colonial South Asia had already experienced racial abuse and feelings of inferiority back home, which contributed to their discomfort in the predominantly white society to which they had come.

But there are decent people everywhere. Some Muslim pioneers recalled positive experiences. For example, Ernest Abas's parents were received kindly by their rural neighbours when they arrived in Hodgson, Manitoba, in 1912. Their religious difference was known but generally accepted by the Christian majority. In other cases, though later, Muslims were given church spaces to say their prayers. In Ottawa in the early 1960s, a Lebanese Christian family gave the first big $500 to the fledgling Muslims who were forming a group and who would go on to build the mosque there. Some men married Christian women who became Muslims. When Dr Fuad Şahin, from Turkey, worked at Kingston's Hotel Dieu Hospital in the 1950s, the nuns took pains to see that he received the food he allowed himself to eat as a Muslim and kept his meals separate from those of the other doctors. For him, this was Lester B Pearson's Canada.

By the 1960s, when Imtiaz Azhar arrived in Kingston from Pakistan, he experienced "zero racism." Neim Sali, the Albanian-born Toronto restaurateur, who, like the early Syrian-Lebanese, made money and went back home to marry, became a real booster of the friendliness of Canadians who accepted them as people and not as a religious group. "I have no complaints about Canada, my beautiful heaven," he said.

Following the fateful destruction of the World Trade Center complex in New York and other coordinated attacks elsewhere in the United States on September 11, 2001, the climate of acceptance changed. All Canadian Muslims fell under a cloud of suspicion and hatred and felt the need to be fearful. The terrorist actions worldwide of al-Qaeda, al-Shabab, the Islamic State, and Boko Haram have only worsened conditions at home for Muslims, further exacerbated by troubles in the wider Middle East, in countries ranging from Libya to Afghanistan and beyond. Canadian Muslims going about their ordinary lives as citizens have been subjects of extremist violence, vilification (sometimes by government ministers), caricatures, discrimination, and public displays of hatred in instances such as name-calling and hijab-snatching. This hostility was enhanced by the rhetoric accompanying the federal Conservative and provincial Quebec governments' attempts to bring about legislation against traditional Muslim female attire (niqab and hijab). It was further enhanced by the rhetoric and actions of US President Donald Trump, who was elected in 2016. On the other hand, the Muslims have produced extremist youth and preachers—especially in Britain and Europe but also to a very small degree in Canada—in response, attracted by the rhetoric especially of al-Qaeda and the Islamic State.

Skills and Education

A crucial aspect of acceptance in a new country is the ability to find and hold a job, ideally in the new immigrant's field of pre-arrival experience and range of talents and skills. The majority of immigrants eventually find work, but not always in their chosen career. The number of well-educated Muslim taxi drivers one meets in the big cities shows that starting at the bottom is still a near-inevitable pattern of immigrant experience, just as peddling was for the earlier generations of Syrian-Lebanese. The points system for immigration was supposed to encourage trained people with some language skills to come here, whatever their national or ethnic backgrounds. That system has worked in some cases and not in others. A chronic problem has been the recognition of immigrants' qualifications, which tend to be discounted unless further training, which often lasts years, is completed in Canada. This has resulted in, for example, doctors running delivery for courier companies, and judges becoming taxi drivers.

After the de-racialization of Canadian immigration laws in the later 1960s, South Asians began to exceed Arabs in numbers of Muslims; they were now, on the whole, a more educated group. Like the Arabs before them, these young men usually arrived without wives. They often came as university students and degree-holders, especially in engineering, and were able to find work quite easily, some becoming eminent in their professions. Other South Asian Muslim immigrants, the Ismailis, Ithnasheris, Bohras, and Sunnis, arrived from East and South Africa;

brought up in the British system of education and fluent in English, they also adapted quickly to life in Canada. The present mayor of Calgary and the Lieutenant Governor of Alberta are from such a background. These examples also show how much Canada has changed since the arrival of the early Arab pioneers.

Marriages

For many of the early Muslim immigrants who were single men, marriage had to wait until they had amassed a suitable amount of money. They then returned home and brought back a much younger wife. For example, Ali Hamdon, when already an established trader in the North, in 1923 went back to Lebanon and married young Hilwie Hamdon. Her marriage to a man she had never seen was arranged when she was seventeen and he forty-one.

For an insight into just how heartbreaking and complex, if sometimes eventually happy enough, the lives and marriages of young Lebanese girls and women were, Nada Awar Jarrar's novel *Somewhere, Home*[170] is well worth reading. Jarrar tells the stories of very young Druse women who were married to much older men making their fortunes in Brazil, Africa, or Australia and who then rarely, if ever, returned to Lebanon.

When a young immigrant man marries a Muslim or non-Muslim bride, his perhaps half-forgotten heritage can either fade completely, or come back with renewed vigour. The latter case can cause problems for family members as the children grow up and make their own ways into the world. Finding a bride, often a close relative from the homeland, was a success in most cases for pioneer Muslims since the women came from traditional backgrounds and sought a way to escape from their troubled homelands. Marrying a relative in an extended family was safe.

Some men found wives in Canada or the United States. Sied Ganam, also known as Sied Ameen Ganam Kadri, who left Lebanon in 1901, met and married Chelsea Pritchard, of Welsh and Irish parents, in South Dakota; she went on to become a committed Muslim. Ed Awid married a woman from Austria-Hungary in Brandon, Manitoba. She had arrived in Canada at the age of one. Much later, in Toronto in 1960, Khaliq Mohamed Khan, from Pakistan, married a young German immigrant, Brigitte Adamaitis, in a service conducted in the London mosque by an Albanian imam from Detroit. My Indian-born wife, Alia, and I, are another example of an interracial Muslim couple.

In modern times, however, the children of Muslims who arrived in the 1970s and later intermarry in significant numbers with or without a conversion of the spouse.

The Roles of Women

For the early pioneers in the west, in places as isolated as Lac La Biche, Alberta, as soon as the wives arrived, they set up Muslim homes; they taught the children the Qur'an, told stories, brought back traditional cuisine, and with other women established communities while accommodating to new ways. There can be little doubt to their foundational roles in Muslim communities.

Some of the women, however, went on to distinguish themselves in the larger society.

Edmonton's Hilwie Hamdon, born in Lebanon in 1905, played a crucial role in the construction of the Al Rashid Mosque in 1938. Her account in this volume speaks for itself. Lila Fahlman, born in Limerick, Saskatchewan, of Syrian and British-origined parents, was an educator and the founder of the Canadian Council of Muslim Women, and she led the cause to save the Al Rashid Mosque from demolition. Soraya Hafez has a public school named after her in Edmonton to commemorate her achievements, as do Hilwie Hamdon and Lila Fahlman. Ayshi Hassan, born in Lebanon, was an activist. Khanom Harris, born in 1910 in Lebanon, ran the family shop in New Glasgow, Nova Scotia, for thirty-six more years after her husband George's death, until she was ninety, a respected matriarch in the town.

But for some of the daughters of the pioneers, much of their initial knowledge about Islam was in the form of the strict limitations placed on them by their parents' ancestral faith and traditions of modesty. It

276 • MINARETS ON THE HORIZON

was rare for girls to be educated, let alone be allowed to attend university. Mary Hafeeza Ahmet, born in Quebec in 1906, recalled that her parents never allowed their children to have a social life, especially with non-Muslim Canadians, despite the initial shortage of available young Muslim men. Mary's marriage at eighteen was arranged: "We said 'hello' and that was all. We were married in the United Church in Windsor." Margaret Banka, born to Albanian Muslim parents, recalled that she was not allowed to date, wear makeup, or talk to boys, and had a strict curfew. Another Canadian-born woman of Albanian background, Fatime Shaben, grew up in Toronto in the late 1930s. She was wed in 1944 in a more-or-less arranged marriage to another Albanian, Sami Kerim. She had not received much Islamic education, but she felt limited by her strict upbringing in terms of clothing, social life, and education.

Today Muslim young women who have grown up in Canada tend to be, on the whole, educated. Many have gone on to become doctors and other professionals, journalists, and even novelists; they may practice their faith or not, cover their heads or not.

The Importance of Their Faith

The earliest pioneer Muslims, from Lebanon-Syria, often single young men alone on the roads peddling, did not practice their faith diligently in terms of regular prayers and fasting. The first priority was to survive. It was also not always easy being devout Muslims in a foreign country; for many, their knowledge of Islam and its practice was traditional and cultural, and sometimes very literal, rather than deeply ingrained by study, thought, and spirituality. Some may have thought they had left it behind. But once they had passed through a period of struggle for self-sufficiency, and settled to some degree, often after getting married, most did open the packs of the traditional Islam they brought from home. The stories told here frequently recount how some scattered individuals coalesced into associations and mosque-builders.

The Islamic faith of early immigrants and their children ranged from not being an issue to a matter of great importance. Some belonging to the second generation simply walked away into mainstream society. Others saw the need to go back to the faith and culture of their forefathers. Canadian-born Saleem Ganam's tale of only finding about Islam during the Depression by reading random books in a public library is surely of significance. Mickey Awid, born in Brandon, Manitoba, recalled that when he was young, going to the Edmonton mosque was not his favourite activity. But his faith crept up on him over time: "All of a sudden, it struck me one day that I was going to all these other churches when my first religion has got them all beat, so I started going back to the mosque when I was about twenty-five and I haven't stopped since then."

In time the building of mosques or Islamic centres and raising minarets became the focus of many Muslim communities across the country. The first mosque in Canada was built in Edmonton in 1938 by a handful of mainly Syrian-Lebanese Muslims. (It was not, however, the first in North America, the Americans taking the lead in 1929.)[171] The second Canadian mosque was started in London in 1957 and the third in Lac La Biche in 1958, both by Syrian-Lebanese Muslims. By this time Muslims had started arriving from South Asia. In 1961, the Muslim Society of Toronto opened an Islamic centre in a store-front property in Toronto's west end for Sunday prayers and meetings, and then opened the much larger Jami Mosque in a converted church in 1969. Then came the Islamic Centre of Quebec (ICQ); it had begun with a small apartment rented as an office in 1958 but moved to a former army barracks in Laval in 1965 and became a mosque.[172] It was expanded in 1973. The spin-off Muslim Community of Quebec (MCQ) built its mosque in Montreal in 1979. Meanwhile, the Islamic Association of the Maritime Provinces opened its mosque in Dartmouth in late 1971. Next, the Ottawa Muslim Association completed a purpose-built domed mosque in 1972, the first in the nation's capital. Other mosques, centres, and prayer rooms soon mushroomed across Canada in the late twentieth century.

The early pioneer Muslims, perhaps because of their small numbers and youth, did not pay attention to sectarian differences whenever they met for prayers. Praying and discussing the Qur'an and its Prophet with fellow Muslims was enough. In Montreal, for example, in the initial stages of Muslim organization, the Ahmadis, now officially declared as non-Muslims and heretics in Pakistan, came to pray alongside other Muslims. Gradually, however, differences began to be felt. The Shi'a opened their own mosques; Saudi-brand of Sunni orthodoxy forced itself into some centres, for example, Toronto. The Ismailis as always had their own prayer houses, called jamatkhanas. Sometimes sectarian and ethnic differences combined to contribute to the separation. Sometimes differences in interpretation and traditions—for example, regarding the roles of women and their place in the mosque during prayers—led to splits. Fortunately these differences have not led to great acrimony.

Now in the early twenty-first century, mosques—with or without iconic minarets—and schools, prayer rooms, bookstores, markets, halal butchers, and Muslim associations sprinkle Canada from coast to coast to coast. In each case, Islamic institutions from associations to mosques and cemeteries usually awaited the spark provided by the arrival of some committed individuals with more formal education and the ability to get things done. The fast-increasing post-1967 Muslim immigration rate spurred on these individuals and provided the money to get institutions up and running, complete with minbars and minarets.

Integration and Assimilation

Anxieties are sometimes raised about "the Muslim question in Canada." A comparative analysis of the history of immigration in North America shows us that such fretting fails to take the long view and is unnecessarily pessimistic. Furthermore, what do we mean by "Muslims" in such a context? It is a broad term and a dangerous generalization.

My approach to the question of the success of the pioneer Muslim generations has been to ask how well they have integrated and assimilated.

By "assimilation" I mean the immigrant's full and willing acceptance of the host society's language, principle values, institutions, and politics in order to benefit from all on offer and avoid discrimination and isolation. If one is young and not too rooted in the soil of the past, it may be easier to embrace the brand new open world offered by becoming "Canadian," whatever that means. However, it can be painful to give up most of one's customs and religion in the interests of success and acceptance.

My second term, "integration," I use specifically to define the situation in which an immigrant or a family retains some of their traditional Islamic religion and culture while joining the mainstream of Canadian society, activities, and thinking. In the mental baggage of all the Muslim immigrants who were interviewed were ideas and attitudes inspired by their religion and culture that led them to a greater or lesser degree to "keep the faith." These self-identified and engaged Muslims did not step out of their beliefs and traditions like old, out-of-fashion clothes. Many retained a more cultural than devotional link to the Islamic tradition in which they were brought up.

But integration includes getting to know neighbours and fellow-workers and joining in local political and social groups or causes. Like assimilation, integration has its aches and pains and no doubt some degree of loss. However, it probably works better in a country that prides itself on its multiculturalism. Integration can mean less of a strain on the individual amidst the many complex challenges of life in Canada. It allows the Muslim to make up his or her mind more independently of religious and family leaders from more paternalistic Muslim homelands.

The pioneer generations, it is fair to say, perforce chose the option of integration once they decided to settle down in Canada. Their stories show that most took the middle path between assimilation and self-isolation. It would have been hard to be isolationist and unfriendly to neighbours in the country in which they found themselves if they were out peddling on the roads, or running a store in the Far North or in small-town Canada, and when they were a tiny minority, during less tolerant times, and with little economic clout.

Two of the early post-pioneer leaders in Saskatchewan, Naiyer Habib and Mahlaqa Naushaba Habib, raise some interesting issues in the introduction to their book, *History of the Muslims of Regina, Saskatchewan, and Their Organizations*: "We adopted the path of integration while maintaining our religious priorities and culture based on Islam. We were flexible and accommodative. We mingled with the society at large and provided them with opportunities to mingle with us."

Isolation may be considered the third position. This, however, is not as problematic as it might appear. Most often, soon after arrival, people of the same faith *and* ethnicity tend to stay together. Speaking a certain language, eating certain kinds of foods, listening to music and watching films, not to say having certain values, lends a level of comfort to displaced families. (People from the East are not likely to come out in bikinis and crotch-tight shorts for the sake of assimilation or integration.) This comfort zone acts as a buffer before the next generation ventures out and seeks its own levels of comfort. Until quite recently, there were suburbs in North America where nonwhites were implicitly or openly kept out by police harassment and real-estate practices. In the United States there was the phenomenon of "white flight," when white people fled to the suburbs when Blacks moved into the cities. After all, not all immigrants want to live close to other immigrants; poor immigrants may be forced to do so also due to cheap housing. And many a wealthy non-white immigrant would have preferred to have a house in Rosedale (Toronto) or Westmount (Montreal).

But while there is comfort for immigrants in living where their food stores, friends and acquaintances, and mosques are at hand, there is a risk in this ghettoization in terms of acceptance. But individuals make their own choices and are free to do so in our democracies. There was once a "Little Syria" in old downtown New York City, as there still is "Little Italy" there, and Brooklyn today is home to masses of Muslims and Orthodox Jews. The so-called "Islamic Republic of Thorncliffe Park" and other areas of Muslim concentration are now found in various parts of the Greater Toronto Area. There are Chinatowns in many Western cities. And there are the Mennonites of Canada and the Amish of Pennsylvania.

At the same time it should not be forgotten that assimilation is a two-way process—the host society, historically white and Christian, also assimilates. At one time Jews were pariahs; now they may be found in government and their novelists belong to the pantheon of American literature. Hasidic Jews, dressed differently and going about their ways, are just another part of our society. In Toronto in the early 1970s South

Asian women were known to be attacked if they came out in saris; now white women have no qualms donning the same attire. The president of the United States may host an Eid luncheon. Ramadan is announced in the mainstream media. And female members of government (Ilhan Omar in the United States, for example) may come out in hijab. And Ginella Massa, also in hijab, has been on Kitchener and Toronto TV starting in 2015 and is (in 2021) heading a new CBC-TV Newsworld program. Times change, and Muslims of any ethnicity have much to contribute to Canada. As pointed out above, many are eminent politicians now, including the popular mayor of Calgary.

Religious Reform for a New Age

In 1983, Earle Waugh, Baha Abu-Laban, and Regula B Qureshi published the results of a 1980 conference as *The Muslim Community in North America*. Some decades later, some of their observations are still valid. Abu-Laban's chapter, "The Canadian Muslim Community: The Need for a New Survival Strategy," was written when Muslims in Canada numbered about 100,000, six out of ten of whom were foreign-born.[173]

Abu-Laban noted that the postwar Muslim immigrants were much more diverse than the original nineteenth- and early twentieth-century Syrian-Lebanese majority, and more diverse in their Islamic roots, from Morocco to Indonesia. Also, they had no significant religious impulse to come to Canada, nor did they need to develop institutions other than mosques, with the related need for imams and benevolent societies.[174] The challenges facing the new Muslim immigrants included the cultural and other differences that they experienced here and the varying public and government attitudes to them, including discrimination. They faced difficulties in reaching their next generations, dealing with the other ethnic groups of Muslim Canadians, and navigating the differences between the Islamic and Canadian law systems. Muslim leaders needed a successful integration strategy. This would involve finding imams knowledgeable in the faith and familiar with North American ways, integrating different groups of Muslims, and "elaborate[ing] Islamic law, in order to reconcile the Islamic faith with the new socio-cultural system."[175] The "innovative survival strategy" that Abu-Laban advocated would facilitate "community cohesion, on the one hand, and successful adaptation to the new Canadian environment on the other."

> Elements of this strategy include the need for Muslim leadership that is capable of addressing the needs of Muslim youth; integrating the diverse Muslim subgroups together; and considering through the revival of the tradition of ijtihad,[176] interpretations of Islamic law that would better reconcile the Islamic faith with the new environment. A main assumption underlying this strategy is that the Muslim leadership has to recognize the social forces that impinge upon individual Muslims in Canada. With this knowledge, Muslim institutions are compelled to compete with other Canadian institutions for the allegiance of individual Muslims, an allegiance that cannot be taken for granted.[177]

Abdolmohammad Kazemipur, professor of sociology at Lethbridge University, in his book *The Muslim Question in Canada: A Story of Segmented Integration*, notes the recent efforts that have been made to bridge the gap between Islam and liberal democracy:

> The shift in the position of the above groups—Catholics, Jews, and Ismaili and Ahmadi Muslims—towards a peaceful coexistence with the mainstream populations in Western countries has not taken place in a vacuum. Indeed, as a result of engagement with the world outside their faith communities, these groups developed new interpretations of their beliefs—interpretations that were more compatible with the three basic principles of liberal democracies . . . Intellectual developments similar to those that have taken place within Roman Catholicism are also happening among Muslims. Over the past two decades, an increasing number of Muslim scholars have begun advocating for a fresh look at Islamic principles in the context of life in a liberal democracy. The conceptual underpinning of these intellectual contributions could be summarized as an effort to bridge the gap between Islam and concepts such as respect for human rights, individualism, democracy, pluralism, and tolerance.[178]

Hamdani in his study for the Canadian Dawn Foundation (2015) also has striking words about opportunities for the larger Muslim community:

> Finally, the Muslim population is changing. The emerging generation is less fixated on ethnicities than their parents or grandparents. Born into diverse ethnicities but bound by their Canadian heritage and a common faith, they come closest to defining that cherished entity called ummah [the larger Muslim community]. A visionary leadership can seize the moment, develop a Canadian Muslim identity and set an example for Muslims in other Western societies. Only a few generations are privileged to have such an opportunity.[179]

Since the 1970s and early 1980s numerous changes have taken place in the Canadian cultural and political landscapes. These include the rise and fall of various Muslim pioneering groups and personalities and the influx of new ideas into the mainstream of Canadian Muslim lives. The intrusion of new political forces from outside Canada have led to new difficulties. Militant extremism, wars, foreign interventions in Muslim countries, and the advent of pervasive and continuously changing media and means of communication have turned the quiet progress of Muslims in Canada and abroad into a daily news topic. In a world of "headline news" practically everyone can react instantaneously, in the heat of the moment, publicly or anonymously via the Internet and social media.

As with almost all things Muslim, the position and rights of women and the application of Islamic laws have highlighted the status of Muslims in the past half-century or so. Reflecting the influx of the money and ideas of the Saudi Arabian and Gulf states in 2003–05, there was a seemingly unstoppable effort by some Muslims to promote the use of *sharia* law into family law in Canada. After much effort (the issue is still controversial among the more militant), this thrust was successfully thwarted after two years by the combined efforts of the Canadian Council of Muslim Women and a wide variety of non-Muslim social groups. The result was a major overhaul of Ontario's arbitration legislation to require *all* family law arbitration to follow Ontario's civil family laws. For Muslims wishing successful integration, and for non-Muslims supporting this move, this was a major milestone in that it made for the inclusion of Muslims into the mainstream of Canadian society.

The issue of what Muslim women should or should not wear continues to agitate Muslims and non-Muslims, in the media and on the Internet as well as in individual Muslim homes. Reaction to each eruption of "news" or opinion on this issue also varies from province to province.

Gordon Jasey of Windsor also suggested regarding the issue of religious reform or interpretation:

> We have to distinguish between Islam, for what it is—it should be the same everywhere and anywhere—and the frills that have been attached or associated with it in the different cultures . . . I think we who belong to the different cultural groups will have to say: "This is Islam, [and] this [other thing] is practiced in this country and it's not contrary to Islam, but it's not Islam and you shouldn't accept it as Islam. If you want to do it, it's fine, and if you don't want to, it's fine."

But hanging over all this is the shadow of recent Islamophobia following 9/11. Hijab-snatching, racial slurs, and continuing suspicion are part of the national scene for Muslims. Negative attitudes in the United States, particularly during the Trump administration, and in Canada during the years of the Harper government, have not helped smooth these troubled waters. Integration and acceptance in the province of Quebec is particularly vexed. The 2017 Quebec City mosque massacre and the passage in June 2019 of the Coalition Avenir Quebec's highly controversial Bill 21, An Act Respecting the Laicity of State, has made matters worse for Muslims and other minority religions. Included in the act is the banning of the wearing of religious symbols by those giving or receiving public services, and challenges of the law's constitutionality have not yet been resolved.

Graeme Truelove's 2019 volume *Un-Canadian: Islamophobia in the True North* is a thought-provoking and detailed study of the issue, with chapters on Islamophobia and politics, the national security apparatus and Muslims, and the infamous Omar Khadr case. In his penultimate chapter, "The Gifts: The Message We're Sending," Truelove states,

To confront the bigotry and discrimination that has been directed toward Muslims in Canada in recent years, non-Muslims must carefully and humbly examine their own behaviour. They also need to hear from Muslims to understand the impact Islamophobia is having on them. Of course, Muslim communities do not speak with one voice. For example, although they appear to be outliers, there are prominent Muslims who have called for a niqab ban themselves and are supportive of efforts to institute one. More broadly, some Muslims have argued eloquently that undue focus on discrimination against Muslims instills a sense of victimhood, which is an impediment to inclusion. However, when speaking with Muslim individuals and organizations generally, an overarching theme becomes clear: "It's not an easy time to be a Muslim in Canada," says Amira Elghawaby, former spokesperson of the NCCM [National Council of Canadian Muslims] . . .

[But] "It's important to keep the damage to the relationship in perspective. Polls show that most Muslims in Canada are pretty satisfied about life here."[180]

The Relevance of Pioneer Muslim History

Pioneer Muslims, those who first came to Canada as Muslims and continued to identify themselves as Muslims, had important stories to tell that are both similar and different from those of other immigrant groups in Canada. On the whole they were happy that they had a chance for a better life in this country and were able to do as well as they did. They did well despite problems of language, culture, and of course religion, which distinguished them from their largely European immigrant and native-born Canadian neighbours. There can be no doubt that their stories are worth retelling and should be part of the history and culture of Canada. These stories should have importance for all Canadians. The acceptance of Muslims and of Islam, and indeed of other groups who may be different than "us," in Canada is a litmus test of the openness and tolerance of our society.

Only by education and personal experience can we ever get to fully know and understand "the other." The acceptance of Muslims, including the thousands of Syrians and others trying to make it to Canada's shores, reflects our "Canadian values."[181] Mean-spiritedness and narrow thinking are not "Canadian values," as shown by the outpouring of sympathy and solidarity with Canadian Muslims following the January 2017 shooting deaths of six men in Le Centre Culturel Islamique de Quebec. These feelings were expressed by Canadians ranging from Prime Minister Justin Trudeau down to the masses of citizens who attended cold winter-night vigils and marched in streets across Canada.

PART III

Glossary

Ahmadi (also Ahmadiyya, Qadiyani) Late-nineteenth-century messianic sect of Islam founded on the teachings of Mirza Ghulam Ahmad (1835–1908) in British India and since spread worldwide.

alhamdolillah Praise be to God (Allah).

Allah God in Arabic, signifying for Muslims the one and indivisible deity, but also used for God by Christians.

asr Mid-afternoon prayer.

Bayram Turkish word for festival and applied to the two Eids.

Bismillah In the name of God, an expression used at the beginning of any action or activity, including recitation of a Qur'anic verse.

Eid al-Fitr Festival of the Fitr (or charitable head tax at the end of Ramadan).

Eid al-Adha Festival of the Sacrifice (the potential sacrifice by Ibrahim or Abraham of his son for the sake of God).

hadith Saying, tradition, or practice of the Prophet Mohammed.

hajj Pilgrimage to Mecca, one of the Five Pillars of Islam.

halal Lawful or permitted, usually applied to ritually slaughtered meat.

halaqa Discussion group on aspects of Islam, often seated in a circle.

haram Unlawful or prohibited.

iftar Meal at the end of the day's fast during Ramadan.

ijtihad Using independent thought in religious questions as opposed to relying on earlier opinions and texts.

imam Prayer leader but often community leader and teacher.

imambarah Twelver Shi'a congregational hall.

insha'allah God willing.

Ismaili A small ethnically and culturally diverse Shi'a community spread across the world whose members owe allegiance to His Highness Prince Karim Aga Khan.

jami Mosque, suggests also Friday congregational prayer site.

jamatkhana   Muslim gathering place, and name for Ismaili mosques.

juma   Obligatory Friday noon prayer.

khutba   Sermon at juma.

minbar   Raised platform where the imam delivers the juma khutba.

muezzin   A person who announces the time for the five daily prayers, usually from a minaret.

qiblah   Direction of prayers towards Mecca from wherever one is.

Qur'an   The collected surahs revealed in Arabic to the Prophet Mohammed by the angel Gabriel, or Gibreel. Can also be spelled Koran

rakas   Units of regular prayers, two, three or four in number.

Ramadan   Arabic lunar month of dawn-to-sunset abstention from food, drink, smoking, sexual relations and addition of greater devotions.

salat   Prayers.

Salat al-Isha   Evening prayers.

Shahada   Bearing witness or declaring one's faith in God and the Prophet Mohammed before witnesses, required for becoming a Muslim.

sharia   The collection of ethical principles taken from the Qur'an and is the basis of Islamic jurisprudence, or fiqh, the human understanding of these principles.

Shi'a   The largest non-Sunni sect of Muslims whose adherents follow the guidance and authority of a series of imams succeeding Ali, the son-in-law of the Prophet Mohammed, stemming from a political-religious dispute of the seventh century.

Sunna, Sunnah   The customs and practices of the Muslim community based on the words and deeds of the Prophet Mohammad and his successors.

Sunni   The majority sect of Muslims follow the guidance of the Qur'an and sunna.

tafseer   Explanation, interpretation, and commentary on the Qur'an.

taraweeh   Voluntary late-night prayers said in pairs of rakas after Salat al-Isha during Ramadan.

ummah   The Muslim community, originally used in Medina, but usually national or international in scope.

Wahabi, Wahabism   Stringent conservative interpretation of Islam, after eighteenth-century movement founder Abd al-Wahab (1703–1792) who made a religious-political pact with Ibn Saud

wudu   Prescribed ablutions before saying prayers.

zuhr (also zohr, dhohr)   Noon prayer time.

Notes

1 *Islam Canada*, "History of Muslims in Canada" September 1979, 10.
2 It was only in the early 1970s that Muslims started arriving in large numbers, thanks to late-1960s reforms to Canadian immigration laws that replaced the quotas on immigration from Asia and Africa and the discretionary powers of the immigration officials who used "criteria emphasizing education, skills and the employability of the applicant." Abdolmohammad Kazemipur, *The Muslim Question in Canada: A Story of Segmented Integration*, UBC Press, 2014, 24, citing Daood Hamdani, "Canadian Muslims in the Eve of the Twenty-First Century," *Journal of Muslim Minority Affairs* 19, no. 2 (1999): 203.
3 Tahir Bokhari died about 2015.
4 Theglobeandmail.com/life/facts-and-arguments/lives-lived-husna-tayyeb-86/article22674998.
5 Hassam Munir, "Early Glimpses of Ramadan in Toronto," www.ihistory.co/ramadan-in-toronto-history, citing the *Globe and Mail*, May 3, 1957, and the *Toronto Star*, April 13, 1959.
6 Sadly, I have forgotten the names of the others, aside from Bosnian Ferid Foco and his brother, behind us, Dr Rahman Syed, to the right, and Moin Ansari, at extreme right of photo.
7 The website states that the foundation was established in 1969, but I think the group started earlier. With a towering dome and minaret, it now is located at Markham Road and Nugget Avenue.
8 The Muslim Students' Association, founded on campuses in the United States in 1963, according to Wikipedia. It was rooted in the Muslim Brotherhood and the Jamaat-e-Islam of India and Pakistan, and can be said to be somewhat political rather than purely devotional. According to its website, MSA spread to Canada in 1964, beginning at the University of Toronto.
9 They included *Ten Lost Years, 1929–1939*, about the Great Depression; *The Pioneer Years, Next Year Country*, about the Canadian West; *Six War Years, 1939–1945: Memories of Canadians at Home and Abroad*; and *The Immigrant Years*, about postwar immigration.
10 Hassam Munir, "Remembering the first Muslims in Canada," www.iHistory.co/first-muslims-in-canada/ Munir is the founder and editor-in-chief of the iHistory.com website. He has produced a number of interesting digital articles, complete with photos.
11 Haselby is a historian and a senior editor at online Aeon. His essay is sub-headed "Muslims came to America more than a century before Protestants,

and in great numbers. How was their history forgotten?" Aeon.co/essays/muslims-lived-in-america-before-protestantism-even-existed.

12   *Servants of Allah*, New York University Press, 1998, 10.

13   Translated and edited by Ala Alryyes: *The Life of Omar Ibn Said*, University of Wisconsin Press, 2011.

14   Laila Lalami, *The Moor's Account*, Periscope, 2015.

15   *Muslims and the Making of America*, Baylor University Press, 2016, 4–5, 114

16   Daood Hamdani, *Canadian Muslims: A Statistical Review*, commissioned by the Canadian Dawn Foundation, presented March 29, 2015. According to the website muslimlink.ca, "The Canadian Dawn Foundation is a registered charity dedicated to inspiring Canadian Muslims to achieve their full potential by actively contributing to our pluralistic society and drawing upon their rich cultural and humanistic heritage to build bridges of understanding and better the world" (https://muslimlink.ca/directory/ottawa/religious/local-orgs/745-cdn-dawn).

17   Hassam Munir, http://www.ihistory.co/first-muslims-in-canada/.

18   Munir, "Remembering," and Hussain, *The Making*, 19.

19   See Hamdani's "Muslims in Canada: A Century of Settlement, 1871–1976," his 1996 talk on Parliament Hill at the Eid al-Fitr dinner; also "Canadian Muslims: An Unnoticed Part of Our History," *Hamdard Islamicus*, 20 no. 3, (September 1997), 97–100, Karachi, Pakistan. In a March 11, 2018, online article by Palvashah Durrani, "Daood Hamdani: Exploring Muslim Canadian History and Demographics," in www.muslimlink.ca/pdf/Canadian-Muslims-A-Statistical-Review-Final.pdf, Hamdani said the Loves were converts. When I visited him in a Kanata retirement residence in May 2018, he was still working on this subject.

20   Munir, "Remembering," For the Loves' children and dates, see Hamdani (1984), "Muslims in the Canadian Mosaic," *Institute of Muslim Minority Affairs Journal* 5, no. 1: 7–16.

21   Baha Abu-Laban, *An Olive Branch on the Family Tree: The Arabs in Canada*, McClelland and Stewart, 1980, 72-5.

22   Abu-Laban, "Arab Canadians," 1, www.thecanadianencyclopedia.ca/en/article/arabs/.

23   Baha Abu-Laban, *Olive Branch*, 55.

24   Ibid, 56–7.

25   Abu-Laban, "Arab Canadians," 2.

26   See Saleem Ganam in chap. 3, Mohammed Fyith in chap. 4, Hanny Hassan in chap. 8.

27   "The Syrian Peddlers," www.mysteriesofcanada.com.

28   See Norman Buchignani's excellent article, "South Asian Canadians," www.thecanadianencyclopedia.ca/en/article/south-asians, May 12, 2010.

29   Patricia E Roy, "Internment in Canada," www.thecanadianencyclopedia/ca/en/article/internment

30   www.cbc.ca/canada/ottawa/remembrance-ceremony-honours-muslim-canadian-in-ww1-1.4396094.

31   Hamdani, *Canadian Muslims: A Statistical Report*, 4.

32   Hamdani, *Canadian Muslims: A Statistical Report*, 4.

33   Usman Ali provided a copy of a December 19, 1977, letter from the BC Interfaith Citizenship Council, 622 Seymour St, Vancouver, to the BC Land

Commission, "Re: Muslim Mosque and Activity Centre," expressing their warm support. It was signed by Rev W L Burnham, chairman of the interfaith council, and Dr William G Black, a chartered member of the council.

34   Ali said that it includes ten mosques, three centres, and two Muslim elementary schools.

35   Gutteridge Books, University of Alberta Press, 2018.

36   Jomha was her maiden name.

37   See Merna Forester, *100 More Canadian Heroines: Famous and Forgotten Faces*, Dundurn, Toronto, 2011, "Hilwie Hamdon: Building Al Rashid," 161–4; *WomenCan Edmonton*: Women behind Al Rashid Mosque," December 18, 2008.

38   Ali Hamdon and Hilwie Hamdon were among the original January 4, 1938, members of the Arabian Moslem Association in Edmonton, which founded the Al Rashid Mosque that year, see Awid, *Muslims in Canada*, 31, and Awid, *Canada's First Mosque*, 42–3 (with photo of them).

39   Richard Awid suggests it was Bedouin Ferran. See also Munir, "'Jew' or 'Black Turk'? The Story of the First Muslim Elected in Canada," www.iHistory.co/peter-baker-first-muslim-elected-canada/.

40   See John Andrew Morrow, chapter "Syrian-Lebanese Settlers in the Dakotas," *Restoring the Balance: Using the Qur'an and Sunnah to Guide a Return to the Prophet's Islam*, Newcastle upon Tyne, 2016. Morrow says Baker was born in Lebanon in 1887 and was elected as a member of the Northwest Territories Legislative Assembly from 1964 to 1967. See also, "Peter Baker (Canadian Politician)," Wikipedia, which suggests Baker escaped the Ottoman draft for a war against the Yemenis and died in 1973.

41   For the record, their children and dates of birth were: Evelyn, January 24, 1924; Lavida, January 22, 1925; Moneer, September 15, 1926; Sidney, February 3, 1928; Helen, December 13, 1929; Lewis, August 11, 1935. Evelyn, Lavida, Sidney and Helen are now deceased.Moneer is now 93 and Lewis is 85.

42   Awid suggests more when children were included.

43   Waugh, 22.

44   Awid notes there were other mosques in Ross, North Dakota (1929), and Cedar Rapids, Michigan, (1934) but whether mayors were involved is less likely.

45   Abdullah Yusuf Ali, later Sir, born Bombay, India, 1872, died Brookwood, Surrey, England, 1953, most famous for his widely used translation, *The Holy Qur'an: Text, Translation and Commentary*, first published in Lahore, India at the time, in 1938. He was on a promotional tour when he came to Canada and helped open the Al Rashid Mosque.

46   Mohammad Ahmed (Sam) Asiff, born in 1904 in Lala, Syria, left home at twenty-seven to earn money to support his widowed mother and two younger children in 1923. He landed in Halifax and eventually reached Edmonton. He became a peddler on foot, later buying a horse and buggy, and later still, a store and rooming house. He helped with the Edmonton mosque's fund-raising, travelling even to Eastern Canada at his own expense. In 1946 he moved to Lac La Biche and started mink ranching. He met and married Malaki Abougoush; they raised seven children. He began raising money for a mosque there which was completed in 1958. He was also the first president of the Lac La Biche Muslim Association, dying in 1980. See "Biography of Mohammad (Sam) Asiff", www.llbleb100.ca/biographies; and Awid,

Canada's First Mosque, 2010, 53–4.

47   Awid suggests that Ali landed in Halifax, travelled to Brandon, Manitoba, and sold goods between Manitoba and Saskatchewan before heading for Edmonton in 1907. He and Sine Alley then went north on foot and finally established a trading post at Fort Chipewyan called Hamdon and Alley Ltd. Awid, *Canada's First Mosque*, 42.

48   Born Rikia Haidar, she came to Canada as a child via Mexico (where she was stranded for five years) and the United States and met and married Mahmoud Saddy (1882–1951), and they farmed, raised a family, and finally moved to Edmonton in 1936 where she became heavily involved in the development of the Al Rashid Mosque. Awid, *Canada's First Mosque*, 46–7. She died in 1990. For a fuller, more personal account, see also "Amina and Rikia," the story of Amina Haidar and her daughter Rikia Haidar Saddy by Rikia's daughter Alia Mohammed Ali, in *At My Mother's Feet: Stories of Muslim Women*, edited by Sadia Zaman. Quarry Press, 1999.

49   Also see "Saleem Ameen Ganam" on the Internet for gravestone image, and obituary, *Edmonton Journal*, June 14, 2003.

50   Richard Asmet Awid, *Through the Eyes of the Son* (2001), 55–6, on the life of Sied Ameen Ganam Kadri and children Saleem, Ameen, and Lila.

51   See Awid, *Through the Eyes of the Son*, 130–32.

52   The gravestone of Al Haj Saleem in Edmonton states 1910, as does his obituary.

53   Habib and Habib includes a short but fascinating history of the Regina Muslims by Dr Anwarul Haque with an addendum by Dr Al-Katib of Davidson about the first Muslim there, a former Ottoman army captain, Muhammad Ali Ta Yahnee, 1864–1982, and of a few early pioneers, Trafford Publishing, 2015, 6–11.

54   Brothers Mohamed and Ahmed Kazeil moved from Brandon to Swift Current in 1912. Awid, *Muslims in Canada*, 52–4.

55   1077–1166; see Wikipedia entries for Gilani, or Jilani, and his Sufi order.

56   Habib and Habib, 4.

57   Waugh, *Al Rashid Mosque*, 67.

58   Awid, *Through the Eyes of the Son*, 55–56, on the life of Sied Ameen Ganam Kadri and children Saleem, Ameen "King" Ganam, and Dr Lila Fahlman.

59   Lila Fahlman's American mother was a great-niece of Zachary Taylor, the twelfth president of the United States, according to Paula Simon's article "In Honouring Strong Muslim Women, Edmonton School Names Send Powerful Message," *Edmonton Journal*, June 22, 2016, about the naming of two K-9 Edmonton schools after them. The schools were the Dr Lila Fahlman School and the Hilwie Hamdon School. Another school, the Soraya Hafez School, was named after Soraya Hafez, the Egyptian-born wife of Richard Asmet Awid. She was the first teacher of the district's Arabic bilingual class at Glengarry School in 1983. *Edmonton Journal*, May 8, 2018.

60   Zaman, ed, *At My Mother's Feet*, 51–70.

61   Ibid.

62   Born in Hanna, Alta, in 1935, Larry Shaben moved to Edmonton in 1940s, attended University of Alberta, married Alma Saddy in 1960, and they had five children. They moved to High Prairie where he bought a general store before entering political politics for the Progressive Conservatives. He won his seat repeatedly in 1975, 1979, 1982, and 1986 until dissolution in 1989. He had been the first Arab

to hold a seat in Alberta and among the first Muslims to hold higher office. Shaben held a series of provincial cabinet posts until he became Minister of Economic Development and Trade before his political career ended. He was badly beaten by a hitchhiker and took up promoting tolerance and understanding of Muslims. He became a citizenship judge in 2005 but died in 2008: Wikipedia.

63   See Awid, *Through the Eyes of the Son*, 123–4; ; Earle Waugh, *Al Rashid Mosque*, 227–8; also Guy Saddy, "The First Little Mosque on the Prairie," *Walrus*, 10/11/15, a very interesting personal reflection on integration and assimilation.

64   Born on July 15, 1883, and sailed to New York in 1900: Richard Asmet Awid, *Muslims in Canada: A Century of Achievement*, 44–7. Also, Daood Hamdani said his research suggested the full name was Mahmoud Saeed el-Haj Ahmed Abi Lamah, shortened by the immigration officer to Mahmoud Saddy. Richard Awid told me Larry Shaben's father signed the charter of the Al Rashid Mosque in 1938 as Mahmoud Saaid El Hage Ahmed.

65   Also spelled Joub Jannine, Jeb Jannine, Djeb Djennin, etc, sixty-plus kilometres from Beirut and just north of another village, Lala, where Saleem Ganam's father came from. It has great archeological interest and now features a large refugee camp.

66   Rikia Haidar left Lebanon as a child with her widowed mother, Amina Shaben Haidar, to join her mother's brothers in the United States in 1912. They landed at Vera Cruz during the Mexican revolution and were stranded there for five years before rejoining her brothers in Sioux City, Iowa, in 1917, and thence all of them moved to Canada, settling in Edmonton. Awid, *Canada's First Mosque*, 46. See also an interesting personal account, "Amina and Rikia," by Rikia's daughter Alia (Aliya) Mohammed Ali, in Zaman, ed, *At My Mother's Feet*, 27–38. Awid states that she was born in 1905 and died in 1990: Awid, *Muslims in Canada: A Century of Achivement*, 45-7.

67   Hamdani suggested four girls. Richard Awid names them Alma, Betty, Jean, and Aliya (Eileen) who married the prime minister of Pakistan, Mohammed Ali Bogra. After he died in 1963, she returned to Edmonton.

68   Awid. *Muslims in Canada: A Century of Achievement*, 45–7.

69   See Awid, *Canada's First Mosque*, 51–2, in which he writes that Esmeil Jamha was born in Lala in 1890 and came to Canada in 1905 with his friend Frank Tarrabain.

70   Or Ahmed Farah, according to Hilwie Hamdon, below. Baker was author of *Memoirs of an Arctic Arab: A Free Trader in the Canadian North—The Years 1907–1927*, (1976). Richard Asmet Awid suggests his name was Bedouin Ferran, see his *Through the Eyes of the Son*, 28–31, and notes he was elected as a territorial councillor in 1964.

71   Waugh, *Al Rashid Mosque*, 227–8.

72   Awid, *Muslims in Canada*, 38–9, and Awid, *Through the Eyes of the Son*, 130–2.

73   The spellings vary, but his name contains similarities to his father's, Ahmed Ali Awid Amerey, above.

74   Shakers were a Christian Arab family. F I Shaker, who was mayor of Hanna, was the MC at the opening of Al Rashid in 1938.

75   For a good account of his life, see Awid, *Muslims in Canada: A Century of Achievement*, 37–8. My account has been amended with some names and other details in brackets and paraphrased or quoted directly from his own account which had been dictated and written by daughters Marie and Lila. See also Awid, *Through the Eyes of the Son*, 33–5. Munir Hassam has also written a very revealing blog, "Meet Ali Abouchadi, the Trailblazing Canadian Muslim," iHistory.co/ali-ahmed-abouchadi/

76 The Lebanese community's website, llbleb100.ca, includes the biography of Alex Hamilton, among others, and photos, put together for their hundredth anniversary in 2010.

77 There are also members of the Tarrabain family in Edmonton. See Awid, *Through the Eyes of the Son*, on Ali Tarrabain, 43–4; Mahmoud Mohammed Tarrabain, 45–6; Sid Hassan Tarrabain, 46, Lila and Frank Tarrabain, and M S (Mike) Tarrabain, 58–9. See also, Awid, *Muslims in Canada*.

78 See a short biography of Mike (Mohammed) Fyith, in www.llbleb100.ca. Also, see Awid, *Canada's First Mosque—The Al Rashid Mosque*, Edmonton, 2010, 54–5.

79 "Biography of Sine Alley Abougoush," www.llbleb100.ca/pdf_files and "Biography of Ameen Sine Abougoush," www.llbleb100.ca/pdf_files organized by the Lac La Biche Lebanese community. Sine Alley returned to Lala in 1930 with his family but returned to Canada in 1932, staying there until 1939, when he went back to Lebanon for good, farmed and was generous to the less fortunate, dying in 1980 at age 92.

80 Asma, 1924; Malaki, 1926; Ameen, 1927; Ali, 1929, "Biography of Sine Alley Abougoush," www.llbeb100.va/pdf_files

81 I had understood the name to be Fayath, as there are a number of spellings, but I am sure Richard Awid is correct in spelling it as Fyith.

82 Lac La Biche Mosque History, and Lac La Biche Museum, on the Internet.

83 Physician and cardiologist from India, who arrived for studies in the United States in 1967 and emigrated to Regina in 1973. His wife was also born in India but her family moved to Pakistan on Partition and took an MA from the University of Karachi in political science. Dr Habib was president in 1977–81, 1984–86, 1989–92, and 1996–98. Habib and Habib, 17–18. Trafford Publishing, 2015.

84 Physician, and ear, nose and throat specialist from Bangladesh, president 1971–77.

85 Physician, and consultant nutritionist from Turkey, president 1981–82.

86 Habib and Habib, 2–8.

87 Ibid, 10.

88 Ibid, 25–6. His sons, Andaleeb and Adnan Qayyum, and their wives, are good friends of my family.

89 "Community profile: The Abas family, the oldest Muslim family in Manitoba," in *Manitoba Muslim*, www.multiculturalcanada.ca/A-Z/a21/3

90 This was the twenty-year guerrilla resistance war led by Omar Al-Mukhtar, who was finally defeated and executed by the Italians in 1931. The 1981 film *Lion of the Desert* portrayed this struggle by the leader of the Senussi Sufi resistance campaign. It ends with a striking shot of vast tented concentration camps in the desert to remind the viewer that this was not just a good Anthony Quinn action film.

91 Hisham Badran, a Palestinian, also became the director of the CMCC-instigated Muslim children's camp for some years.

92 Zaman, *At My Mother's Feet*, 80

93 Nina Karachi-Khaled added, "I remember our library in the house having so many George Bernard Shaw books and plays and finding out that he learned English by reading those books. He would try to learn a number of new English words each day and push himself to expand his vocabulary."

94 Dr Thomas Ballantyne Irving, whom we all knew in Toronto, lived from 1914 to

2002. He was a Canadian-American scholar, a convert to Islam in the 1950s and produced *The Qur'an: First American Version*, in 1985. He also published a number of books on Islam and also wrote about Islam and Muslim Spain in Spanish.

95   For the sake of brevity here, Hussain stated in his abstract: "Canadian Islam offers an important window through which to view a future role for Islam to play in the world. Muslims in Toronto are engaged in creating distinct religious lives for themselves. This thesis argues that Islam in Toronto is not simply a collection of diaspora Islams, but instead is its own local manifestation of Canadian Islam." And I should add I am honoured that he quoted the whole of an account I wrote for him in 1993 about those years.

96   Fatime's parents, father Sabri Feizo, 1898 to 1959, and mother Xhevahire Feizo, 1900 to 1985, from their eldest granddaughter Eileen Spencer, December 2017.

97   Now Eileen Spencer, who resolved a lot of small mysteries for me.

98   Maureen Merieme (Kerim) Temple, a teacher for thirty-four years, who died at the age of fifty-nine in 2008.

99   Followed by Doreen, and lastly Lori in 1959, born on the day their father, Sami Kerim, died.

100   The cousins were Sami Kerim's brothers Gervat Kerim, 1895–1968, and Talha Kerim, 1893–?

101   Eileen Spencer asserts that Regep Assim, her father, Sami Kerim, and Neim Sali registered the Albanian Muslim Society of Toronto in 1954, not Zakria Malik.

102   In Quebec for many years Muslims could only be married in a church by a willing minister until when?

103   Recorded July 4, 1979.

104   Recorded July 4, 1979.

105   Ruth Foley, 1936–86, and Jean Coram, 1938–.

106   According to son Luan Banka of Oshawa, when they were married on Aug. 25, 1949, by Imam Vehbi Ismail, it was his first marriage ceremony.

107   Sami, Gevat, Talha, Sabri, and Seitali Kerim.

108   Recorded August 2017.

109   Ahmed went to work at another uranium mine near Blind River, Khan added, and also ended up sometime about 1965 in the City of Toronto planning department. Another friend of Khan was Quasi Saeed, also from Aligarh University, who arrived in 1960, attended OISE, and taught education planning there for the rest of his life.

110   In 1950, according to son Vezi Tayyeb. For Ali and his wife Husna's lives, see note 4.

111   Founded in 1969 it began on Rhodes Avenue and is now housed in a large mosque at 441 Nugget Avenue in Scarborough.

112   Email from Badrul Hasan, Aug. 28, 2017.

113   Ayube Ally was another of the leading figures in the Muslims Society of Toronto in the 1960s. He was born in Guyana on February 6, 1922, and married Shamyoon McDoom on June 8, 1947. They migrated to Canada in May 1962 with their four children, Jean, Joan (married to Luan Banka, son of Margaret and Rizvan Banka, above), Farida and Jaleel Kayam (JK).

114   Daood Hamdani tells his own story later in the Newfoundland chapter.

115   Muneeb Nasir is the chair of the Olive Tree Foundation, a public endowment

foundation, a former board member of the Islamic Foundation of Toronto, and long-time member of various committees, including the program committee. Mohamed Nasir was a Guyanese businessman who arrived in Toronto in 1973 and was soon involved with the Jami Mosque and the Islamic Foundation. According to Muneeb Nasir's articles, Mohamed Nasir led the development of the foundation's Nugget Avenue mosque, was president of its board of directors for nearly two decades, and was instrumental in establishing in Toronto both Rabitat al-Alam al-Islami offces and ISNA's Canadian headquarters.

116　Amjad Syed, email of November 9, 2019.

117　Dr Ahamd Sakr, founding member and president of the Muslim Students Association of the United States and Canada, a Muslim Brotherhood off-shoot, and involved in the Saudi-backed Muslim World League, died in November 2015.

118　Azhar gave me two handwritten pages dated February 13, 2015, entitled "Humanity, Race and Colour," vehemently defending Canada for its lack of racial discrimination—in his case, at least.

119　From Hafiz Rahman, long-time off-and-on president.

120　The ground-breaking was in June 1995; Hafiz Rahman.

121　The Qur'an, 2: 187, states: "And eat and drink, until the white thread of dawn appears to you distinct from its black thread; then complete your fast till the night appears." There are differing interpretations of this line.

122　The others were Imam Gamal Solaiman, 2001–07, and Imam Khaled Abdul-Hamid Syed. Jennifer Green, *Ottawa Citizen*, May 2, 2009, "Ottawa Mosque Holding Steady as It Sails into Winds of Dissent."

123　This was a particularly segregated women's balcony, where most of the women could not even see the imam down below, let alone the male congregants, and certainly none of the men could see any of them. Traditonally, women have prayed behind the men, although not on the pilgrimage. The position of women in prayers is one of the greater gender issues in modern Islam.

124　See previous note.

125　Formerly Camp Al-Mu-Mee-Neen, now Camp Deen, at Long Bay Campground on Bob's Lake, near Westport, Ontario. Qasem Mahmud was the long-time manager of the site for a consortium of Muslims. Tragically, I was up at Long Bay Campground in July 2017, checking on supplies for the following month's camp, when his daughter appeared out of the mess hall and told me she'd just learned her father had died. I had been arranging in those weeks to meet him for an interview for this book.

126　Incorporated in 2000, previously called the Canadian Council on American-Islamic Relations, the original CAIR being American.

127　As I did in November 2017.

128　Religious study circle.

129　Abu-Laban, *Olive Branch*, 4.

130　Statistics Canada, 2016 Census.

131　Ibid, 5.

132　See canadianarabcommunity.com/historyofrecentimmigrationtocanada.php, 2, Copyright 2008 Windsor Public Library.

133　*Muslim Communities in North America*, Yvonne Y Haddad and Jane Smith, eds, State University of New York Press, 1994.

134   Ibid, 318.

135   Hamdani, *Canadian Muslims*, 17.

136   Hamdani (1984), "Muslims in the Canadian Mosaic," Institute of Muslim Minority Affairs. Journal, 5:1, 7–16, DOI: 10.1080/02666958408715874, Table II, Muslim Population of Canada, by Province.

137   Government of Canada. Statistics Canada (2013–05–08) "Statistics Canada: 2011 National Household Survey Profile," www12.statscan.gc.ca

138   Mumtaz Haque Rehman, "The Story of Indo-Pakistani Muslim Community in Montreal, Quebec," published on the Montreal Religious Sites Project website (http://mrsp.mcgill.ca/reports/html/MuslimHistory/index.htm), is hereafter cited as Rehman 2004.

139   Spelled Panjab for the university, not Punjab as used elsewhere.

140   Smith, 1916–2000, was a professor of comparative religion. He wrote a shelf of books starting with three on India and Pakistan, then *Islam in Modern History: The Tension between Faith and History*, and many others.

141   Bill 194 (Private), An Act to incorporate the Islamic Centre of Quebec— El-Markaz Islami, assented to August 6, 1965, Legislative Assembly of Quebec.

142   For more details, see Rehman 2004, 4.

143   Ibid, 9.

144   Ibid, 8.

145   Wikipedia's lengthy article suggests the name means "society for spreading Islam," and begins by suggesting it is "a non-political, global Sunni Islamic mission- ary movement that focuses on urging Muslims to return to primary Sunni Islam, and particularly in matters of ritual, dress, and personal behaviours." The majority are South Asians and commit to touring countries doing *dawah* or preaching. They like to visit mosques and move in for periods of time as well as visiting individual Muslim homes.

146   *Globe and Mail*, April 1, 2017, "Muslim Acceptance Still a Delicate Matter," A3.

147   www.cbc.ca/news/canada/montreal/muslim-cemetery-referendum-sainy- apollinaire, posted July 16, 2017

148   www.montrealgazette.com/news/two-years-after-quebec-citys-mosque-attack- muslim-cemetery-remains-unbuilt.

149   The Islamic Community Centre of South Shore, and Masjid Qutb, or Centre communautaire Islamique de Brossard.

150   Rehman mentioned him above in connection with the early Pakistani commu- nity in Montreal, Izhar Mirza's older brother and co-survivor of the attack that killed their parents in India in 1947.

151   Dr Ketene retired as a professor of otolaryngology at Dalhousie University, Halifax.

152   See www.islamnovascotia.ca/history. The article, written by Syed M Ali, was published in 2002 by the Association of Canadian Educators of East Indian Origin, Dartmouth, Nova Scotia, in the book *The Quiet Nation Builders*, Schooner Books, 2000.

153   Robert Stanfield was the successful premier of Nova Scotia, 1948–67 and then leader of the Progressive Conservative Party of Canada and Leader of Her Majesty's Loyal Opposition until 1976.

154   Murray Joseph's son, London lawyer Faisal B Joseph, added in January 2017: "My dad's oldest brother was Kamal Joseph, who served in the Royal Canadian Navy

during the Second World War. Next was Jamal (Bam) Joseph, businessman and expert bridge player. Hummet (Hum) Joseph was drafted by the Boston Red Sox and played semi-pro baseball in the Maritimes and the United States. He is also in the Sports Hall of Fame of Nova Scotia. Hum was also in the Canadian navy. There is a photo of him with baseball star Ted Williams, taken in Miami about 1958. Shakeeb (Sheeb) Joseph moved away to Miami in early 1960s and became a millionaire businessman. Alec (Ali) Joseph, got polio when he was about four years old and lived on crutches the rest of his life, but still became an independent businessman and denturist in Truro Nova Scotia. He also became a high level Mason as a way of giving back to the Shriners for the medical care they gave him as a child, as the Joseph family was very poor. All the boys were well respected businessmen."

155   The Registrar of the Civil Status Department of Rashaya, dated May 26, 1997. However, despite this evidence, there is some confusion, because George Harris's tombstone gives his lifespan as 1893 to 1954. His passport stated his birth as in 1893.

156   A plaque in Mdoukha in Arabic attests to this waterpipe contribution by Hajj Hussein Jabara. Jabara was apparently a nickname suggesting he was a person who fixed things, and the date 1935. The honorific Hajj confirms that he had made the pilgrimage to Mecca.

157   There is family uncertainty about the timing and reason for the name change.

158   The Islamic Association of Nova Scotia website www.islamnovascotia.ca/history.php—formerly the Islamic Association of the Maritime Provinces (IAMP)—suggests the cemetery was founded in 1944 and the adjoining mosque in 1971. However, a poster in Truro headed "The Moslem Cemetery in Bible Hill," states that it was established in 1941, and that "some of the individuals involved were Joseph Moorby, A R Joseph, M S Awad, all of Truro, and George Harris of Westville."

159   The children of Wayne and Fran Harris were Renda, Dwain Murray, Nadine, and Reaud Murray, all surnamed Harris.

160   Eaglesfuneralhome.com/tribute-ajax/print-obituary.

161   Sam Hamod, quoted in "The World Comes Together: Dual Identity in the Poetry of Sam Hamod," by Anna L Cates, *Fringe Magazine*, no. 17, probably 12 January 2008.

162   Louis de Bernieres, *Birds Without Wings*, Vintage 2005, 225.

163   Abu-Laban, *Olive Branch*, 75.

164   "History of the Jews in Canada," https://en.wikipedia.org/wiki/History_of_the_Jews_in_Canada. For further reading, see Irving Abella and Harold Troper, *None Is Too Many: Canada and the Jews of Europe 1933–1945*, and books by the late Queen's University professor of history, Gerald Tulchinsky.

165   Naturalization   Records,   1915–1951,   www.bac-lac.gc.ca/eng/discover/immigration/citizenship-naturalization-records-1915-1951/.

166   Canada, Parliament, House of Commons, *House of Commons Debates: Official Report, Third Session—Twentieth Parliament*, vol. 3 (Ottawa: King's Printer and Controller of Stationery, 1947), 2645–46.

167   Ibid.

168   Abu-Laban, *Olive Branch*, 83–4; William Duncan Scott, *Dictionary of Canadian Biography*, vol. 15 (1921–1930) online.

169   Abu-Laban, *Olive Branch*, 85–8.

170   William Heinemann 2003, Harper Collins 2011. She is also author of *Dreams*

of Water, and *A Good Land*.

171 Syrian-Lebanese built the first North American mosque in tiny Ross, North Dakota, in 1929 but it later fell into disrepair. Then the Moslem Temple, also known as the Mother Mosque of North America, was built in 1934 in Cedar Rapids, Iowa, which has a noted Syrian population. It was followed by the Al Rashid Mosque in Edmonton, in 1938.

172 Mumtaz Haque Rehman, telephone conversation, 24 June 2019.

173 Abu-Laban, "The Canadian Muslim Community: The Need for a New Survival Strategy," in *The Muslim Community in North America*, 76n8, referring to the estimates of Muslim scholars of the day. For the record, I too have an article in it: "Socio-Religious Behaviour of Muslims in Canada: An Overview."

174 Ibid, 76–80.

175 Ibid, 80–8.

176 In the very simplest terms, *ijtihad* is the Arabic for independent thought, among other things—usually opinions by scholars but potentially by individuals trying to adjust to the modern world and its ways—as opposed to living by the opinions of scholars of 1,000 years or more ago. Martin Luther argued that Christians did not need to seek redemption for their sins from the Roman Catholic Church but that "every man is his own priest," a thought that could find resonance among critical Muslims.

177 Abu-Laban, *Muslim Community*, 88–9.

178 Kazemipur, UBC Press, 2014,180.

179 Hamdani, *Canadian Muslims*, summary, ix.

180 Truelove, *Un-Canadian: Islamophobia in the True North*, Nightwood Editions, 2019, 187–8.

181 *The Report on Canadian Values of the Canadian Race Relations Foundation* of 19 November 2014 lists a number of values such as the general ones of freedom, equality, and democracy, with the more specifically Canadian additions being federalism, bilingualism, and multiculturalism. It also mentions the Canadian Charter of Rights and Freedoms as including freedoms of conscience, thought, belief, opinion, expression, association, and peaceful assembly.

Select Index

Acknowledgements

Following a 2011 arson attack on our home, which also destroyed all my tapes and papers, this book would never have been restarted nor completed in recent years without one man's skills. Our son-in-law John Douglas Henson was somehow able to retrieve from cyberspace what interviews I had earlier and rather randomly typed into my computer. Next, I must thank my long-time friend from school and university days and noted editor Peter G K Carver for encouraging me to pick up these pioneer interviews again and to inject my story into the lead to explain how an average white Canadian became a Muslim in the mid-1950s, and hence how all this collection came into being. Then I must thank my first editor, Maureen Garvie, a fellow former *Kingston Whig-Standard* veteran, for organizing and improving my first attempts at this project.

This book also owes its inception to Muin Muinuddin (1928-98), a leading spirit and ideas man of the Council of Muslim Communities of Canada, which, sadly like him, is no more. There have also been so many people I have known for a lifetime who in recent hours of need have helped me via email or telephone with information about lives, photos, or clarifications. I am embarrassed that I will have forgotten some, so please forgive me.

However, I must thank a variety of people for their encouragement over the last few years. They include the late Daood Hamdani, who was the source of our Muslim statistics and always interested and helpful during this book's progress, and Edmonton and Alberta Muslim pioneer historian Richard Asmet Awid and University of Alberta emeritus sociology professor Baha Abu-Laban. Among the younger generation I must also thank Jan Raska of the Canadian Museum of Immigration at Pier 21, in Halifax, Hassam Munir for his iHistory internet articles on many Muslim pioneers and subjects, and theological studies professor Amir Hussain of Loyola Marymount University in Los Angeles. Others are dear friends professors emeritus Elizabeth Whitmore of Carleton University and retired University of Toronto Canadian history professor Arthur Silver, of Kingston, for reading the text in its earlier stage.

Recently, Noor Al-Henedy, communications director at the Al Rashid Mosque in Edmonton, was very helpful regarding the early photo of Canada's first mosque. Fisal Asiff, born in Lac La Biche and now of Edmonton, was also of great help with the cover photo of his father, Mohammad (Sam) Asiff, and of the early Lac La Biche mosque. And for future services I will now thank my webmaster, Yusuf Khaled, of Burlington. I will also thank all those pioneer Muslims and their families who recalled for me their lives, and sometimes their ancestors' lives, in so many emails and long-distance telephone calls.

This book is not comprehensive in any way because there are, or were, so many pioneers whose stories are equally valuable and interesting who I never knew or heard of in time. Interviewing Mr Regep Assim, "Effendi" and imam at the original Muslim Society of Toronto, would have been very interesting if he had lived until 1979, as would have been Qasem Mahmud of Ottawa, whom I was arranging to interview just before he died. I wish I had been able to do more, but others must carry on this project while pioneers are still alive and well.

Most importantly, I must really sincerely thank both of Mawenzi House's award-winners, publisher Nurjehan Aziz and thoughtful editor and novelist MG Vassanji, for taking such a risk in accepting my manuscript and for making it what it is now. I also want to thank publishing assistant Sabrina Pignataro for helping to deal with all my on-going mistakes and last-minute second thoughts. Of course, any errors, omissions and misjudgements are my responsibility alone.

Murray Hogben

MURRAY HOGBEN was born in Toronto in 1935 and grew up in Ottawa. In 1957 he earned a bachelor's degree in English literature and then a journalism degree at Carleton University. There he met an Indian Muslim student, Alia Rauf, duly became a Muslim in 1956, and they married in 1959. Working for the CBC in Toronto, he became secretary in 1960 of the new Muslim Society of Toronto for years. Also, starting in 1965, he began to earn a doctorate in history from the University of Toronto, graduating in 1973. He then taught at the Royal Military College of Canada in Kingston and then at le College militaire royal de Saint-Jean, in Quebec. Murray then joined the *Kingston Whig-Standard* in 1979 as a reporter and columnist until 2000. Meanwhile, he had also become secretary of the Islamic Society of Kingston, a volunteer Muslim chaplain at several prisons, secretary of the Kingston Police race relations advisory committee, and for decades canoeing instructor and arts and crafts director at a camp for Muslim girls and boys. Murray and Alia live on their hobby farm near Kingston, close to their children and grandchildren.